Introduction to Pentecostal Doctrine

An Independent-Study Textbook
by Zenas Bicket

Third Edition

Berean School of the Bible,
a Global University School

1211 South Glenstone Avenue
Springfield, MO 65804 USA

1-800-443-1083
Fax: (417) 862-0863
Email: berean@globaluniversity.edu
Web: www.globaluniversity.edu

GLOBAL
UNIVERSITY

Dr. Zenas Bicket is a retired president of Berean University, the school that merged in 1999 with ICI University to become Global University (in Springfield, Missouri). He has served Assemblies of God ministries in additional capacities: as a professor and an academic dean of Evangel College (now Evangel University), as a professor at Central Bible College (now Evangel University), and as chair of the AG Doctrinal Purity Commission from 1989–2002. Bicket has authored or contributed to several books, including *The Effective Pastor*, *The Pentecostal Pastor*, *Walking in the Spirit*, *The Spirit Helps Us Pray*, and *We Hold These Truths*.

Licensed with the Assemblies of God in 1957 and ordained in 1985, Bicket has an Ed.B. from Wisconsin University, Whitewater; an M.A. and a Ph.D. from the University of Arkansas; and a Th.B. from Central Bible College.

Global University
Springfield, Missouri, USA

PN 03.21.01

ISBN 978-0-7617-1463-7

Printed in the United States of America

Table of Contents

Digital Course Options

This independent-study textbook (IST) represents only one of the ways you can study through Global University's Berean School of the Bible (BSB). Global University offers electronic delivery formats that allow you to complete courses without using printed material.

You may choose one or more of these course delivery options with or without the printed IST.

Digital Courses

- <u>Online Courses</u>. Complete your entire ministry training program online with fully interactive learning options.

    You can complete your chapter reviews, unit progress evaluations, and final exam online and receive instant results, even if you use print or other digital study versions.

- <u>Logos Bible Software</u>. Purchase an entire digital library of Bibles and Bible reference titles and the Berean courses specifically created to function inside these digital library environments.

- <u>Electronic courses</u>. Check Global University's website for additional electronic course versions (for e-readers and other devices) and their availability.

Enrollment Policies and Procedures

Enrollment policies and procedures are provided in the most current Berean School of the Bible Academic Catalog. An electronic version of the catalog is available at the Global University website.

Contact Global University for Enrollment Information

Phone: 1-800-443-1083 (9 a.m. to 6 p.m., CST, Monday–Friday)

Spanish language representatives are available to discuss enrollment in Spanish courses.

Email: berean@globaluniversity.edu

Web: www.globaluniversity.edu

Fax: 417-862-0863

Mail: 1211 S. Glenstone Ave., Springfield, MO 65804

How to Use Berean Courses

Independent study is one of the most dynamic and rapidly growing educational methods. Although different from traditional classroom study, the goal is the same—to guide you, the student, through a systematic program of study and help you gain new knowledge and skills. Berean courses are independent-study courses. Some students may participate in a Berean study group, where a facilitator enhances the learning experience for a group of Berean students. Other options include studying the courses online and/or purchasing digital study tools made possible through Berean's partnership with Logos Bible Software.

All Berean courses are printed in a comprehensive independent-study textbook (IST). The IST is your teacher, textbook, and study guide in one package. Once you have familiarized yourself with the course components, explained below, you are ready to begin studying. Whether you are studying for personal growth or working toward a diploma, the Berean faculty, advisers, and student service representatives are available to help you get the most out of your Berean program.

General Course Design

- Each course is based on course objectives.
- Each course is composed of several units.
- Each unit is composed of several chapters.
- Each chapter is composed of two or more lessons.
- Each lesson contains one or more lesson objectives.
- Each lesson objective corresponds to specific lesson content.

Course Objectives

Course objectives represent the concepts—or knowledge areas—and perspectives the course will teach you. Review these objectives before you begin studying to have an idea of what to focus on as you study. The course objectives are listed on the course introduction page.

Unit Overview

A unit overview previews each unit's content and outlines the unit development.

Chapter, Lesson Content, Lesson Objectives, and Numbering System

Each *chapter* begins with an introduction and outline. The outline presents the chapter's lesson titles and objectives. Chapters consist of short lessons to allow you to complete one lesson at a time (at one sitting), instead of the entire chapter at one time.

The *lesson content* is based on lesson objectives.

Lesson objectives present the important concepts and perspectives to be studied in the course.

Each chapter, lesson, and objective is uniquely numbered. This numbering system is designed to help you relate the lesson objective to its corresponding lesson content. Chapters are numbered consecutively throughout the course. Lessons are numbered within each chapter with a two-digit decimal number. For example, Lesson 2 in Chapter 3 is numbered 3.2. The first number is the chapter (3), the second number is the lesson (2) within the chapter.

Lesson objectives are tagged with a three-digit decimal number. For example, Chapter 1, Lesson 1, Objective 1 is identified as Objective 1.1.1. Chapter 1, Lesson 2, Objective 3 is Objective 1.2.3. The first number is the chapter, the second is the lesson, and the third is the objective. The numbering system is to assist you in identifying, locating, and organizing each chapter, lesson, and objective.

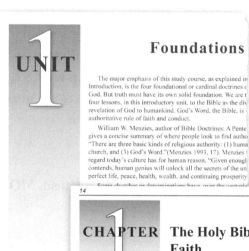

UNIT 1

Foundations

The major emphasis of this study course, as explained in Introduction, is the four foundational or cardinal doctrines of God. But truth must have its own solid foundation. We are to four lessons, in this introductory unit, to the Bible as the div revelation of God to humankind. God's Word, the Bible, is authoritative rule of faith and conduct.

William W. Menzies, author of Bible Doctrines: A Pente gives a concise summary of where people look to find autho "There are three basic kinds of religious authority: (1) huma church, and (3) God's Word."(Menzies 1993, 17). Menzies regard today's culture has for human reason. "Given enough contends, human genius will unlock all the secrets of the un perfect life, peace, health, wealth, and continuing prosperity

14   In

CHAPTER 1

The Holy Bible—Our Fou Faith

Jesus closed His Sermon on the Mount with a st built his house on the sand (Matthew 7:24–27). He man who built his house on a rock. Of course, the c the house that did not have a solid foundation, while firm in spite of the driving wind and rain. He likene would hear His teachings and obey them.

The Word of God provides us with the firm foun our lives and our belief system. We must begin with is indeed the Word of God, and every doctrine must of the Sixteen Fundamental Truths taught by the Ass on the inspiration of Scripture. Since we get all of o through the Bible, a proper view of it is the basis fo

The principles taught in this course are firmly ba foundation can never be changed or destroyed. "Hea away, but my words will never pass away" (Matthe political, or philosophical attacks, God's Word will built on it.

Lesson 1.1   The Need for Sound Doctri

Objectives
1.1.1   Describe Bible doctrine.
1.1.2   Point out how the four foundational or card Bible doctrines.
1.1.3   Explain the differences between doctrine an

The King's Background, Birth, and Early Years

The Background of

Take time to study this first section. Like a pic Gospels. Consider some important events God or

Political History Between

In the Bible, the New Testament is just a pa Testament. However, those pages represent a h book in the Old Testament had been written, fo the events in the book of Matthew and vast cha took the place of Hebrew as the language of Pa **Pharisees, Sadducees**, and **Scribes**—guided r (small places of worship, study, and socializati Jews were ruled by the powerful and hated Ro years under the cultural influence of the Near E completely. What had happened?

1.1.1
OBJECTIVE
Relate specific ways that God historically and politically prepared the earth for Christ's coming.

The Greek Period

The Persian Empire was in power at the end and Nehemiah rebuilt Jerusalem's wall and the Alexander the Great conquered the Persian Emp world, including what remained of Israel and Ju

1 About how many years passed between the end of the Old Testament and the events in the book of Matthew?

took the place of Hebrew as the langu
Pharisees, Sadducees, and **Scribes**—
(small places of worship, study, and so
Jews were ruled by the powerful and h
years under the cultural influence of th
completely (Scroggins 2003, 328).

The Greek Period

The Persian Empire was in power a
and Nehemiah rebuilt Jerusalem's wal

  Test Yourself

Circle the letter of the *best* answer.

1. Why are only two chapters of the entire Bibl devoted to the never-ending eternity?
a) Eternity will be a constant repeat of regular activity, so no more space is needed.
b) The eternal fate of the wicked should not be given any more attention
c) Greater details of New Jerusalem would be meaningless.
d) The purpose of Scripture is to encourage hc living now

2. What happens to the present heaven and eart make way for new heaven and earth?
a) They are gradually cleansed and changed in

What to Look for in the Margins

Left margins contain numbers for units, chapters, and lessons. In addition, margins contain two learning tools—*lesson objectives with their respective numbers* and *interactive questions* that focus on key principles. Read, understand, and use these two learning tools to study the lesson text.

Interactive questions relate to specific lesson content and specific lesson objectives. Interactive questions, along with lesson objectives, will help you learn the concepts and perspectives that are tested in exam questions. Interactive questions are numbered consecutively within each chapter. Once you understand what the interactive question is asking, search for the answer as you study the lesson's related content section. You can compare your responses to our suggested ones at the back of each chapter.

Lesson objectives present the key concepts. These tips on using lesson objectives will help you master the course content and be prepared for exams:
- Identify the key concept(s) and concept perspectives in the objective.
- Identify and understand what the objective is asking you to do with the key concept(s).
- Think of the objective as an essay test question.
- Read and study the lesson content related to the objective and search for the answer to the "essay test question"—the objective.

Lesson Titles and Subheads
Lesson titles and subheads identify and organize specific lesson content.

Key Words
Key words are presented in **boldface** print and defined in the glossary of this IST; they are words that are used with a specific meaning in the lesson.

Reference Citations
Outside sources are documented using in-text citations in parentheses. These sources are compiled in more detail in the reference list at the end of the IST.

Test Yourself
The Test Yourself section concludes the chapter with multiple-choice questions based on the lesson objectives, interactive questions, and their supporting lesson content. Test Yourself answer keys are in the Essential Course Materials at the back of this IST.

Glossary and Reference List
A *glossary* (which defines key words) and *reference list* (works cited in each chapter) follow the last chapter of the IST.

Recommended Reading Textbook
An optional textbook is recommended for use with each course. The textbook recommended to accompany this course is listed on the course introduction page. Some courses may provide additional suggested reading lists following the *reference list*.

Essential Course Materials in the back of this IST contain the following:
- Service Learning Requirement (SLR) Assignment and SLR Report Form
- Unit Progress Evaluation (UPE) Instructions and UPEs
- Answer Keys for Test Yourself quizzes and UPEs
- Forms: Round-Tripper (as needed) and Request for a Printed Final Examination (if needed)

Two Requirements to Receive a Course Grade:
To receive a grade for this course, you must:
1. Submit your SLR Report Form. The instructions for the SLR assignment are in the Essential Course Materials at the back of this IST. The report is required, but not graded.
2. Take a closed-book final examination. Your course grade is based on the final exam. The Berean School of the Bible grading scale is 90–100 percent, A; 80–89 percent, B; 70–79 percent, C; and 0–69 percent, F.

Checklist of Study Methods

STUDY METHODS	√	If you carefully follow the study methods listed below, you should be able to complete this course successfully. As you complete each chapter, mark a √ in the column for that chapter beside each instruction you followed. Then continue to study the remaining chapters in the same way.																
1. Read the introduction in the Independent-Study Textbook (IST) to learn how to use the IST.																			
2. Study the Table of Contents to familiarize yourself with the course structure and content.																			
CHAPTERS		1	2	3	4	5	6	7	8	9	10	11	12	13	14	15	16	17	18
3. Pace yourself so you will study at least two or three times each week. Plan carefully so you can complete the course within the allowed enrollment period. Complete at least one lesson each study session.																			
4. Read Scripture references in more than one translation of the Bible for better understanding.																			
5. Underline, mark, and write notes in your IST.																			
6. Use a notebook to write additional notes and comments.																			
7. As you work through each chapter, make good use of reference tools, such as a study Bible, a comprehensive concordance, a Bible dictionary, and an English dictionary.																			
8. Complete all interactive questions and learning activities as you go.																			
9. In preparation for the Test Yourself, review the objectives for each lesson in the chapter and your notes and highlights to reinforce the key principles learned in the chapter.																			
10. Discuss with others what you are learning.																			
11. Apply what you have learned in your spiritual life and ministry.																			
UNIT EVALUATIONS																			
Review for each Unit Progress Evaluation by rereading the																			
a. lesson objectives to be sure you can achieve what they state.																			
b. questions you answered incorrectly in Test Yourself.																			
c. lesson material for topics you need to review.																			

Student Planner and Record

*This chart is for you to record your personal progress in this course. Be sure to keep it **up to date** for quick reference.*

In the boxes below, record the unit number, the date you expect to complete each chapter, the date you do complete the chapter, and the date of review.

Unit Number	Chapter Number	Expected Completion Date	Actual Completion Date	Date Reviewed
	1			
	2			
	3			
	4			
	5			
	6			
	7			
	8			
	9			
	10			
	11			
	12			
	13			
	14			
	15			
	16			
	17			
	18			

UNIT EVALUATIONS	Date Completed
Unit Evaluation 1	
Unit Evaluation 2	
Unit Evaluation 3	
Unit Evaluation 4	
Unit Evaluation 5	
Unit Evaluation 6	

WRITTEN ASSIGNMENTS & FINAL EXAM	Date Completed
Service Learning Requirement (SLR) Report	
Final Examination	
SLR report & closed-book final exam materials submitted (The SLR report does not apply to the internship courses.)	

The Four Foundational, or Cardinal, Doctrines

The world has many religions. Most of them lack a divine Savior like Jesus Christ. Their adherents consider the Bible to be a religious book, but not necessarily God's inspired, infallible, and authoritative Word for humans to follow in all cultures and times. Pentecostals, however, and especially the Assemblies of God, have strong convictions about the Bible and its declaration of God's design for the human race. We firmly hold that the Scriptures, both the Old and New Testaments, are verbally inspired of God and are the revelation of God to mankind, the infallible, authoritative rule of faith and conduct (1 Thessalonians 2:13; 2 Timothy 3:15–17; 2 Peter 1:21).

As Pentecostals, we hold most biblical truths in common with born-again evangelicals. As the Assemblies of God and other Pentecostal groups came into existence early in the twentieth century, certain biblical truths were considered as needing greater emphasis in our ministry of bringing the lost to Christ. Four of these were identified as the Foundational (or Cardinal) Doctrines. Jesus is (1) our Savior, (2) our Baptizer in the Holy Spirit, (3) our Healer, and (4) our soon returning King. In this course, these four points are treated as the doctrines of (1) Salvation, (2) Baptism in the Holy Spirit, (3) Divine Healing, and (4) the Second Coming of Christ.

The effective Pentecostal minister or witness must know these doctrinal truths with great certainty. "Cardinal" means something is so significant that we cannot do without it. These four truths are essential to the empowered ministry for which Pentecostals are noted. May the Lord anoint your mind and heart as you study these truths so essential to our faith and practice.

Course Description   THE114 Introduction to Pentecostal Doctrine (5 CEUs)

An examination of the four cardinal doctrines of the Assemblies of God: The Salvation of Man, The Baptism in the Holy Spirit, Divine Healing, and The Second Coming of Christ or "The Blessed Hope." After an introductory unit on the importance of doctrine, there is a unit of study on each of the doctrines. This course is essential to the further understanding of the complete Pentecostal message as presented in other courses.

In addition to using your Bible we also recommend that you use *What the Bible Says about the Holy Spirit*, Revised Edition, by Stanley Horton to enhance your learning experience.

Course Objectives

Upon completion of this course, you should be able to

1. Explain the importance of an inspired and inerrant Bible as the basis for sound doctrine.

2. Define the meaning of salvation, and describe how it restores a personal relationship with God.

3. Explain to a sinner the steps to receiving God's gift of salvation, using supporting Bible verses.

4. Indicate why all believers who wish to be used by God in effective ministry to others need the baptism in the Holy Spirit.

5. List and explain the nine gifts of the Spirit (1 Corinthians 12), and show how the Holy Spirit is not limited to working only through these gifts.

6. Describe the many other gifts the Spirit bestows on Spirit-filled believers in addition to the traditional nine gifts.

7. Explain from the Scriptures how the fruit of the Spirit along with the gifts of the Spirit mark a Spirit-filled life.

8. Describe what the Holy Spirit can do in the personal life of the Spirit-filled believer, in addition to imparting power for anointed ministry.

9. Summarize from biblical references possible reasons for physical suffering and illness, pointing out how healing is included in Jesus' atonement for our sins.

10. Explain to a person suffering physically how to trust God for healing and how to live in faith even after the healing comes.

11. Write a summary chart of end-time events from the Rapture to the New Heavens and Earth.

12. Identify reasons for our glorious anticipation of reigning with Christ in His eternal Kingdom.

BEFORE YOU BEGIN

Successfully completing this course requires that you apply content you study in a ministry activity. The instructions for this Service Learning Requirement (SLR) are found in the Essential Course Materials in the back of this IST. Please take time now to become familiar with these instructions so that you can be planning your SLR activity throughout your study of this course.

UNIT 1

Foundations

The major emphasis of this study course, as explained in the Course Introduction, is the four foundational or cardinal doctrines of the Assemblies of God. But truth must have its own solid foundation. We are therefore devoting four lessons, in this introductory unit, to the Bible as the divinely inspired revelation of God to humankind. God's Word, the Bible, is our infallible and authoritative rule of faith and conduct.

William W. Menzies, author of *Bible Doctrines: A Pentecostal Perspective*, gives a concise summary of where people look to find authority for their beliefs. "There are three basic kinds of religious authority: (1) human reason, (2) the church, and (3) God's Word." Menzies then observes the high regard today's culture has for human reason. "Given enough time, the rationalist contends, human genius will unlock all the secrets of the universe and lead to perfect life, peace, health, wealth, and continuing prosperity" (Menzies 1993, 17).

Some churches or denominations have, over the centuries of their existence, placed church leaders and their additions to church doctrine above the authority of Scripture. However, Bible believing churches, like the Assemblies of God, hold the Bible to be the highest authority for our beliefs and for the way we live.

Chapter 1   The Holy Bible, Our Foundation for Faith

Lessons
1.1   The Need for Sound Doctrine
1.2   Bible Doctrine: A Guide for Daily Living
1.3   Confronting Alternative Belief Systems
1.4   The Holy Bible: The Basis for True Doctrine

CHAPTER 1

The Holy Bible: Our Foundation for Faith

Jesus closed His Sermon on the Mount with a story about a foolish man who built his house on the sand (Matthew 7:24–27). He contrasted him with a wise man who built his house on a rock. Of course, the coming storm utterly destroyed the house that did not have a solid foundation, while the house on the rock stood firm in spite of the driving wind and rain. He likened the wise man to one who would hear His teachings and obey them.

The Word of God provides us with the firm foundation we need for building our lives and our belief system. We must begin with the assumption that the Bible is indeed the Word of God, and every doctrine must be measured by it. The first of the Sixteen Fundamental Truths taught by the Assemblies of God focuses on the inspiration of Scripture. Since we get all of our information about God through the Bible, a proper view of it is the basis for all other doctrine.

The principles taught in this course are firmly based on the Bible. That foundation can never be changed or destroyed. "Heaven and earth will pass away, but my words will never pass away" (Matthew 24:35). In spite of cultural, political, or philosophical attacks, God's Word will stand—as will the doctrines built on it.

Lesson 1.1   The Need for Sound Doctrine

Objectives
1.1.1   Describe Bible doctrine.
1.1.2   Point out how the four foundational or cardinal doctrines relate to other Bible doctrines.
1.1.3   Explain the differences between doctrine and theology.

Lesson 1.2   Bible Doctrine: A Guide for Daily Living

Objectives
1.2.1   Indicate why there is a great need for doctrinal study.
1.2.2   Describe the value of doctrine for everyday living.

Lesson 1.3   Confronting Alternative Belief Systems

Objectives
1.3.1   Explain why natural law is not the standard for righteous living.
1.3.2   Explain why human philosophy is not the standard for restored relationship with God.
1.3.3   Describe how some religions relate to Christianity.

Lesson 1.4   The Holy Bible: The Basis for True Doctrine

Objectives
1.4.1   Explain what we mean when we say the Bible is inspired and inerrant.
1.4.2   Explain why belief in the inspiration and inerrancy of Scripture is essential.

LESSON 1.1

1 Why spend valuable time studying doctrine?

1.1.1
OBJECTIVE
Describe Bible doctrine.

The Need for Sound Doctrine

Sinners are dying daily and going to hell. You have been touched supernaturally by God's Spirit. Your salvation experience is powerful and life changing. You want to share it with others and do it right now. Even the newly converted believer can and must share his or her experience with Jesus Christ, but at the same time you must learn many things so that winning others to Christ is effective and lasting. Biblical truths must be learned if we are to see God's dynamic work in the lives of those to whom we witness.

The apostle Paul knew the importance of sound doctrine. In his letters to young pastors Timothy and Titus, Paul uses the words four times. The first refers to lifestyles that are contrary to sound doctrine (1 Timothy 1:10). But then he proclaims the absolute need for sound doctrine. "For the time will come when men will not put up with sound doctrine. Instead, to suit their own desires, they will gather around them a great number of teachers to say what their itching ears want to hear" (2 Timothy 4:3). To Titus, Paul repeats the importance of sound doctrine in the pastor's ministry: "He must hold firmly to the trustworthy message as it has been taught, so that he can encourage others by sound doctrine and refute those who oppose it" (Titus 1:9). Then Paul says again to Titus, "You must teach what is in accord with sound doctrine" (Titus 2:1).

Systematic Instruction

Doctrine literally means "something taught" or "teaching and instruction." **Bible doctrine** is a framework of fundamental biblical truths arranged in a systematic form. Bible scholars study the entire Bible to determine all it says about a particular subject. They then arrange those biblical statements into a comprehensive statement on a subject. The end result is an outline of the prominent subjects of Christian doctrine. Some of the more common areas of doctrine are the doctrine of angels (angelology), the doctrine of Jesus Christ (christology), the doctrine of last things or prophecy (eschatology), the doctrine of the church (ecclesiology), and the doctrine of the Holy Spirit (pneumatology).

These and other doctrines are treated in great detail in theology textbooks that sometimes exist in many volumes. This course, however, does not treat all the doctrines of the Bible, just the ones most predominant in the ministry of Pentecostals. There are four that stand out as the foundational doctrines of the Assemblies of God and other Pentecostal groups.

- Salvation through the death and resurrection of Jesus Christ
- The Holy Spirit and His dynamic work in Spirit-filled Christians
- Divine healing as part of the atonement
- The Second Coming of Jesus Christ

The systematic study of doctrine also protects us from unbalanced and wrong interpretations of Scripture. A single verse can be taken out of the entire Bible context and applied improperly. "All Scripture is God-breathed and is useful for teaching, rebuking, correcting and training in righteousness, so that the man of God may be thoroughly equipped for every good work" (2 Timothy 3:16–17). The emphasis should be on all Scripture. It is true that the Bible is God-inspired from Genesis 1:1 to Revelation 22:21. Yet to be sure that we fully understand what God is saying to us through any particular verse or passage, we must consider all the verses and passages in Scripture dealing with the subject being studied. Comprehensive study leads to sound doctrine. Only when we know everything the Bible says about how we should live can we be taught and trained in righteousness and be properly equipped for doing God's work.

The Four Cardinal Doctrines

The Assemblies of God Statement of Fundamental Truths contains sixteen points (The official scholarly treatment of the sixteen points is from Menzies' *Bible Doctrines: A Pentecostal Perspective*). The preamble to the statement adopted in 1916 says, "This statement of Fundamental Truths is not intended as a creed for the church, nor as a basis of fellowship among Christians, but only as a basis of unity for the ministry alone (i.e., that we all speak the same thing, 1 Corinthians. 1:10; Acts 2:42)" (Menzies 1993, 11). The Statement has come to be recognized as the guideline for our faith and practice, for what we believe and how we are expected to live.

1.1.2
OBJECTIVE
Point out how the four foundational or cardinal doctrines relate to other Bible doctrines.

Four of the sixteen points are the four foundational doctrines we are about to study. These four cardinal doctrines are The Salvation of Man (5), The Baptism in the Holy Spirit (7), Divine Healing (12), and The Second Coming or "The Blessed Hope" (13). Yet, the other twelve points are vitally related to the four cardinal doctrines, thus indicating their importance. Consider the total list of sixteen points making up the Statement of Fundamental Truths.

1. The Scriptures **Inspired**
2. The One True God
3. The Deity of the Lord Jesus Christ
4. The Fall of Man
5. The Salvation of Man
6. Ordinances of the Church
7. The Baptism in the Holy Spirit
8. The Initial Physical Evidence of the Baptism in the Holy Spirit
9. Sanctification
10. The Church and Its Mission
11. The Ministry
12. Divine Healing
13. The Second Coming or "The Blessed Hope"
14. The Millennial Reign of Christ
15. The Final Judgment
16. The New Heavens and the New Earth

Next, we must consider how the remaining twelve points of the Statement of Fundamental Truths relate closely to the four foundational doctrines.

2   What are the four cardinal doctrines found among the sixteen doctrines in the above list?

The Scriptures Inspired (1) provides the foundation for all of our doctrine. The Scriptures, both the Old and New Testaments, are verbally inspired of God and are the revelation of God to man, the infallible, authoritative rule of faith and conduct (1 Thessalonians 2:13; 2 Timothy 3:15–17; 2 Peter 1:21).

The One True God (2) emphasizes the unity of the Father, Jesus Christ, and the Holy Spirit, providing for our salvation and our daily walk with God.

The Deity of the Lord Jesus Christ (3) confirms the truth that the death of Jesus Christ, the divine Son of God, provides salvation, something that no human could provide.

The Fall of Man (4) explains why a plan of salvation was necessary to restore fellowship between God and humankind.

The Ordinances of the Church (6) include water baptism and the Lord's Supper. Water baptism commemorates salvation as the burial of past rebellion against God and resurrection to a new life of fellowship with God. The Lord's Supper or Communion commemorates Christ's great sacrifice for our salvation.

The Initial Physical Evidence of the Baptism in the Holy Ghost (8), or speaking in tongues, is the biblical pattern for entry into an empowered Spirit-filled life.

Sanctification (9) relates to the foundational doctrines of salvation and baptism in the Holy Spirit. A Christian is instantly sanctified in God's sight at salvation, but the Holy Spirit then begins a lifelong work of making the believer more and more Christlike.

The Church and Its Mission (10) and The Ministry (11) describe the functions of the Body of Christ (the church) in fulfilling Christ's Great Commission to carry the message of salvation into all the world.

The Millennial Reign of Christ (14), The Final Judgment (15), and The New Heavens and the New Earth (16) all deal with future events that take place following the Second Coming of Jesus Christ.

Relationship between Doctrine and Theology

1.1.3
OBJECTIVE
Explain the differences between doctrine and theology.

Doctrine literally means "teaching or instruction." Theology means "the study of God" or our understanding of God and His relations with humankind. So doctrine and theology are closely related words and often used with the same meaning.

Some theologians, however, make a distinction. One who specializes in the study of theology is a theologian, but we do not have a corresponding word for one who studies doctrine. Originally a doctor was an educated teacher of doctrine. But *doctor* now means "a medical specialist or learned specialist in any field of study."

One possible distinction is that theology is the thought of individuals, while doctrine is the recognized thought of a church. The original Statement of Fundamental Truths was drafted by theologians who expressed their understanding of Scripture. A recognized body of members then approved the Statement, making it the doctrine of the Assemblies of God. Theologians may express interpretations that are not covered by the Statement, but in becoming credentialed ministers of the group, they express their agreement with the doctrinal statements of the church.

Questions of faith and practice not covered in the Statement of Fundamental Truths may later arise. In the Assemblies of God, a Doctrinal Purity Commission (composed of theologians, pastors, and church leaders to give balanced views) is asked to produce position papers on assigned subjects, all within the previously approved truths of the Statement. The result of their work is presented to church leadership bodies that approve or disapprove of the results of their study. If approved, the paper becomes a further guideline, with less strength than the *Statement of Fundamental Truths*, for the faith and practice of members.

LESSON 1.2

1.2.1
OBJECTIVE
Indicate why there is a great need for doctrinal study.

Bible Doctrine: A Guide for Daily Living

The Need for Doctrinal Study

The Assemblies of God is committed to a strong belief that the Bible is God's inspired Word, showing all people the way of salvation and righteous living. When we consider whether or not all Christians share that same firm commitment, the answer might be found in looking at what teenage children in Christian homes know about the Bible. What do the following actual responses of high-school-age students reveal about the success the church is having in grounding its youth in biblical truth? Though the survey was taken a number of years ago by a Sunday school teacher, it would be hard to claim that the church is doing better today. (The following passages quote the King James Version for the references given.)

"His name shall be called . . . the (Justice) of Peace" (Isaiah 9:6)

Jesus was baptized by (Moses).

Jesus was in agony in the Garden of (Eden).

"Ye seek Jesus . . . He is not here: for he is (dead)" (Matthew 28:5–6).

"Charity" in the King James Version of 1 Corinthians 13 means (to give).

"I have fought a (losing) fight . . . I have kept the faith" (2 Timothy 4:7).

Jacob wrestled all night with (insomnia).

The wise sayings in Proverbs are generally attributed to (parents).

3 Who is to blame for this lack of a real understanding of the Bible and its doctrines?

We can speculate on a number of possibilities for the current lack of understanding regarding the Bible and its doctrines. The family altar, including Bible reading, may have been neglected because of a busy lifestyle. Sunday school may be becoming less important for families with children. Or Sunday school leaders and teachers may emphasize entertainment rather than learning in order to encourage better attendance. Finally, daily Bible reading and private prayer and devotions may not be sufficiently encouraged for our children and youth. In some cases, the teachers and workers with youth may need a stronger foundation in biblical study, memorization, and application.

Whatever may be the reason for lack of Bible knowledge in our youth and adults, this course is prepared to help remedy the lack and to help the student faithfully pass on to others the basic truths of the Bible. In some instances, this course is required as preparation for the ministry to which God is calling you. Your diligence in becoming a worker who does not need to be ashamed of his or her understanding of God's Word and who correctly handles the word of truth (2 Timothy 2:15) will make you a more effective witness.

1.2.2
OBJECTIVE
Describe the value of doctrine for everyday living.

Doctrine and Everyday Living

Studying the doctrines of the Bible may not sound like the most exciting way to spend your time. But it is much like falling in love. If you love a potential partner, or want to know that person better, time spent together is enjoyable and passes quickly. Falling in love with Jesus means wanting to be with Him, hearing His words in the Gospels, and listening to His heartbeat throughout the rest of the Bible. Studying the Bible as God's personal love letter to us is a blessed experience.

God's love letter is more than a row of red hearts around the words, "I LOVE YOU!" God really loves us and wants what is truly for our best. So instead of giving us everything we would at the moment ask for, He gently corrects, counsels, and shows us the path that will bring us fulfillment as we follow His leading. His ultimate goal is to make sure we have companionship with Him throughout eternity.

Doctrine is

- a series of road signs on our discipleship journey.
- a safeguard against error.
- the basis for our conduct and behavior.
- the basis for our service to God and others.

Doctrine is a series of road signs on our discipleship journey. Jesus said to His disciples, "If you hold to my teaching, you are really my disciples. Then you will know the truth, and the truth will set you free" (John 8:31–32).

Some colleges and universities have the words of verse 32 on their official seal, "You will know the truth, and the truth will set you free." Some educators use the verse out of context and take it to mean that knowledge will free people from all the things that make life an unhappy experience. But its true meaning grows out of verse 31 because of the word *and* (or *then* in some translations) that connects the two verses. Jesus was saying that only disciples really know the truth that will set them free. And the way to be His disciple is through obedience to the teachings, or doctrine, of Christ.

So doctrine is extremely essential. It is God's instruction or teaching for the greatest good of His people. He has spoken through His Son Jesus and the inspired writers of the Old and New Testaments. We must certainly obey the doctrine delivered to us, but we cannot obey it completely unless we first understand it. Hearing or understanding comes by and through study of the Word (Romans 10:17).

Doctrine is a safeguard against error. Our eternal salvation could depend on a right understanding of biblical doctrine. Peter warned against false teachers who from greedy motives exploit unsettled Christians with untrue stories (2 Peter 2:3) and seduce unstable persons with their deception (v. 14). Self-centered sinners, in blindness and disobedience, perceive God far differently from who He really is. These errors lead to paganism, humanism, and rejection of the truth of Scripture.

Some people arrogantly claim that all religions will lead to heaven if the seeker is sincere. But error in doctrine can lead us away from God rather than toward Him. Our doctrine must be solidly based on the Bible, God's inspired Word, for our spiritual well-being.

Doctrine is the basis for our conduct and behavior. Strong doctrinal beliefs are absolutely essential for the full development of strong Christian character. The stronger the belief, the more trustworthy and upright the character will be. We need only observe the actions of the many who refuse to believe there is a God who tells His human creation how to live. Though they claim moral beliefs, their behavior reveals shifting standards that place self-satisfaction above obedience to a divinely prescribed standard of conduct. If children are to grow up to be men and women of character and integrity, the teachings and doctrines of God's Word must be firmly planted in their minds and hearts.

Every individual has a conscience created by God. "Indeed, when Gentiles, who do not have the law, do by nature things required by the law, they are a law for themselves, even though they do not have the law, since they show that the requirements of the law are written on their hearts, their consciences also bearing witness, and their thoughts now accusing, now even defending them" (Romans 2:14–15).

Even those who reject the existence of God and the Bible as God's message to humankind still have a conscience. Their conscience functions, however, on what they have individually determined to be right or wrong. When we see the wanton mistreatment of human beings in our world today, we are powerfully reminded of the need for God's standard of love and respect for each other. That is a vital part of Christian doctrine.

Doctrine is the basis for our service to God and others. After three and a half years with His disciples, Jesus was about to leave. His mission was almost completed. Those years with the Twelve had been years of preparation. The messenger is as valuable as the message. The example of the messenger must match the words of the messenger. After the truths of the doctrine had changed the lives of the messengers, the commission was delivered:

"All authority in heaven and on earth has been given to me [Jesus]. Therefore go and make disciples of all nations, baptizing them in the name of the Father and of the Son and of the Holy Spirit, and teaching them to obey everything I have commanded you. And surely I am with you always, to the very end of the age" (Matthew 28:18–20).

We cannot share our faith successfully until we can tell others about it. And that personal experience must match the pattern described in Scripture and promised by God to all men and women. "Always be prepared to give . . . the reason for the hope that you have" (1 Peter 3:15). This study of the four foundational doctrines is part of that preparation.

Confronting Alternative Belief Systems

People have always sought an explanation for their existence and that of the world around them. They try to find or to make a standard by which they can live together with other people. As we seek to bring such persons to the only true belief system found in God's Word, we should know some of their thinking as we present the biblical view of reality.

Most adults come to know Christ personally because they have faced a crisis in their lives. Introducing them to Jesus as the One who can bring peace into their troubled lives and give victory over a personal crisis often blesses their lives. But knowing something about the religious background or non-religious mind-set of the person is always helpful. The Holy Spirit can and will work supernaturally in such instances, but the soul winner should always be prepared to be used effectively.

Some people believe in one God, some in many gods, and some in no god at all. Even if they believe God exists, they often hold different views of how God relates to human beings. Some believe there is life after death; some do not. Some believe there is evil in the world, while others believe that all people are basically good and will treat each other kindly if they are taught to respect others.

Some of these views are associated with various religions. Others are based solely on the world adherents see around them, which they interpret from their own perspective. Absolute truth is outside their willing acceptance. We cannot in a single course deal with all the world's religions, or even the different interpretations of the Bible among professing Christian groups. But before dealing with our understanding of Holy Scripture, which will help us recognize some interpretations that have departed from faithful application of biblical truth, we will look at alternative belief systems that do not acknowledge a God who has spoken to humankind through the Holy Bible.

1.3.1
OBJECTIVE
*Explain why natural law
is not the standard for
righteous living.*

Natural Law Versus Righteous Living

The first paragraph of the United States Declaration of Independence, adopted in 1776, includes a reference to "the laws of nature and of nature's God."

When in the Course of human events, it becomes necessary for one people to dissolve the political bands which have connected them with another, and to assume among the Powers of the earth, the separate and equal station to which the Laws of Nature and of Nature's God entitle them, a decent respect to the opinions of mankind requires that they should declare the causes which impel them to the separation.

The phrase "the laws of nature and of nature's God" can be interpreted in two ways, satisfying those who believe in a God and those who do not. Christians understand "the laws of nature" to be part of God's laws as contained in the Bible. Those who do not believe in a God who created and rules His universe can interpret the phrase to mean two different and optional kinds of law: natural law and the Bible. Many today still reject the Bible as moral authority and choose natural law. Unfortunately, there is no single source that defines natural law.

Those who believe in natural law, as opposed to the moral declarations of the Bible, believe that all persons have access to natural law through human reason. They teach that one knows right from wrong by observing the realities of the physical world. Some even go so far as to declare that natural law is better than biblical definitions of right and wrong, making biblical revelation unnecessary.

The presence and strength of this false belief today is seen everywhere. Modern societies are moving fast toward a completely secular view of life. Religion, and especially Christianity, is viewed as an outdated system of belief. It is accused of bias, even hatred, toward behaviors condemned by the Bible, but those behaviors are given growing acceptance in today's world.

The Bible does acknowledge natural law. However, it is part of God's law, not separate from it.

All who sin apart from the law will also perish apart from the law, and all who sin under the law will be judged by the law. For it is not those who hear the law who are righteous in God's sight, but it is those who obey the law who will be declared righteous. (Indeed, when Gentiles, who do not have the law [God's law], do by nature things required by the law, they are a law for themselves [natural law], even though they do not have the law, since they show that the requirements of the law [God's law] are written on their hearts, their consciences also bearing witness, and their thoughts now accusing, now even defending them.) (Romans 2:12–15)

Natural law does not provide salvation. It serves only to condemn the sinner and direct him or her to Christ as the Creator of nature. It cannot serve independently as a substitute for God's revealed law.

Inadequacy of Human Philosophy

1.3.2
OBJECTIVE
*Explain why human
philosophy is not the
standard for restored
relationship with God.*

Closely related to natural law is the arrogant belief that human reason can put together a philosophy or value system that can satisfy the spiritual needs of all cultures and ethnic groups in the world. This belief system is based on the assumption that all people are basically good and that human reason can tell the difference between right behavior and wrong behavior. Like those who believe only in natural law, these who idolize human reason conclude that there is no afterlife. Denying the existence of a God to whom humans are accountable goes along with no rewards or punishment after a person dies. Morality then becomes what is best for me first, and then best for everyone else. Each person becomes a rule or standard to him- or herself. There is no need for an external guide to right belief or behavior. Human reasoning, no matter how trained and perfected, is no match for God's wisdom. God's message to the most brilliant human mind is "'My thoughts are not your thoughts, neither are your ways my ways . . . As the heavens are higher than the earth, so are my ways higher than your ways and my thoughts than your thoughts'" (Isaiah 55:8–9). The secular world resists the concept of an evil Satan violently opposing God and righteousness. One of Satan's greatest accomplishments is influencing and darkening the minds of those trained in human wisdom. To the worldly wise, it is all flesh, blood, and intellect. But God has declared, "For our struggle is not against flesh and blood [and the minds of flesh and blood creatures], but against the rulers, against the authorities, against the powers of this dark world and against the spiritual forces of evil in the heavenly realms. Therefore put on the full armor of God, so that when the day of evil comes, you may be able to stand your ground, and after you have done everything, to stand" (Ephesians 6:12–13). Satan is still very much alive and well on planet Earth.

1.3.3
OBJECTIVE
Describe how some religions relate to Christianity.

Friends and Foes of the Cross

Christian belief has many varieties. Some have asked why Christians cannot all come together in unity, all believing the same thing. Those who express that idea usually are asking, "Why do not all the other church groups change their understanding of doctrine and join our fellowship?" Some churches even believe that one must be a member of their church in order to go to heaven. This belief, however, is an identifying characteristic of a cult.

Though we desire that all Christians believe in salvation and the baptism in the Holy Spirit as we do, we do not claim to be the only church that teaches the true plan of salvation. "For it is by grace you have been saved, through faith—and this not from yourselves, it is the gift of God—not by works, so that no one can boast" (Ephesians 2:8–9). If we add anything besides faith in Jesus Christ and the sacrifice He made for our salvation, we do wrong. Likewise, if anyone describes a different requirement than faith, that too is wrong. We must not be misled by groups that claim to be Christian, but add other requirements besides faith.

Unfortunately, there are religions that oppose Christianity, sometimes persecuting and even killing Christians. In various parts of the world, Christians are giving their lives for their belief. Yet beginning with Stephen, the first martyr, the blood of the martyrs has been the seed from which the church of Jesus Christ has grown. We do not know what the future holds for Christians now living in peaceful lands. But God is faithful. His promise will always be true: "God has said, 'Never will I leave you; never will I forsake you.' So we say with confidence, 'The Lord is my helper; I will not be afraid. What can man do to me?'" (Hebrews 13:5–6). Even when Satan uses other religious beliefs to attempt to destroy Christianity, God is still on the throne.

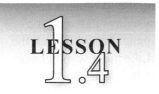

The Holy Bible: The Basis for True Doctrine

Pentecostals, as well as all Christians, should be known as people of the Bible. If we get our understanding of the Bible solely through the interpretations of others, we are headed for disaster theologically. We must be like the noble Bereans who "examined the Scriptures every day to see if what Paul said was true" (Acts 17:11). If Paul's hearers searched the teachings of the great apostle, we should do the same with those whose message we receive. And as ministers of the gospel, we should encourage our hearers to search the Scriptures on their own to verify the truths that we are sharing. In the past, some churches have not encouraged their people to study the Word on their own, possibly fearing that they would recognize teachings not found in Scripture. But if we truly desire to lead our hearers to a closer walk with our Lord, we should urge them to go to God's Word for themselves. The minister's task is not to teach new ideas, but to encourage followers to drink at the Fountain of Life for themselves.

God's Inerrant Word

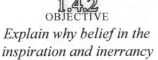

1.4.1
OBJECTIVE

Explain what we mean when we say the Bible is inspired and inerrant.

The secular world views the Bible as just another book on the library shelf. But the Bible is different from all other books. It is the only book in the world wholly inspired by God. The Holy Spirit of God is the divine Author of the Bible, using willing human instruments He chose: "For prophecy never had its origin in the will of man, but men spoke from God as they were carried along by the Holy Spirit" (2 Peter 1:21).

This divine inspiration applies fully to all of the sixty-six books, the historical and poetical as well as the doctrinal and pastoral. Every word is inspired and without error in the original manuscripts. Because of many copyings by scribes before printing was invented, a few minor inaccuracies have appeared in translations. No vital doctrine has been affected, however. God has preserved the truth and meaning of His desired relationship with all humans. Some of the minor variations are being cleared up by more recent discoveries of older manuscripts.

4 How important is this high regard for the Bible?

Inerrant means "free from error." It is generally used as a synonym for infallible, which means "incapable of error." The Statement of Fundamental Truths of the Assemblies of God calls the Bible "the infallible rule of faith and conduct . . . and superior to conscience and reason." Like the doctrinal statements of other evangelical groups, the Statement of Fundamental Truths does not use the word inerrant, but we believe that the Bible is both infallible and inerrant.

The Importance of Believing in the Bible's Inspiration and Inerrancy

1.4.2
OBJECTIVE

Explain why belief in the inspiration and inerrancy of Scripture is essential.

When we declare in our Statement of Fundamental Truths that the Bible is "superior to conscience and reason," are we going a little too far? Sinful, arrogant humankind, determined to allow no authority above its own, objects strongly to our belief that the Bible is superior to human reason. These persons believe that their academic degrees from prestigious secular universities qualify them to judge right from wrong and to define what constitutes truth. But the inspired Word describes a time when ancient people held the same view.

In describing a sinful person, the Psalmist wrote, "There is no fear of God before his eyes. For in his own eyes he flatters himself too much to detect or hate his sin. The words of his mouth are wicked and deceitful; he has ceased to be wise and to do good" (Psalm 36:1–3). There is vast difference between wisdom and knowledge. Academic degrees indicate the mastery of knowledge. However, true wisdom comes from God, and the person who has declared there is no God, lacks the most basic wisdom.

Wisdom has been defined as "knowledge guided by understanding" (cf. Proverbs 10:13, 23), especially understanding grounded in moral integrity. The world has not produced a moral guideline comparable to the divinely inspired Holy Bible. "The fear of the Lord is the beginning of wisdom, and knowledge of the Holy One is understanding" (Proverbs 9:10). Fear in this context means "profound reverence and awe" (Webster's 2002, online) especially toward God.

The Bible is God's Word to sinful humans. God himself must be true and infallible—without error. To accept that there is error in God's Word casts doubt on the very character of God. To believe that the original Word of God had error in it, just because humans had a part in writing the actual words, denies the full meaning of inspiration. It reduces the Bible to the level of any book on moral goodness published today.

Some critics of biblical inerrancy will accept infallibility in matters of faith and practice but refuse to accept it in matters of science or history. The Bible is not a science textbook, yet it records historical and scientific events with the same infallible authority with which it treats doctrine and practice. Unless we accept this view we are faced with a major question. Whose decision determines what parts of the Bible are true and what parts are in error?

Because of our high regard for the Bible, some opponents of inerrancy claim that **evangelicals** and Pentecostals worship a book rather than the Christ who is portrayed in the Book. They further claim that Christians should place final authority in Christ, not in a book recording God's dealings in a dated past time. But the Bible is the only way we have of knowing about Jesus Christ and His authority and work on our behalf. If the Bible that reveals Christ to us is subject to error, it may not be accurate in describing Him as the human-divine Savior that He is. The whole framework of Christian faith rests on the inerrancy of the Scriptures.

> The Assemblies of God position paper, "The Inerrancy of Scripture," can be found on the Internet or in the complete collection of position papers, Where We Stand: The Official Position Papers of the Assemblies of God (Springfield, Mo.: Gospel Publishing House, 2003.) The Internet paper can be found at www.ag.org, and then follow the "Beliefs" and "Position Papers" buttons.

Trusting God's Word

We cannot deny that there are some unanswered questions concerning the historical, chronological, and scientific statements of the Bible. An article in *Christianity Today* reported that almost five thousand original-language manuscripts of Scripture exist today, and no two copies are exactly alike. We have no evidence that the orthodox church attempted to alter the manuscripts to make them exact; so we can believe the original-language copies are still authentic (Witherington 2004, 30). In recent years, there have been enough answers uncovered for previously unsolved Bible questions to assure us that we can trust God's Word. When all the explanations have been revealed, the inspired Word will stand true and without error.

Unfortunately, in the face of unanswered questions some "scholars" choose to trust the fallible, human mind rather than the inerrant Word of an infallible God. The reliability of the Bible has been proven beyond any reasonable doubt. On the other hand, the unreliability and limitations of human reason have been proven with the same consistency.

T Test Yourself

Circle the letter of the *best* answer.

1. The apostle Paul expressed the importance of sound doctrine by
a) quoting Jesus' references to sound doctrine.
b) using the words sound doctrine four times in his pastoral letters to Timothy and Titus.
c) appealing to the Old Testament prophets in support of sound doctrine.

2. Which of the following is one of the cardinal doctrines of the Assemblies of God?
a) The Deity of Jesus
b) The Baptism in the Holy Spirit
c) Sanctification

3. The official document of the Assemblies of God that is our basis for unity is called the
a) Bylaws of the General Council of the Assemblies of God.
b) Amendment for Doctrinal Unity.
c) Statement of Fundamental Truths.

4. The word theology means literally
a) "the study of God."
b) "the study of religions."
c) "the study of doctrines."

5. The study of Bible doctrine serves four purposes. Doctrine is a guard against error, a series of road signs on our discipleship journey,
a) a guide for conduct, and a reason for emotional response.
b) a source for judging others, and a basis for Christian service.
c) a guide for conduct, and a basis for service to God and others.

6. Two secular belief systems that do not accept any religious faith or doctrine are
a) communism and Islam.
b) natural law and human philosophy.
c) atheism and Catholicism.

7. According to the Bible, natural law
a) belongs to the kingdom of Satan.
b) is a part of God's law and is not separate from it.
c) is a secondary means of salvation.

8. Human philosophy opposes God by
a) elevating human reason above the rules given by a God.
b) requiring a defense of God's character.
c) seeking to prove that God's Word is a reflection of human thinking.

9. To accept that there is error in the salvation message of the Bible
a) is not a problem because God can speak to us through nature.
b) gives people a reason to live in any way they please.
c) casts doubt on the existence and character of God.

10. Belief that the Bible is inspired and inerrant is important because
a) God is trustworthy; human reason is fallen and unreliable.
b) no one would read the Bible if it were not inspired and inerrant.
c) the many other inspired and inerrant books do not tell us about God.

Responses to Interactive Questions

Chapter 1

Some of these responses may include information that is supplemental to the IST. These questions are intended to produce reflective thinking beyond the course content and your responses may vary from these examples.

1   Why spend valuable time studying doctrine?

Understanding sound doctrine makes us effective and strengthens our faith. What is true? Why do we hold an idea as truth? What makes our truth different from myth and fantasy? Doctrine is valuable.

2   What are the four cardinal doctrines found among the sixteen doctrines in the above list [16 points of the *Statement of Fundamental Truths*]?

The Salvation of Man (5); The Baptism in the Holy Spirit (7); Divine Healing (12); and The Second Coming or "Blessed Hope" (13).

3   Who is to blame for this lack of a real understanding of the Bible and its doctrines?

For those of Christian background it is a failure to 'follow through' and for others it is the struggle to 'come to' a proper place in Christ. Christians with a Christian heritage may lack diligence in their personal discipleship. Those without a Christian heritage may have a distorted or incomplete worldview.

4   How important is this high regard [belief in Bible inspiration and inerrancy] for the Bible?

The Bible is a message from God to man (inspiration). The Bible is a reliable presentation of God's Word and desire (inerrancy). It is empty arrogance to say that our belief is above the beliefs of others if this was not definitely true.

UNIT PROGRESS EVALUATION 1

Now that you have finished Unit 1, review the lessons in preparation for Unit Progress Evaluation 1. You will find it in Essential Course Materials at the back of this IST. Answer all of the questions without referring to your course materials, Bible, or notes. When you have completed the UPE, check your answers with the answer key provided in Essential Course Materials. Review any items you may have answered incorrectly. Then you may proceed with your study of Unit 2. (Although UPE scores do not count as part of your final course grade, they indicate how well you learned the material and how well you may perform on the closed-book final examination.)

UNIT 2

Salvation as Restored Relationship with God

Forgiveness, assurance, acceptance, hope, liberation, deliverance, freedom, and liberty—all are words describing the desires of every human soul. Yet so many souls live in bondage, rejection, despair, spiritual slavery, and feelings of guilt.

God knew this would be the sad condition of humankind after sin put its blemish on His perfect creation. So He implemented a plan to restore fellowship with all humans. God's response to the terrible cancer of sin was not an afterthought. The Bible tells us that Jesus was chosen before the creation of the world to provide for our salvation. "It was not with perishable things such as silver or gold that you were redeemed from the empty way of life handed down to you from your forefathers, but with the precious blood of Christ, a lamb without blemish or defect. He was chosen before the creation of the world, but was revealed in these last times for your sake" (1 Peter 1:18–20). The plan of salvation was drafted even before sin made clear the need for humankind's redemption.

In greater detail, this unit on salvation (the first foundational doctrine) brings together the biblical teachings on God's perfect creation, the entry of sin in the fall of Adam and Eve, the sacrifice of Jesus Christ for our salvation, how salvation changes an individual's life, and how the church keeps our attention on this primary doctrine.

Chapter 2   Salvation: The Only Cure for Fallen Humanity

Lessons
2.1   God's Love for His Fallen Creation
2.2   The Fall of Adam and Eve
2.3   The Power and Ugliness of Sin

Chapter 3   Jesus Christ: God's Gift for Our Salvation

Lessons
3.1   God's Plan for Restoring Fellowship with Fallen Humans
3.2   Jesus: the Sacrifice that Provides Our Salvation
3.3   Our Salvation and Christ's Death, Resurrection, and Ascension
3.4   Salvation Means Regeneration, Justification, and Repentance
3.5   Sanctification, Assurance, Reconciliation, and Redemption

Chapter 4   Affirming and Maintaining Salvation

Lessons
4.1   Declaring and Remembering Our Salvation
4.2   The Security of the Believer and Warnings against Falling

Salvation: The Only Cure for Fallen Humanity

Two men went for a boat ride. The boat had two life jackets, but one of the men felt he did not need the jacket. He could swim, and the boat had never capsized before. The river was swift from spring rains. Hitting a hidden rock, the boat overturned, throwing both men into the river. The man wearing the life jacket quickly rose to the surface and was rescued. But his friend lost his life.

Our world is like a fast-moving, dangerous stream. Christ's death for our sins is our life jacket, yet many do not feel the need to be prepared for eternity. We do not know if the surviving man felt any guilt for not insisting that his friend use his life jacket, but he well could have. Do we feel any concern or responsibility for those we know who are going through life without Jesus as their Savior?

Repenting and becoming a Christian takes less time than it does to put on a life jacket. But the consequences are far greater. It is truly tragic for one to lose his or her life for not taking time to put on the jacket. But it is many times more tragic for one not to accept God's offer of free salvation. An eternity without Christ makes the loss of a few years on earth of little importance. After all, every person is appointed to face physical death at some time. Dying without accepting Christ as Savior is a choice that lasts for eternity.

Lesson 2.1   God's Love for His Fallen Creation

Objectives

2.1.1   Indicate the basis for believing there is a God and that He reveals himself to humans.

2.1.2   Point out why it is necessary to believe Jesus is the Son of God.

2.1.3   Explain how God's plan of salvation guards and regains His creation.

Lesson 2.2   The Fall of Adam and Eve

Objectives

2.2.1   Indicate why it is important to believe Adam and Eve actually existed.

2.2.2   Define what it means to be "made in the image of God."

2.2.3   Explain Satan's role in Adam and Eve's sin.

Lesson 2.3   The Power and Ugliness of Sin

Objectives

2.3.1   Describe various characteristics of sin as it relates to human behavior.

2.3.2   Describe the similarity between the first sin and sin today.

2.3.3   Point out how God can hate sin but still love the sinner.

2.1.1
OBJECTIVE

Indicate the basis for believing there is a God and that He reveals himself to humans.

1   Why did God who inspired the Bible not give us a reasoned proof of His existence?

2   Why would the supreme Creator of our world give us choice in responding to His love?

God's Love for His Fallen Creation

Salvation is needed because creation is fallen. We have already studied in the introductory chapter the importance of the Bible, recognizing that God inspired it. Brief mention was made concerning critics who do not accept the Bible because they do not believe there is a God to whom all humans are accountable.

Belief in God Is Reasonable

For most of the inhabitants of planet Earth, there is an inner consciousness that something or someone must have made the fantastic universe and world we see around us. A person does not need a college degree to look into the heavens and know that a Power or Intelligence greater than anything on earth brought the sun, moon, and distant stars/suns into existence.

Some who refuse to accept the existence of God may say something like "I will believe there is a God when you show me the evidence in a test tube." That response demonstrates the limited view that reality exists only in what we can touch with our hands or see with our eyes. For them, a spiritual, non-material world does not exist. The absurdity of such a conclusion is that learning more results in knowing less. Trying to understand the physical world without acknowledging a Creator eliminates a vital part of life and our reason for living. We need Christian scholars who excel academically without losing their understanding and relationship with a personal God.

The Bible makes a direct statement about linking the realities of the physical and spiritual worlds. "And without faith it is impossible to please God, because anyone who comes to him must believe that he exists and that he rewards those who earnestly seek him" (Hebrews 11:6). Everyone has faith in something. Unfortunately, faith in the contents of the test tube does not solve the problems of human **sin** and self-centeredness. Science and human philosophy lack the capacity to deal with spiritual realities.

God's Self-Revelation to Humans

God created humans with a **free will**. We are not puppets or lifeless pawns whose choices are made for us by God. God is all-powerful and controls the universe. But He has given humans choice in one vital matter—whether or not they want to have a relationship with Almighty God.

God knows that a forced relationship involves no exchange of love. The apostle John captured this personal relationship beautifully. "And so we know and rely on the love God has for us. God is love. Whoever lives in love lives in God, and God in him" (1 John 4:16).

In spite of God's generosity in giving humans free will, self-centered people have misinterpreted this gift. Aware that they can make decisions and choose between alternatives every day, they wrongly conclude there is no higher power than themselves, no one to whom they must answer for their conduct.

God, a spirit Being, has revealed himself (1) through the historical events recorded in the Old and New Testaments, (2) through the recorded miracles in the life of Jesus, and (3) through the wise moral teachings of Scripture that lead to fulfilled lives when obeyed. We may never convince atheists that there is a God, but the eyes of faith can see evidence of God all around them and within their innermost being. The Bible speaks eloquently of the presence of God in human history, but it never once attempts to prove God exists. "In the beginning God . . ."

(Genesis 1:1). That is the extent of the proof. But the reality for the Christian is the daily walk with a God who loves and cares.

Jesus, the Divine Son of God

2.1.2
OBJECTIVE
*Point out why it is
necessary to believe Jesus
is the Son of God.*

The biblical account of salvation is easy to understand if the reader believes that Jesus is the divine Son of God who willingly came to earth to die as a sacrifice that our sins might be forgiven. If Jesus were only a man, His death would have no more significance than that of any other man. But the death of a virgin-born, God-in-flesh Savior makes a difference.

3   Why did the Father allow His Son to be disgraced and brutally killed?

Allowing His Son to be disgraced and killed was the central part of God's plan to redeem humankind. In doing what Jesus did for our salvation, He became the example for all those for whom He died. "Your attitude should be the same as that of Christ Jesus: Who, being in very nature God, did not consider equality with God something to be grasped, but made himself nothing, taking the very nature of a servant, being made in human likeness. And being found in appearance as a man, he humbled himself and became obedient to death—even death on a cross!" (Philippians 2:5–8). There was total agreement among the Trinity. The three members of the Godhead were agreed on redeeming sinful humans, no matter what the cost.

God's Created World

Though there are on earth many beauty spots we love to see—a beautiful sunset, a rainbow during a rainstorm, or mountains or lakes in the distance—that beauty is nothing like the beauty of God's creation. We can only imagine the glory of God's creative handiwork. Out of darkness, out of nothing, God created through the Word of His Son a dazzling, beautiful world. The light created by the first act of power provided a perfect promise of what was to follow. Another "Let there be" rolled the moisture-rich heavens apart from the water below. The third act of creation formed dry land where humans could live. Plants and all forms of vegetation brought great beauty to the bare earth. There were yet no weeds to spoil the beauty.

Then God moved back through His beautiful but empty spaces and filled them with great variety. In the heavens He placed the sun, the moon, and the stars. All kinds of flying birds filled the skies, and fish filled the seas. In His crowning acts He created animals and formed and breathed life into the first man. Can you see in your mind's eye the brightness and shine of that perfect creation—still untouched by the stain of sin?

Some people today teach that the world evolved from a chance beginning, over millions of years, without any divine involvement. This belief is called **atheistic evolution**. But the theory denies the existence of God, making the story of salvation difficult for them to understand or believe. If God did not begin it all, humans have no escape from their sinful and lost condition.

Yet many have preferred the fiction of atheistic evolution to the fact of God's creative acts. Rebellious humans search for explanations apart from God at work. But by refusing to admit God exists, they close the door of salvation. Thus, they lose their only opportunity to escape their sinful natures, both in this life and in life beyond the grave. God is! And He made everything.

2.1.3
OBJECTIVE
*Explain how God's plan
of salvation guards and
regains His creation.*

Guarding His Creation

Paul wrote to the Roman Christians, "We know that the whole creation has been groaning as in the pains of childbirth right up to the present time" (Romans 8:22). But the redemption of creation, including our salvation, has now been paid in full. We now just wait until God announces that time is no more. He then binds Satan permanently and restores creation and humankind as He first created them. Even between the time of Adam's fall and the sacrifice of the last Adam Christ (1 Corinthians 15:45), God was guarding His creation and looking forward to the fulfillment of the salvation plan. We have been redeemed! Spiritual death no longer prevails. Physical death is just a breath away from meeting our loving Savior.

LESSON 2.2

The Fall of Adam and Eve

Terrorists kill women and children without any sense of right and wrong. In fact, when they cruelly kill innocents, they claim they are fulfilling a call to take over the world for their political or religious convictions. The words of Jesus to His disciples seem to apply to what is happening today.

You will hear of wars and rumors of wars, but see to it that you are not alarmed. Such things must happen, but the end is still to come. Nation will rise against nation, and kingdom against kingdom. There will be famines and earthquakes in various places. All these are the beginning of birth pains. Then you will be handed over to be persecuted and put to death, and you will be hated by all nations because of me. At that time many will turn away from the faith and will betray and hate each other, and many false prophets will appear and deceive many people. Because of the increase of wickedness, the love of most will grow cold, but he who stands firm to the end will be saved. (Matthew 24:6–13)

4   How did the world come to be in this mess?

Can anybody help us make things better? Unfortunately, Jesus' prediction of the end times does not give much hope. He promises only "the increase of wickedness" as we approach the end of time. But there is a reason to face the future without fear: "He who stands firm to the end will be saved." Standing firm does not mean fighting back, though nations do have to respond to aggression. But Christians stand firm as they confess Christ as Savior and trust their eternal lives to His care.

2.2.1
OBJECTIVE
*Indicate why it is
important to believe Adam
and Eve actually existed.*

Adam and Eve: Real People

Some would say the story of Adam and Eve is a myth. But the reality of an Adam and an Eve, as two distinct persons, is vital to an understanding of God's plan of salvation. Paul made the point very clear: "For since death came through a man, the resurrection of the dead comes also through a man. For as in Adam all die, so in Christ all will be made alive" (1 Corinthians 15:21–22). Jeremiah stated that every person has a leaning toward sin: "The heart is deceitful above all things and beyond cure" (Jeremiah 17:9).

All humans are born under this spiritual and moral handicap because Adam, the father of the race, sinned and brought the penalty into our basic nature. This is what we call "original sin." Original sin, with its universal effect on all descendants, cannot be explained by the theory of evolution. All races and every person in each race are born with a tendency toward sin.

5   Why did God not immediately restore Adam and all of his descendants?

If God would have immediately restored Adam and all of his descendents, we would never have known Jesus as our Savior, who came to earth and died so we can all have fellowship with Him. Also, the idea that humans have free will would still have been the test for each person who ever lived. God knew what He was doing, and His plan was best.

Made in His Image

2.2.2
OBJECTIVE

Define what it means to be "made in the image of God."

God made humankind so we might bring glory to Him (Ephesians 1:12). He made His crowning creation perfect in body, soul, and spirit. Created by God, Adam was a son of God. Unlike the animal creation, Adam and Eve possessed reason and moral awareness. They knew right from wrong. The divine likeness in human form was a rich treasure in a temple of clay. But the perfect work was soon marred by the blot of sin.

We have no problem understanding that Adam and Eve were created in the image of God (Genesis 1:26–27). The phrase "in our likeness" helps explain the meaning of "in our image." But what about the descendents of Adam and Eve, and what about those born today into a world so affected by sin? The same words are used in describing the birth of Adam's son Seth, although the likeness was related to Adam's image (Genesis 5:3). The likeness could be taken to mean the fallen nature of Adam, but instead it refers to something passed down from Adam's creation before the first sin. That meaning is seen in the statement on capital punishment found in Genesis 9:6: "Whoever sheds the blood of man, by man shall his blood be shed; for in the image of God has God made man."

6   What then is the likeness to God that all humans have?

Some say our likeness to God lies in our superior intellect. Others say humans, like God, serve as managers of created nature (Genesis 1:26–28; Psalm 8:5–8). Still others take the words to mean that humans can have fellowship with God and with one another. The *Evangelical Dictionary of Biblical Theology* puts these three views together as the full meaning of "in the image of God." "Humans are like God in that they are uniquely gifted intellectually (and in many other ways) so that they may relate to God and to each other as they live as stewards of the world God has given them to manage" (Turner 1996, 366). Of course, since God does not have a body, the likeness is not physical.

7   What if Adam and Eve had never sinned?

As redeemed believers we strive to be like Jesus, who represented in human form what God is like. Paul described Christ as "the image of God" (2 Corinthians 4:4). The goal of every Christian should be to be like Jesus. The fruit of the Spirit—love, joy, peace, patience, kindness, goodness, faith, meekness, and self-control—are certainly godlike attributes we should exhibit.

Origin of the Fall of Adam and Eve

2.2.3
OBJECTIVE

Explain Satan's role in Adam and Eve's sin.

We can only imagine what life would be like today if sin had never entered our world. Yet we must live with the reality. Satan's rebellion was an event of eternal significance, and it occurred before Adam and Eve's temptation. Satan became the tempter. After Adam disobeyed, he blamed Eve. Eve blamed the serpent. The serpent might have blamed Satan for using it to tempt Eve.

The Bible is silent on many hard questions regarding the fall of Satan and the fall of humanity. But there is no doubt about the reality of sin. We can only tell the story of Satan's fall and consider briefly how it might have begun.

8   Who or what tempted Satan while he was still in heaven?

All scholars do not agree on the meaning of Ezekiel 28 and Isaiah 14. However, evangelicals commonly agree that the passages have two applications: (1) the historical kings of Tyre and Babylon, and (2) the pride and fall of Lucifer

(Satan). Satan is not mentioned by name in Ezekiel 28, but the description moves at times beyond any possible human application: "perfect in beauty" (Ezekiel 28:12); "You were in Eden" (v. 13); "You were anointed as a guardian cherub" (v. 14); and "You were blameless in your ways from the day you were created till wickedness was found in you" (v. 15). These without doubt look beyond any human figure.

Isaiah 14:12–14 describes Lucifer. Sin actually began with pride, and that led to rebellion. Lucifer said, "I will make myself like the Most High" (v. 14). From that rebellious beginning grew discord and open warfare against Almighty God. Other angels joined the rebellion and became the wicked spirits who assist Satan in his evil opposition to God's kingdom of righteousness.

Satan was no match for God. He failed in his attempt to take control of heaven. But his defiance found a new setting to carry on the conflict. The perfect creation that God had so recently completed became the site where Satan attempted to do what he had not been able to do in heaven.

9   Was God not able to defeat Satan here on earth as He had banished him from heaven?

God could have destroyed Satan, taking from him the possibility of tempting and afflicting Adam and Eve. God never loses control of events, either in human history or in the spirit world. Just as He makes the wrath or evil of humans to praise His name (Psalm 76:10, KJV, NKJV), so God turned the rebellion of Satan to His own purpose: to prove the voluntary love and obedience of His children. Having fallen from his perfect state as an angel in heaven, Satan became an adversary and deceiver, but God has never relinquished His own authority and power—anywhere!

Accepting Responsibility

Genesis 3 recounts the first sin of Adam and Eve. The thing we must remember is that Adam and Eve were created with all they needed to remain free from sin. They knew right from wrong and possessed adequate reason and understanding. God's command not to eat of the Tree of Knowledge of Good and Evil (Genesis 2:9) was not beyond their comprehension. Adam and Eve were given dominion over the earth; their fall was not caused by fear or weakness. Just as Satan was accountable for his pride and disobedience, so Adam and Eve had to answer for their rebellion.

Every act in our lives has some consequence. But no act has had the consequence of this first human disobedience. Sin ruined everything. All of natural creation felt the effect of the curse. Labor, sorrow, sickness, and death came to distress the human race.

The divine image in human beings was marred even though it was not lost entirely. All descendents of Adam and Eve have been born as sinners and have been guilty of committing actual sin. "For all have sinned and fall short of the glory of God" (Romans 3:23). Friendly relationships that God desired to exist between all His children were shattered by inner discord and outward conflict. Removing these spiritual and moral defects is what the plan of salvation is all about. Thank God, He had a plan!

LESSON 2.3

The Power and Ugliness of Sin

Sin is ugly. Satan disguises it to make it appear more attractive. When we see it as it really is, as God sees it, it is repulsive and vile. Solomon knew this:

"There is a way that seems right to a man, but in the end it leads to death" (Proverbs 16:25).

The Bible does not give a single definition of sin, but has several words with slightly different perspectives that help us understand sin (Kuizenga 1956, 2798–2802). In the Hebrew OT, there are words that mean "rebellion," "transgression," "perversion," "evil disposition," and "impiety." The Greek NT has words meaning "missing the mark," "transgression," "unrighteousness," "violation of law," "depravity," and "desire for what is forbidden, or lust."

10 What is sin? Do humans define it, or does God's Word define it for us?

With this long list some might wrongly choose one of the meanings as defining sin. We frequently hear that sin means, "missing the mark." That seems to please some because it does not sound as harsh as some of the other definitions. But instead of choosing one of the meanings, we should consider all of the meanings to be essential to a full understanding of sin. In this lesson, we will look at the true nature of sin.

2.3.1
OBJECTIVE
Describe various characteristics of sin as it relates to human behavior.

More Than Wrong-doing

Sin is voluntary; we can never say, "The devil made me do it." Breaking God's moral law is sin, but wrong attitudes and wrong desires are also sin. The acts of adultery and murder are sins, but so are the feelings that prompt the actions. Jesus said, "'You have heard that it was said, 'Do not commit adultery.' But I tell you that anyone who looks at a woman lustfully has already committed adultery with her in his heart'" (Matthew 5:27–28). John writes, "Anyone who hates his brother is a murderer, and you know that no murderer has eternal life in him" (1 John 3:15). There is a difference between temptation and sin, but failing to deal with the temptation immediately with the help of the Holy Spirit may lead to a sinful act.

Careless Christians have a false sense of safety when they avoid the physical act but still allow lust or hate to dwell in their hearts. Nor can we justify hate by calling it something else. Our relationships and feelings toward others, even those who mistreat or hurt us, should be Christ-like. The unity of the body of Christ is vital. When sinners mistreat us, we should follow the example of Christ: "But if you suffer for doing good and you endure it, this is commendable before God. To this you were called, because Christ suffered for you, leaving you an example, that you should follow in his steps. 'He committed no sin, and no deceit was found in his mouth.' When they hurled their insults at him, he did not retaliate; when he suffered, he made no threats. Instead, he entrusted himself to him who judges justly" (1 Peter 2:20–23). To our carnal hearts, that sounds unreasonable. We have our rights. But when we see our actions and attitudes as God sees them, we will not behave like the evil one who still opposes God.

Unbelief and disobedience are sins. But so is an attitude of indifference and lack of concern about spiritual matters. God's true children seek to answer His call to holiness and to serve Him wholeheartedly. Our thoughts and our words are as important as our commitment not to break any of the Ten Commandments.

2.3.2
OBJECTIVE
Describe the similarity between the first sin and sin today.

From Temptation to Sin

Some have suggested that Adam and Eve did not clearly understand God's command and the consequences of their disobedience. Satan through the serpent planted doubt about God's prohibition in Eve's mind. What could possibly be wrong with eating desirable fruit and gaining wisdom? Where was the lie in Satan's temptation? There was no actual poison in the fruit, and Eve did not immediately die when she ate the fruit. In one sense, Satan told no lies; he just did not tell all that was involved in disobeying God. Both Adam and Eve, after their disobedience, knew they had done wrong rather than right. Satan was right in saying that God knew the difference, but he distorted the truth in saying that they would be like God. In one sense they gained a godlike knowledge, yet their innocent God-given nature was gone forever. And the death punishment, though not immediate, was set in motion with their sin. But God's love did not leave them.

All living humans face temptation in the same way today. What can possibly be wrong with involvement in some of the actions the Bible tells us to avoid? Lying that produces a good end and stealing from someone who has so much more than he or she really needs—human reason tells us that good can come from a little compromise once in a while. But such an attitude toward the commands of God, as laid down in Holy Scripture, destroys the very core of our relationship with God. Obeying His instructions for living is far safer than letting the mind of every person rationalize what is right and what is wrong. The conflicts of the world and of individuals result from every person doing what is right in his or her own eyes. The Bible records a time in the history of Israel when God's people neglected God's commandments: "In those days Israel had no king; everyone did as he saw fit" (Judges 17:6, 21:25). Lawlessness and disrespect for authority go hand in hand. Societies around the world seem headed in an anti-authority direction.

The real nature of Adam and Eve's sin was deeper than just eating the fruit and disobeying a command of God. Instead, the temptation was directed at their belief and trust in God. Adam and Eve knew that God existed.

They had no doubt communed with Him as He walked with them in the Garden of Eden. But this time, in the cool of the day right after their disobedience, they hid from God. Their eating of the fruit did not frustrate God, but their doubts about His instructions and their failure to trust Him as their greatest Companion and Friend did disappoint Him. Their punishment was not handed down out of revenge, but out of divine justice and love that demands a proper response. God's love did not leave them even after their sinful act. Nor has His love for the whole world changed one bit. He had already set in motion the means of restoring fellowship with the entire human race.

Sin: Failure To Do Good

2.3.3
OBJECTIVE
Point out how God can hate sin but still love the sinner.

James writes, "Anyone, then, who knows the good he ought to do and doesn't do it, sins" (James 4:17). These are called the "sins of omission." The Bible is full of positive things that our faith should lead us to do. James gives examples of the good deeds that demonstrate our faith: "Religion that God our Father accepts as pure and faultless is this: to look after orphans and widows in their distress and to keep oneself from being polluted by the world" (James 1:27). Fulfilling the Great Commission or reaching the lost for Christ is another of the many "goods" a true believer should demonstrate. So putting together all the biblical teaching on sin, we come to a definition of sin: Sin is willful or voluntary rebellion against God's holy law. It can be found in what we are (mind, heart, and attitudes), what we do (sinful acts), and what we fail to do (falling short in doing right).

Limits to Satan's Freedom

At times it seems like Satan has the upper hand in our world. He seems so successful in making sin attractive, in leading proud humans to think more highly of themselves than they should, and in deceiving more and more people into thinking there is no God who requires accountability. Satan does not even care if people do not believe in his existence, as along as he succeeds in discrediting the idea of a Creator God.

The Christian is provided with a way of victory over Satan's deceit. Jesus told Peter, "Simon, Simon, Satan has asked to sift you as wheat. But I have prayed for you, Simon, that your faith may not fail" (Luke 22:31–32; see also James 4:7, 2 Corinthians 2:10, 11, and Ephesians 6:11). With our trust placed in our loving Savior, we need not fear Satan. Though Satan is more powerful than any human, he is not **omnipotent** like God. Though he has a keen, devious intellect, Satan is not **omniscient**, as God is. Satan, also, is not **omnipresent**. He must send out his assisting demons, since he cannot, like God, be everywhere at the same time. Satan's power is limited. Yet when men and women refuse to believe that God exists, their minds and hearts are fertile ground for Satan to sow his evil seed. As noted before, God allows Satan a limited freedom to work his deceit so each person has a choice to make: to serve God or self and Satan. God is in control even when Satan seems to be so active.

God Hates Sin But Loves the Sinner

Since God is holy, He must look on sin with wrath and judgment. "The wrath of God is being revealed from heaven against all the godlessness and wickedness of men who suppress the truth by their wickedness" (Romans 1:18). And again, "The present heavens and earth are reserved for fire, being kept for the day of judgment and destruction of ungodly men" (2 Peter 3:7). But God still loves the sinner and seeks to separate every sinner from the sin that brings judgment. Though sin is a blight and curse on our world, God is still on the throne. He reigns in the heavens, our world, and the universe. Glory to His holy name!

T Test Yourself

Circle the letter of the *best* answer.

1. When we say God is omnipotent, we are saying He is
a) all-knowing.
b) all-powerful.
c) everywhere present.

2. Because God is spirit rather than human, evidence of His existence comes through
a) mental telepathy.
b) philosophy.
c) faith.

3. When we say humans are created with a free will, we mean
a) we have a choice in our eternal destiny.
b) humans can do anything they wish to do.
c) we are not subject to the will of a sovereign God.

4. In addition to the magnificent creation around us, God has clearly revealed himself through
a) a living human voice in every generation.
b) humanly inspired books and films describing "The Passion of Christ."
c) the historical events and recorded teachings of the Bible.

5. Salvation requires that a person believe
a) the Bible is the greatest book ever written.
b) the teachings of Jesus surpass the best of human philosophy.
c) Jesus is the divine Son of God.

6. Atheistic evolution teaches that
a) God does not actually exist.
b) all living creatures came from earlier life forms, which were created by God.
c) a theistic view of life has evolved from a prehistoric search for answers.

7. Our understanding of the origin of sin is based on the fact that
a) Adam and Eve were real people who committed the first human sin.
b) the Bible defines original sin at the end of the story of Adam and Eve.
c) Adam and Eve did not originate the human tendency to sin.

8. God turned the rebellion of Satan to His purpose by using it to
a) identify all enemies of God's righteous Kingdom.
b) condemn all Satan's followers to eternal punishment.
c) prove the love and obedience of God's children.

9. Sin can be defined as
a) the result of honest mistakes.
b) wrong attitudes and wrong actions.
c) the temptation that Satan brings against a person.

10. Satan's temptation of Adam and Eve
a) spoke true facts but did not tell all of God's truth.
b) was one lie after another.
c) was not foreseen by God.

Responses to Interactive Questions
Chapter 2

Some of these responses may include information that is supplemental to the IST. These questions are intended to produce reflective thinking beyond the course content and your responses may vary from these examples.

1   Why did God who inspired the Bible not give us a reasoned proof of His existence?

The Bible makes a direct statement about linking the realities of the physical and spiritual worlds. "And without faith it is impossible to please God, because anyone who comes to him must believe that he exists and that he rewards those who earnestly seek him" (Hebrews 11:6). God desires that his human creatures relate to Him in faith. God could have overwhelmed us with proof of His existence. Such proof would eliminate faith, thus eliminating what God has established as a crucial ingredient in responding to Him.

2   Why would the supreme Creator of our world give us a choice in responding to His love?

Real and true love is not forced. A loving relationship, which is His desire, is not mechanical or automatic. We are unique individuals that develop and mature—or are supposed to.

3   Why did the Father allow His Son to be disgraced and brutally killed?

Allowing His Son to be disgraced and killed was the central part of God's plan to redeem humankind. In doing what Jesus did for our salvation, He became both the atoning sacrifice and the example for all those for whom He died.

4   How did the world come to be in this mess?

Student's answer will vary, but could include a discussion of Jesus' prediction that wickedness will increase. It is the world's own wickedness that created the mess and continues to make it worse.

5   Why did God not immediately restore Adam and all of his descendants?

If God would have immediately restored Adam and all of his descendents, we would never have known Jesus as our Savior who came to earth and died so we can all have fellowship with Him. And the idea that humans have a free will would still have been the test for each person who ever lived. God knew what He was doing, and His plan was best.

6   What, then, is the likeness to God that all humans have?

Humans are like God in that they are uniquely gifted intellectually (and in many other ways) so that they may relate to God and to each other as they live as stewards of the world God has given them to manage.

7   What if Adam and Eve had never sinned?

We can only imagine what life would be like today if sin had never entered our world. Yet we must live with the reality. Still, there also is the reality of a restored future, "But in keeping with his promise we are looking forward to a new heaven and a new earth, the home of righteousness" (2 Peter 3:13).

8   Who or what tempted Satan while he was still in heaven?

The Bible is silent on this. But there is no doubt about the reality of sin. We can only tell the story of Satan's fall as we infer it from the Scriptures and consider briefly how it might have begun.

9   Was God not able to defeat Satan here on earth as He had banished him from heaven?

God has already appointed Satan's end. There is a time and a purpose, consider Revelation 20:1–3 and 7–10 which show that it is Satan that is not able to defeat God.

10 What is sin? Do humans define it? Or does God's Word define it for us?

The Bible does not give a single definition of sin, but there are several words with slightly different perspectives that help us understand sin. We frequently hear that sin means "missing the mark." That seems to please some because it does not sound as harsh as some of the other definitions. But instead of choosing one of the meanings, we should consider all of the meanings to be essential to a full understanding of sin. Breaking God's moral law is sin, but wrong attitudes and wrong desires are also sin.

CHAPTER 3

Jesus Christ: God's Gift for Our Salvation

An understanding of Jesus Christ is the foundational doctrine of the Christian faith. People who believe that Jesus Christ is the divine Son of God are called *Christians*. *Christianity* as a world religion includes all churches that declare Jesus Christ as the way of salvation. Unfortunately, the terms *Christian* and *Christianity* have been shamefully misused. The United States and many other countries are frequently called Christian nations. But true Christians living in those countries know sadly that what may have been true in past years is very different today. Christianity has been losing ground as a religion or belief that guides the leaders and citizens of the countries. Secularism, or the rejection of religion, turns its back on the Christian foundations and beginnings of countries. Christianity is often singled out for greater opposition than other religions because of the large numbers who call themselves Christians. True, committed Christians are in short supply. We are living in end-time days when "Because of the increase of wickedness, the love of most will grow cold" (Matthew 24:12).

Your study of this course on the four foundational doctrines is not just one of many other things you might be doing. God is calling you to be one soldier in an army that is growing daily. As society turns its back on Jesus Christ, God does not give up on those who are rejecting Him. He still loves all sinners. And you, as a true Christian, are called to take the message of salvation to all who will listen. That is the Great Commission given by Christ to His church.

Lesson 3.1   God's Plan for Restoring Fellowship with Fallen Humans

Objectives
3.1.1   State the basis for God's plan to restore fellowship with disobedient sinners.
3.1.2   Describe the importance of Old Testament sacrifices in God's salvation plan.

Lesson 3.2   Jesus: The Sacrifice that Provides Our Salvation

Objectives
3.2.1   Identify the Old Testament prophecies that look forward to Jesus.
3.2.2   Describe the nature of Jesus, and explain why He was the perfect sacrifice.

Lesson 3.3   Our Salvation and Christ's Death, Resurrection, and Ascension

Objectives
3.3.1   Explain how salvation is the basic doctrine of the four cardinal doctrines.
3.3.2   Describe why Christ's resurrection is so important.
3.3.3   List the evidences that prove Christ rose from the grave.
3.3.4   Describe how sinners seek to redefine sin, but still need God's salvation.

Lesson 3.4   Salvation Means Regeneration, Justification, and Repentance

Objectives
3.4.1   Describe regeneration as a contrast between life before and after salvation.
3.4.2   Explain justification as it relates to God's nature.

Lesson 3.5 **Sanctification, Assurance, Reconciliation, and Redemption**

Objectives

3.5.1 Explain the nature of sanctification.

3.5.2 Point out how reconciliation turns God's enemies into His children.

1 Did God have a plan and purpose in speaking the world into existence?

God's Plan for Restoring Fellowship with Fallen Humans

Some have suggested that in the endless eternity of God, before time began, God became lonely. So He created some things He could enjoy and some human beings He could love. But loneliness is not, and never has been, one of the characteristics of God. Loneliness is not a plan.

The creation account in Genesis does not even suggest a reason for God's creative acts. Nor does He have to explain or give answers to questions we may have. Yet we can look at a characteristic of God that suggests why He created the world, why He created Adam and Eve, and why He sent Jesus to die for our sins. First John 4:16 states, "And so we know and rely on the love God has for us. God is love. Whoever lives in love lives in God, and God in him." Timothy George expresses it this way: "Within the being of God himself there is a mysterious living love, a dynamic reciprocity of surrender and affirmation, of giving and receiving, among the Father, the Son, and the Holy Spirit. The Maker of heaven and earth is at once the Triune God of holiness and love" (George 2000, 224).

God's boundless, unselfish love cannot be understood by humans who usually see only self-centered love, love that gives so it may receive something. God did not create humans because He needs their love. He desires a love relationship, but He gives far more love than we could ever return to Him. "God so loved the world that he gave his one and only Son" (John 3:16). We can never repay that love, not even by giving our lives for Him. Yet God places in the heart of each one who accepts His Son as Savior the desire to love Him as much as we humanly can. God created humans as beings on whom He can shower His unlimited love, not to receive in return their love for His **self-gratification**. The Bible calls on believers to love God. But that command is for our own good, not to fill a void in God's personality.

A Plan of Restoration

3.1.1
OBJECTIVE
State the basis for God's plan to restore fellowship with disobedient sinners.

The tragic story of sin's entry into God's perfect creation is heartbreaking. First there was the beauty of the original creation. But Satan pushed that beautiful lamp of God's perfect creation off the table and onto the floor, where it was smashed into thousands of pieces.

Some people think of the plan of salvation as God's bottle or tube of glue, by which He sweeps up the shattered fragments and patiently and methodically glues the many broken pieces together. But a rebuilt lamp is never as good as the original.

God does more than restore broken lives to their original condition. He is and has always been in control of His creation. He is not a frustrated adult running around after Satan picking up the damaged pieces and trying to make the best of a bad situation. No, He forces the wrath of Satan, like the wrath of humans, to bring praise to His name (cf. Psalm 76:10). The new creation fashioned by His plan of restoration is better than the original was in its perfect state. The new creature (2 Corinthians 5:17, KJV) has been tested and declared a child of God—redeemed and filled with the grace and love of Christ himself. How much more He is pleased by our worship, and how much more we are blessed by our Savior, after we have been delivered from the bondage of sin.

A poet in the fourteenth century became so captivated by the excitement of his restored relationship with God that he wrote a poem called "Oh Happy Sin" (Medieval theologians, writing in Latin, called it "*O felix culpa*"). The theme of the poem was that we would never have known Jesus as our Savior and close Friend if Adam and Eve had not sinned. No sin should ever be called happy or good, but the feelings of the poet should remind us that God has never been outdone by Satan. What He has made available to us, both in this life and the next, as a result of Jesus' sacrificial death, is a thrilling and magnificent blessing.

God and Sinner Active in Personal Salvation

God does not force His salvation on anyone. He simply offers it to everyone. Because of this truth, some people wrongly conclude that anyone who does accept God's salvation has actually done something to save him- or herself. Others go to the other extreme, saying that God does it all and we have no choice. If God wants to save a person, he or she will be saved whether or not the person wants to be saved. Neither of these extreme positions is correct. Those who believe individuals can accept or reject God's free offer of salvation are called **Arminians**. Those who deny that people have any free will or choice in the matter are called **Calvinists**.

Many verses in the Bible stress the **security of the believer**. The words of Jesus in John 10:28–29 are often noted: "I give them eternal life, and they shall never perish; no one can snatch them out of my hand. My Father, who has given them to me, is greater than all; no one can snatch them out of my Father's hand." Another favorite passage of Calvinists is Romans 8:38–39—"For I am convinced that neither death nor life, neither angels nor demons, neither the present nor the future, nor any powers, neither height nor depth, nor anything else in all creation, will be able to separate us from the love of God that is in Christ Jesus our Lord." In both instances there is no mention of a believer deliberately turning away from God, removing him- or herself from God's hand. We believe in the security of the believer with that one exception. Hebrews 6:4–6 defines **apostasy** as turning away from God after knowing Him personally. That does not mean, however, that one immediately loses salvation when a sin is committed. But refusing to ask God's forgiveness as soon as one is aware of the sin may put one on the road to possible apostasy.

> It is impossible for those who have once been enlightened, who have tasted the heavenly gift, who have shared in the Holy Spirit, who have tasted the goodness of the Word of God and the powers of the coming age, if they fall away, to be brought back to repentance, because to their loss they are crucifying the Son of God all over again and subjecting Him to public disgrace. Hebrews 6:4–6

In support of the Arminian view, there are many Scriptures, in addition to Hebrews 6:4–6, warning God's people against carelessness and deliberate sin after salvation. Typical verses include: "My brothers, if one of you should wander from the truth and someone should bring him back, remember this:

Whoever turns a sinner from the error of his way will save him from death and cover over a multitude of sins" (James 5:19–20). Also, the writer of Hebrews instructs, "See to it, brothers, that none of you has a sinful, unbelieving heart that turns away from the living God. But encourage one another daily, as long as it is called Today, so that none of you may be hardened by sin's deceitfulness" (Hebrews 3:12–13).

2   Why are there so many verses in support of both the Arminian and Calvinistic positions?

Throughout Scripture the Christian is warned of failing to remain in Christ (John 15:6), being taken captive by the devil (2 Timothy 2:24–26), being entangled with and overcome by the world (2 Peter 2:20–21), and forsaking his or her first love (Revelation 2:4–5).

We cannot explain away the verses that support the interpretation that is different from our own. It may be that God knew there would be Christians who needed at various times one emphasis or the other. For those who are concerned that they have committed a sin and if Jesus were to come at that moment, they would miss the Rapture, the assurance verses are needed. For those who become careless in their confidence that they cannot lose their salvation, there are verses of caution and warning. The altar of **repentance** is always a good place to go, but one does not lose salvation at every failure or violation of God's Word. He is faithful to forgive and cleanse again from all unrighteousness (1 John 1:8–9). God's love always finds a way.

A Sacrifice, Essential to God's Plan of Salvation

3.1.2
OBJECTIVE

Describe the importance of Old Testament sacrifices in God's salvation plan.

3   Why did the plan of restoration include a sacrifice?

We cannot fully understand it, but God's Word declares that a sacrifice was essential to restoration. "Without the shedding of blood there is no forgiveness" (Hebrews 9:22). The Old Testament says the same thing. "For the life of a creature is in the blood, . . . it is the blood that makes atonement for one's life" (Leviticus 17:11). The Jews had for centuries slaughtered and sacrificed animals as commanded by the Law. But Jesus, as the divine Son of God, was the perfect Sacrifice offered "once for all" (Hebrews 10:10).

LESSON 3.2

Jesus: the Sacrifice that Provides Our Salvation

Begin this lesson by imagining that you are having a face-to-face meeting with Jesus, like Zacchaeus had, as recorded in Luke 19. Jesus has invited himself to your home and is having a meal with you, just the two of you. What feelings are going through your mind, causing your heart to beat faster? You know that Jesus knows everything about you, without your telling Him anything. He even knows what you did yesterday, and He knows what you are thinking right now. Would you be filled with anxiety or dread? Or would you be filled with joy? Some people would be very uncomfortable in Jesus' presence, but hopefully not you. What do you think the immoral Samaritan woman (John 4) felt when she met Jesus face-to-face at the well and He told her all about her unpleasant past? The conversation she had with Jesus shows He was a friend of sinners. He made her feel comfortable in His presence. No matter what our past may be, Jesus comes alongside, making us feel the warmth of His presence. He is right beside you as you study this lesson. Take a moment to read John 4:5–30.

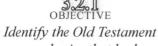
OBJECTIVE

Identify the Old Testament prophecies that look forward to Jesus.

Old Testament Prophecies About a Coming Savior/Messiah

The most striking confirmations that Jesus was divinely sent by God to be the Sacrifice for our salvation are the many Old Testament prophecies looking forward to the life, death, and purpose of His earthly ministry.

Birth of Jesus Micah (ca. 700 BC)	"But you, Bethlehem Ephrathah, though you are small among the clans of Judah, out of you will come for me one who will be ruler over Israel, whose origins are from of old, from ancient times . . . He will stand and shepherd his flock in the strength of the Lord, in the majesty of the name of the Lord his God. And they will live securely, for then his greatness will reach to the ends of the earth. And he will be their peace" (Micah 5:2, 4, 5).
Triumphal Entry Zechariah (ca. 500 BC)	"Rejoice greatly, O Daughter of Zion! Shout, Daughter of Jerusalem! See, your king comes to you, righteous and having salvation, gentle and riding on a donkey, on a colt, the foal of a donkey" (Zechariah 9:9).
Betrayal of Jesus Zechariah (ca. 500 BC)	"I told them, 'If you think it best, give me my pay; but if not, keep it.' So they paid me thirty pieces of silver. And the Lord said to me, 'Throw it to the potter'—the handsome price at which they priced me! So I took the thirty pieces of silver and threw them into the house of the Lord to the potter" (Zechariah 11:12-13).
Death of Jesus Zechariah (ca. 500 BC)	"And I will pour out on the house of David and the inhabitants of Jerusalem a spirit of grace and supplication. They will look on me, the one they have pierced, and they will mourn for him as one mourns for an only child, and grieve bitterly for him as one grieves for a firstborn son" (Zechariah 12:10).
Passion of Christ Psalm (ca. 1000 BC)	"I am poured out like water, and all my bones are out of joint. My heart has turned to wax; it has melted away within me. My strength is dried up like a potsherd, and my tongue sticks to the roof of my mouth; you lay me in the dust of death. Dogs have surrounded me; a band of evil men has encircled me, they have pierced my hands and my feet. I can count all my bones; people stare and gloat over me. They divide my garments among them and cast lots for my clothing" (Psalm 22:14-18).
Christ's Suffering and Ministry Isaiah (ca. 700 BC)	"Surely he took up our infirmities and carried our sorrows, yet we considered him stricken by God, smitten by him, and afflicted. But he was pierced for our transgressions, he was crushed for our iniquities; the punishment that brought us peace was upon him, and by his wounds we are healed. We all, like sheep, have gone astray, each of us has turned to his own way; and the Lord has laid on him the iniquity of us all. He was oppressed and afflicted, yet he did not open his mouth; he was led like a lamb to the slaughter, and as a sheep before her shearers is silent, so he did not open his mouth . . . He was assigned a grave with the wicked, and with the rich in his death, though he had done no violence, nor was any deceit in his mouth . . . After the suffering of his soul, he will see the light of life and be satisfied; by his knowledge my righteous servant will justify many, and he will bear their iniquities. Therefore I will give him a portion among the great, and he will divide the spoils with the strong, because he poured out his life unto death, and was numbered with the transgressors. For he bore the sin of many, and made intercession for the transgressors" (Isaiah 53:4-7, 9, 11-12).

Such fulfilled prophecies and insights into the future, at various times some five hundred to one thousand years before the events actually happened, confirm the divinity of Jesus as God coming down to our world to lift us eventually to the heavenlies of His abode.

3.2.2
OBJECTIVE
Describe the nature of Jesus, and explain why He was the perfect sacrifice.

4 Can you describe Jesus Christ, the Sacrifice for the sin of all humankind?

Jesus, a Unique Combination of Human and Divine Natures

Jesus is the one and only Son of God (John 3:16). At the same time He was also the Son of Man by virtue of being born into this world through the Virgin Mary. The first word of His name, *Jesus,* means Savior (Matthew 1:21). The word *Christ* means "the Anointed One" or "the Messiah." He was both human and divine during His years on earth. His Father is our Heavenly Father, God himself. His mother was Mary.

With this parentage, Jesus was fully human and fully divine. This may seem like a paradox, but it simply means that we can identify with Him completely as a human being, knowing that He was just as human as we are, although never sinning (Hebrews 4:15). At the same time, we can look to Him as the all-powerful, miracle-working Person of the divine Godhead, knowing that He is able and desires to use His divine power and authority to make us sons and daughters of God, conformed to His image.

Jesus, the Perfect Sacrifice

Animals were used as sacrifices in the Old Testament. Human sacrifice, including young children, was practiced in many ancient cultures. Yet God went a step further. He sent His one and only Son to die as a sacrifice for our sins. Christianity is the only religion in which the god of that religion became a sacrifice as a means of dealing with sin for the entire human race.

Jesus was the perfect sacrifice in another way. Not only was He part of the Godhead, but He was also sinless. The gods of other religions were often viewed as *super humans*. They had to a greater degree all the bad traits, as well as the good traits, of living men and women. But to have a sinless representative of the God "who does not change like shifting shadows" (James 1:17) is unheard of in the history of the pagan or secular world.

Jesus, More Than a Sacrifice

Many editions of the Bible have the words of Jesus printed in red. What an appropriate color choice! The One who shed His lifeblood for our salvation also teaches us the way of salvation and holy living. He came to earth "to give his life as a ransom for many" (Mark 10:45). The prophet Isaiah spoke of a future time when God's people would hear a voice behind them saying, "This is the way; walk in it" (Isaiah 30:21). Though Jesus did not use those exact words, His teaching spoke that truth. To some He said, "Go now and leave your life of sin" (John 8:11). To others He said, "Love your enemies" (Luke 6:27). We need not quote here the entire Gospels. As the sacrificial Lamb of God, Jesus became our blessed Savior. But He also spoke the words of heaven to sinners and saints alike.

Someone has said that Jesus is God's way of spelling himself out in a language we can understand. If a man wanted to speak to a hive of bees, he would have to speak their language. In our natural world, that is impossible. Yet God knew we could not understand His mind or speech. So He came down as one member of the Trinity, spoke a human language, and shared His love in terms we can understand. Thank God for a Master Teacher who models love and teaches us the way of salvation.

Our Salvation and Christ's Death, Resurrection, and Ascension

Two young men went through law school as close friends. Upon graduating, their lives took strangely different paths. One became a greatly respected judge on a prominent court. But the other, facing some family disappointments, became an alcoholic and wasted his great potential.

Some years later, the unfortunate friend was arrested for a crime, charged, and brought before a judge. As strange as it may seem, the judge was the lawyer friend from university days. When the fact became known, the lawyers in the community wondered what the judge would do with his former colleague. To their surprise, the judge applied the heaviest penalty the law would allow. But the story does not end there. The judge then paid the large fine himself and set his old friend free.

We have all sinned against God and His law. When Abraham pleaded with God to spare Lot and his community from destruction, he asked, "Will not the Judge of all the earth do right?" (Genesis 18:25). Like the judge in the story, God has already done right. His justice demands a penalty, and He has handed down the heaviest penalty He could—a death sentence for every sinner. But then, showing mercy, He stepped down from the Judge's role and took the sinner's place before His empty chair, taking the full penalty upon himself. "God was reconciling the world to himself in Christ" (2 Corinthians 5:19). Notice that it was not *through Christ* but *in Christ*. It was God himself who came to earth to bring us salvation.

Salvation, the Bedrock of Christian Faith

New life begins with salvation. Before salvation, a person is spiritually dead (Ephesians 2:1). There is no Spirit-filled life (Foundational Truth 2) before salvation. Divine healing (Foundational Truth 3) is God's provision for His followers. Finally, there is no glorious future of seeing Jesus face-to-face (Foundational Truth 4) and living with Him throughout eternity without first experiencing God's free offer of salvation. It all begins at the Cross.

Salvation saves us from sin, guilt, bondage, fear, despair, spiritual death, and a meaningless life. It provides peace with God (forgiveness), a redeemed life, personal access to God's presence, supernatural strength in suffering, and opportunity for a Spirit-filled life. All this is available through the sacrificial death and supernatural resurrection of Jesus Christ as our Savior.

Resurrection and Crucifixion

It is true that Christ died for our sins. That is the sacrifice part of our salvation, but without the resurrection, the death of Jesus would have been no different from the horrendous death of some other person claiming to be God's messenger. Or at best, it would have been like an Old Testament sacrifice that had to be repeated regularly. We live "a new life" because we participate in Christ's death *and* resurrection. "We were therefore buried with him through baptism into death in

3.3.1
OBJECTIVE
Explain how salvation is the basic doctrine of the four cardinal doctrines.

5　Of all the doctrines of the Christian faith, why is salvation the most important? Or, why is it the most important of the four foundational doctrines we are studying?

3.3.2
OBJECTIVE
Describe why Christ's resurrection is so important.

order that, just as Christ was raised from the dead through the glory of the Father, we too may live a new life" (Romans 6:4). After Jesus took on the appearance of a man (Philippians 2:8), the presence of deity was proven in His resurrection.

Salvation through the death of Christ is an inward, spiritual miracle. But the outward, physical miracle, the great miracle on which Christianity rests, is the resurrection of Jesus Christ. Once the historical truth of this event is accepted, all the miracles of the biblical record are believable. And the miracle of salvation is authenticated. The entire Christian faith stands or falls on this central miracle of Christ's resurrection. The earthly life of Jesus ended, not with the question mark of death, but with the exclamation point of resurrection!

Evidences of the Resurrection

3.3.3
OBJECTIVE
List the evidences that prove Christ rose from the grave.

Evidences of the resurrection are well established and dependable—except to the skeptic who decides before the evidence has been heard that he or she will not believe. The written sacred record is more reliable than all the other histories that have been written about the event from that day to the present. The tomb was empty. The precautions taken by the Romans to make sure nothing improper was done to the body point clearly to the reality of the resurrection of Jesus. The testimony of the disciples who saw Jesus after His resurrection is powerful evidence. Four contemporaries to the actual resurrection appearances record the event in the Gospels we read today. It all adds up to one conclusion: Up from the grave He arose . . . a victor over sin!

Because of the resurrection, we know that Jesus is all that He claimed to be: the Son of God, our Savior, and our Lord. The death of Christ, coupled with His resurrection, describes the atoning work of God. But one more event, as supernatural as the resurrection, points to another of the foundational doctrines. Just as Christ's entrance into the world was supernatural, so was His departure. Death would have been natural. Just disappearing would have invited much speculation. But many saw Him as He ascended into heaven where He is now seated at the right hand of the Father (Romans 8:34). As Jesus was leaving the disciples, two men dressed in white, most likely angels, stood beside the disciples, telling them this was not a final goodbye. "'Men of Galilee,' they said, 'why do you stand here looking into the sky? This same Jesus, who has been taken from you into heaven, will come back in the same way you have seen him go into heaven'" (Acts 1:11). Jesus is coming again, the second time. Not as a baby in a manger this time. He will rapture all believers, both living and dead, to meet Him in the air, and then "we will be with the Lord forever" (1 Thessalonians 4:17). This return of Jesus is one of our four foundational doctrines.

But in the meantime, until He does return, He is doing something very special for those who have accepted the salvation He came to earth to provide. As He sits at the right hand of the Father, He is "interceding for us" (Romans 8:34). He does not save us and then leave us to struggle alone. Every believer is on His prayer list. The One who prayed with compassion and urgency in the Garden of Gethsemane prays today for those who struggle with spiritual and physical problems.

3.3.4
OBJECTIVE
Describe how sinners seek to redefine sin, but still need God's salvation.

Salvation, Still a World Need

The world is busy redefining sin. It does so by substituting innocent-sounding names for behavior the Bible distinctly calls sin (Kennedy 2004, 6–7). And Christians can sometimes be lulled into thinking the evil behaviors are not as bad as they have thought them to be. Some examples include:

Instead of *pornography*, it is called "adult entertainment."

Instead of *abortion*, it is called "the right to choose."

Instead of *adultery*, it is called "an affair."

Instead of *lust*, it is "sexual liberation."

Instead of *strippers*, they are called "exotic dancers."

Instead of *strip joints*, they are called "gentlemen's clubs."

Instead of *pedophiles*, the act is called "intergenerational intimacy."

Instead of *inappropriate nudity*, it has been called "a wardrobe malfunction."

There is more involved in such euphemisms (substituting a pleasant term for one that has negative meaning) than seeking to avoid offending people. Christians and Christian beliefs are being ruthlessly attacked around the world. In some cases it is a militant religion that seeks to replace Christianity. But more frequently it is secularism that wants to abolish all religion. Christians must be especially alert to the subtle use of pleasant sounding words in place of words and behaviors the Bible describes as sin.

The Bible describes and condemns this hypocrisy. "Woe to those who call evil good and good evil, who put darkness for light and light for darkness, who put bitter for sweet and sweet for bitter. Woe to those who are wise in their own eyes and clever in their own sight" (Isaiah 5:20–21). We must keep focused on Jesus and His hatred of sin and His love for holy living. The words of an old chorus are so true: "Turn your eyes upon Jesus, look full in His wonderful face; and the things of earth will grow strangely dim in the light of His glory and grace" (Lemmel 1950).

Salvation Means Regeneration, Justification, and Repentance

Theological terms are often confusing. To rattle off a few Rs, what are **regeneration**, **reconciliation**, **redemption**, and repentance? How do they differ from each other? Before we begin the study of the next two lessons, when these terms will be fully discussed, take a piece of scratch paper and write in a few words (no more than a sentence each) expressing what you think the four words mean. You need not look for a comprehensive answer. We will come to that in our study. But there is value in trying your own definition first and then seeing how it compares with dictionaries and word studies. These preliminary definitions are for your eyes only. You will not be asked to share them with anyone.

Understanding Regeneration

OBJECTIVE

Describe regeneration as a contrast between life before and after salvation.

To the secular world, being "born again" sounds strange, maybe even bizarre. Why does a living person need to go through the birth process again? When an evangelical Christian is elected to a government position, critics ridicule the person by saying, "Oh, you are one of those born-again persons!"

Jesus himself is the source of this term. "I tell you the truth, no one can see the kingdom of God unless he is born again" (John 3:3). The soul of a sinful person, dead in trespasses and iniquity, needs a new life. This new and higher life is imparted at salvation by a divine act of regeneration. Regeneration is not the gaining of additional knowledge, pledging moral or ethical improvement, being baptized in water, or joining a church. It is not something added to what we are. It is a complete change—an exchange of the old life for a new one.

The New Birth

At salvation, each person becomes a child of God. This act of grace is truly a new birth. The terms "adoption" (KJV, ASV) and "full rights of sons" (NIV) are ways of describing our being brought into God's family at salvation.

A New Creature

Regeneration is the change brought about by the Spirit of God, making a person a new creature in Christ. "If anyone is in Christ, he is a new creation; the old has gone, the new has come!" (2 Corinthians 5:17). In saving us, God does not simply energize the old creation with new ability and power. The God who created humans in the first place, only to see them fall into sin, recreates us at salvation by the operation of His Holy Spirit. The practical result is a radical change in the nature, character, desires, and motives of the transformed person.

Justification and the Mercy of God

3.42
OBJECTIVE
Explain justification as it relates to God's nature.

The word *justify* is a judicial or legal term meaning "to acquit" or "to declare righteous." **Justification** is the easiest of these theological terms to define because in English it can be remembered as *just as if* I had never sinned. At the moment of salvation, the guilty sinner stands before God, the righteous Judge; but instead of a sentence of condemnation, he receives a sentence of acquittal. (Recall the story where the judge pronounced judgment on his former law school friend, but then paid the price to set him free from the penalty.) We receive acquittal only because of the atoning death of Christ.

Justification involves our relationship with God. It has nothing to do with our personal righteousness or spiritual condition. It makes no one a holy or righteous person. Rather, it is God's declaration that we are righteous, in spite of the sin and disobedience that filled our lives before the supernatural miracle of God's grace.

All sin is disobedience against God, and sin must be judged. But when sinful humanity comes to the Great Judge and asks forgiveness for disobedience, the Judge says, "I declare you to be righteous." The past is forgiven and forgotten, and our relationship to God is restored to what it was intended to be before the Fall. All guilt, condemnation, and separation are removed by the act of justification. "Who will bring any charge against those whom God has chosen? It is God who justifies" (Romans 8:33).

Justification is more than a pardon. A pardoned criminal is not regarded as being righteous. He or she is only pardoned from the penalty of his or her crime. But the Christian is declared righteous. Justification goes beyond forgiveness. It declares one to be righteous and then lovingly responds to the justified person, "You are just as righteous as if you had never sinned." Such love! Such mercy!

Justification and the Supernatural Grace of God

Some churches teach that justification is the complete eradication of sin. We do not find in Scripture any statement supporting that view. Though justification forgives all past sins, it does not guarantee that no sins can or will be committed in the future. "If we claim to be without sin, we deceive ourselves and the truth is not in us . . . If we claim we have not sinned, we make him out to be a liar and his word has no place in our lives" (1 John 1:8, 10).

6   There is another side of grace. Can we forgive and demonstrate grace to fellow humans who offend or mistreat us?

Justification, or absolute forgiveness, is the best proof of God's grace. "Undeserved favor" is the simple definition of *grace*. One expositor on the subject of grace wrote, "It may be the most important word in the Bible, the heart of the gospel" (Yancey 1997, 14). Being justified and forgiven, when we do not deserve such grace, is beyond our mental grasp. But with great thankfulness we accept it, along with the love that motivates it.

A prostitute was deep in sin and poverty. She allowed others to abuse her two-year-old daughter. There seemed no way out of her messed up life. When asked if she had ever thought of going to a church for help, her response was dramatic. "Church! Why would I go there? They would just make me feel worse" (Yancey 1997, 14.).

Are church members with that reputation missing something? Do they not understand that the grace we receive from God should be passed on to others? Or are such church members just faithfully standing up for righteousness and strongly opposing all forms of sin? We are called to denounce sin. But like God, we are to love the sinner. It takes a real burden for the lost to so love their souls—denouncing sin but not in a way that drives them away from their only hope for deliverance.

7   Do we find it hard to forgive? Do we have rights that others should not violate?

There are situations in which sinners become so committed to their sinful behavior that they defiantly reject the message of love and deliverance shared with them. But the invitation to receive God's forgiveness and grace must still be presented with the help of the Holy Spirit. We must not hear the words the master spoke to one of his servants, "I canceled all that debt of yours because you begged me to. Shouldn't you have had mercy on your fellow servant just as I had on you?" (Matthew 18:32–33). As faithful servants of our Lord, we have great responsibility for the souls of those whose lives we touch.

Rights are civil and secular concepts. The Bible nowhere tells Christians to stand up for their rights in human relationships. We are to resist the devil (James 4:7), but to our fellow humans, even when they may be prompted by the devil, we are to turn the other cheek (Matthew 5:39). Jesus was our great example; even when His executioners physically abused Him. "He was led like a sheep to the slaughter, and as a lamb before the shearer is silent, so he did not open his mouth" (Isaiah 53:7; Acts 8:32). There are Christians around the world being martyred for their faith. Can we not accept with God's grace the fact that others seem to ignore some of our so-called rights? God's mercy is greater than all our sins. Is our mercy towards others the same?

Beyond Remorse

A criminal is likely to be sorry when caught and sentenced to serve time in prison. But the criminal's sorrow may be for the wrong reason. The apostle Paul commended the Corinthian Christians because their sorrow led to something good. "I am happy, not because you were made sorry, but because your sorrow led you to repentance . . . Godly sorrow brings repentance that leads to salvation and leaves no regret, but worldly sorrow brings death" (2 Corinthians 7:9, 10). Repentance is a godly sorrow for sin followed by a sincere effort to forsake sin. "[The Lord] is patient with you, not wanting anyone to perish, but everyone to come to repentance" (2 Peter 3:9).

LINCOLN'S PRAYER PROCLAMATION

In 1863, during the American Civil War, Abraham Lincoln called the nation to repentance, to confession of national sins, and to a turning back to God. In a world today caught up in conflict between nations and within nations, a similar call would bring more peace and prosperity than wars or treaties can provide.

A Proclamation for a National Day of Prayer

Whereas, the Senate of the United States, devoutly recognizing the supreme authority and just government of the Almighty God in all the affairs of men and of nations, has by a resolution requested the president to designate and set apart a day for national prayer and humiliation.

And whereas, it is the duty of nations as well as of men to own their dependence upon the overruling power of God: to confess their sins and transgressions in humble sorrow, yet with assured hope that genuine repentance will lead to mercy and pardon; and to recognize the sublime truth, announced in the Holy Scriptures and proven by all history, that those nations only are blessed whose God is the Lord:

And insomuch as we know that by His divine law nations, like individuals, are subjected to punishments and chastisements in this world, may we not justly fear that the awful calamity of civil war which now desolates the land may be but a punishment inflicted upon us for our presumptuous sins, to the needful end of our national reformation as a whole People? We have been the recipients of the choicest bounties of Heaven. We have been preserved, these many years, in peace and prosperity. We have grown in numbers, wealth, and power as no other nation has ever grown; but we have forgotten God. We have forgotten the gracious hand which preserved us in peace, and multiplied and enriched and strengthened us; and we have vainly imagined, in the deceitfulness of our hearts, that all these blessings were produced by some superior wisdom and virtue of our own. Intoxicated with unbroken success, we have become too self-sufficient to feel the necessity of redeeming and preserving grace, too proud to pray to the God who made us:

It behooves us then, to humble ourselves before the offended Power, to confess our national sins, and to pray for clemency and forgiveness:

All this being done in sincerity and truth, let us then rest humbly in the hope authorized by the divine teachings, that the united cry of the nation will be heard on high, and answered with blessings no less than the pardon of our national sins, and the restoration of our now divided and suffering country to its former happy condition of unity and peace.

"Blessed is the nation whose God is the Lord" (Psalm 33:12). When the people of a nation repent and ask for God's mercy, that nation is truly blessed.

LESSON 3.5

Sanctification, Assurance, Reconciliation, and Redemption

An American newspaper columnist once wrote, "Americans have always been able to handle austerity and even adversity. Prosperity is what is doing us in" (Reston 1974). Though he was speaking about the values and morality of the general population, the principle holds true for spiritual commitment as well. Prosperity has given many people the feeling that they do not need God, if indeed He exists. They see no need for salvation. They can make it on their own.

We must remember this fact as we seek to share salvation with a lost and dying world. The growth of Christianity in many other countries far exceeds the growth in America and other materially prosperous countries.

There can be a strong temptation to share the gospel with successful members of society. The poor and disadvantaged do not promise to add much respectability and financial support to the church. Yet it takes a greater effort to persuade the prosperous of their need for salvation. Most down-and-outers are just waiting for someone to bring the word that will help them out of their terrible condition. After mentioning the sexually immoral, adulterers, prostitutes, homosexual offenders, thieves, greedy persons, drunkards, and swindlers, Paul says, "And that is what some of you were. But you were . . . justified" (1 Corinthians 6:9–11). The atheist Karl Marx called Christianity the "opiate of the people," implying that strong and independent people do not need religion (Wolff 2003). But his communistic beliefs are on the ash heap of history while Christianity purposefully marches on.

Jesus came to seek and save the lost (Luke 19:10). We must go "out into the highways and hedges, and compel *them* to come in" (Luke 14:23, NKJV). No economic or social level is excluded. The lost may not be won by telling them about the blessings of **sanctification**, regeneration, redemption, and all the other theological terms that we are now studying. But the soul winner must know what the blessings of salvation are, and then present Christ as the answer to every need the sinner may have. In this lesson, we study some of the many blessings that come through salvation, blessings that help us understand the wonderful continuing benefits of salvation in our lives and in the lives of those we lead to Christ.

3.5.1
OBJECTIVE
Explain the nature of sanctification.

Sanctification: Immediate AND Progressive

Salvation is sanctification! And the initial salvation experience begins the process of sanctification! No, those statements are not contradictions. Unless we remember the two-fold meaning of sanctification, our understanding of how it applies to our spiritual life is not complete. Some churches teach that sanctification is a distinct work of grace after salvation. For them sanctification is the eradication or elimination of sin. After one has been sanctified, according to this teaching, he or she can no longer sin. But then follows the struggle of explaining what actually goes on in the spiritual life of a believer.

There are definite verses that teach sanctification at the moment of salvation. "But you were washed, you were sanctified, you were justified in the name of the Lord Jesus Christ and by the Spirit of our God" (1 Corinthians 6:11). In this meaning, sanctified is related to justification. Like justification, sanctification is God's declaration of righteousness. But the emphasis of justification is release from the guilt of sin. The emphasis of sanctification is breaking the bondage of sin. They both happen at the same time: washing, sanctifying, and justifying.

In justification we receive a new standing before God: imputed or divinely given righteousness. In sanctification we receive the spiritual life of Christ that changes our character and conduct. Sanctification, though complete in one sense at salvation, continues throughout this earthly life and is finally completed when Jesus returns. "We are children of God, and what we will be has not yet been made known. But we know that when he appears, we shall be like him, for we shall see him as he is" (1 John 3:2). There are actually three stages of sanctification, two of which concern our earthly lives. Sanctification involves (1) an initial declaration, (2) a progressive growth, and (3) final perfection. Right now we "are being transformed into his likeness with ever-increasing glory, which comes from the Lord, who is the Spirit" (2 Corinthians 3:18).

As in the act of *instantaneous* sanctification, the Holy Spirit is the primary Agent in helping us *progressively* become like Jesus. His work of sanctification should be greatly accelerated when the believer remains filled with the Spirit after experiencing the baptism in the Holy Spirit. We will study this aspect of sanctification in a later lesson. But for now, remember that the process of sanctification is growth in right attitudes and behavior.

The original meaning of the word *sanctify* is "separation or being set apart." To be made holy sets us apart from what we were before salvation. The Bible speaks of persons and places being sanctified. Whatever was sanctified was set apart for God's possession and use. The seventh day was set apart for rest and worship. "Then God blessed the seventh day and sanctified it" (Genesis 2:3, NKJV). "Remember the Sabbath day by keeping it holy" (Exodus 20:8). A house or a field could be sanctified (KJV) or dedicated "as something holy" (Leviticus 27:14–17).

Another key aspect of sanctification is *purification*. The presence of the Holy Spirit in our hearts will purify our thoughts, desires, motives, and actions. God desires holiness to touch and affect our entire being—body, soul, and spirit. The sanctification that comes at salvation permeates and affects every part of us. We are not only declared to be righteous, but we also begin to become the holy beings God desires us to be.

Sanctification, however, is more than a doctrinal concept. It must be applied to every action of every day. One area of life is appropriately highlighted by one expositor.

Sexual purity is a frequently mentioned application in Scripture of a properly functioning sanctified life (1 Corinthians 6:18–20; 1 Thessalonians 4:3–8). This is so, in part, because marriage is the most revealing context from which to understand Christ's sanctifying purpose for the Church (Ephesians 5:25–30). Believers' bodies are sanctified by controlling them in such a way that God's purposes are being fulfilled by them (Romans 6:19, 22; 12:1–2; 1 Thessalonians 4:4) (Mullen 1996, 712).

Maintaining a sanctified life calls for constant vigilance. The Holy Spirit helps, but we must heed the caution of Scripture, "Be self-controlled and alert. Your enemy the devil prowls around like a roaring lion looking for someone to devour. Resist him, standing firm in the faith" (1 Peter 5:8–9).

The Assurance of Personal Salvation

Life in this world is filled with worry and uncertainty. Human beings with feelings and emotions may at times feel unsure about their salvation. But assurance is a beautiful gift God provides for His children. Though a moment of depression may bring questions about our eternal destiny, the doubt is from Satan, not from God. Our salvation is not based on our abilities or our feelings, but on confidence in God's promises given us in His Word. Even in times of doubt, God's promise still is true, "'Never will I leave you; never will I forsake you'" (Hebrews 13:5). The promise is clinched firmly by the words of Jesus: "'I give them [my sheep] eternal life, and they shall never perish; no one can snatch them out of my hand. My Father, who has given them to me, is greater than all; no one can snatch them out of my Father's hand'" (John 10:28–29). Both the Father and the Son hold us securely. Nothing external can take us out of those hands. Only we have the power to leave those secure hands. And that is difficult because those hands of love hold us firmly. The question of eternal security will be discussed in detail in Chapter 4.

Assurance of our salvation must never be confused with material prosperity or getting answers to our prayers. Some Christians begin to doubt when a sincere prayer for healing is not answered as they had hoped and prayed. Life in a fallen world has pain, sorrow, and tragedy; and Christians are not exempt. But even in these times of trials that test our faith, God provides an anchor of hope and encouragement (Hebrews 6:18–19). So you can cast all your care and anxiety on him "because he cares for you" (1 Peter 5:7).

3.5.2
OBJECTIVE
Point out how reconciliation turns God's enemies into His children.

God's Reconciliation with Sinners

Reconciliation is needed when two Christians are not able to get along together. But reconciliation between a sinner and God is even more important. In reconciling human relationships and differences, either party can begin the process, though both must participate in the reconciliation. However, in a sinner's reconciliation with God, God is always the One who makes the first offer of reconciliation.

The need for reconciliation implies a breakdown in a relationship. In our relationship with God, sin has caused that breakdown. Paul notes that sinners cannot initiate reconciliation: "You see, at just the right time, when we were still powerless, Christ died for the ungodly" (Romans 5:6). Then he concludes the passage with Christ's work of reconciliation: "For if, when we were God's enemies, we were reconciled to him through the death of his Son, how much more, having been reconciled, shall we be saved through his life!" (Romans 5:10).

On one occasion Jesus said to His disciples, "But if you do not forgive, neither will your Father in heaven forgive your trespasses" (Mark 11:26). The same truth is contained in the reconciliation principle. "All this is from God, who reconciled us to himself through Christ and gave us the ministry of reconciliation: that God was reconciling the world to himself in Christ, not counting men's sins against them. And he has committed to us the message of reconciliation" (2 Corinthians 5:18–19). We have a ministry of reconciliation and a message of reconciliation—God has reconciled the world to himself in Christ's sacrifice; He no longer counts our sins against us if we accept His offer. We are declared righteous and can have God's peace in our hearts.

The Beauty of Redemption

Redemption is more than a theological term. It had a variety of legal and religious uses in Bible times. It could include releasing a person from a binding agreement, setting one free from slavery or captivity, buying back something lost, and paying a ransom to regain someone or something. Each of these definitions portrays the beauty of our salvation. When we sin, we pledge allegiance and enter into a binding agreement with the enemy of our soul; salvation releases us from the bondage. Sinners are captives of the devil (2 Timothy 2:26), but believers have been set free. We have been bought at a great price (1 Corinthians 6:20), not of "silver or gold . . . but with the precious blood of Christ" (1 Peter 1:8–19).

T Test Yourself

Circle the letter of the *best* answer.

1. God's plan to restore fellowship with wayward sinners was

a) to pick up the pieces Satan had damaged.

b) conceived after Satan succeeded in bringing sin into the world.

c) to pay the penalty himself for the sins of the world.

2. Apostasy is defined as

a) committing the unpardonable sin.

b) turning one's back on God after knowing the reality of His personal presence.

c) refusing to accept God's offer of salvation.

3. Jesus had to die as a sacrifice for our sins because

a) without the shedding of blood there is no forgiveness.

b) the animal sacrifices of the Old Testament were not pleasing to God.

c) God had to die like an Old Testament sacrifice to provide salvation.

4. Christ's suffering for our salvation (led like a lamb to slaughter) was predicted by

a) David.

b) Isaiah.

c) Malachi.

5. Jesus was like no other person who has walked on earth in that He

a) gathered many followers during His three and a half years of ministry.

b) was human at birth but became divine when He was baptized in water.

c) was both fully human and fully divine.

6. Jesus was more than a sacrifice for our sins; the Bible also portrays Him as

a) a great Teacher showing us how to live.

b) a great Prophet who warned about Antichrist.

c) the most important member of the Trinity.

7. The bedrock or most important truth of our Christian faith is

a) divine healing.

b) the baptism in the Holy Spirit.

c) salvation.

8. Christ's resurrection is essential to our faith because

a) Easter is more important than Good Friday.

b) without the Resurrection, Christianity could have no miracles.

c) without the Resurrection the miracle of salvation would lack its power.

9. Salvation as "regeneration" means being

a) adopted.

b) born again.

c) justified.

10. Sanctification is both instantaneous (or immediate) and also

a) progressive.

b) impossible to achieve.

c) regressive.

Responses to Interactive Questions

Chapter 3

Some of these responses may include information that is supplemental to the IST. These questions are intended to produce reflective thinking beyond the course content and your responses may vary from these examples.

1   Did God have a plan and purpose in speaking the world into existence?

The Creation account in Genesis does not even suggest a reason for God's creative acts. Nor does He have to explain or give answers to questions we may have. Yet we can look at a characteristic of God that suggests why He created the world, why He created Adam and Eve, and why He sent Jesus to die for our sins. First John 4:16 says, "And so we know and rely on the love God has for us. God is love. Whoever lives in love lives in God, and God in him." Timothy George expresses it this way: "Within the being of God himself there is a mysterious living love, a dynamic reciprocity of surrender and affirmation, of giving and receiving, among the Father, the Son, and the Holy Spirit. The Maker of heaven and earth is at once the Triune God of holiness and love."

2   Why are there so many verses in support of both the Arminian and Calvinistic positions?

It may be that God knew there would be Christians who needed at various times one emphasis or the other. Both positions have elements of truth that are essential to the gospel and the Church. Remember that Arminianism and Calvinism are human system of interpretation. The Bible is coherent and cohesive in its teaching. Human interpretation introduces paradox and conflict.

3   Why did the plan of restoration include a sacrifice?

Disobedience is sin and sin has its consequences, a sentence of death. God gave Jesus as a blood-sacrifice substitute to cover our sins. Consider Revelation 13:8, "In the book of life belonging to the Lamb that was slain from the creation of the world."

4   Can you describe Jesus Christ, the sacrifice for the sin of all humankind?

Jesus is the one and only Son of God (John 3:16). At the same time he was also the Son of Man by virtue of being born into this world through the virgin Mary. The first word of His name, Jesus, means "The Lord Saves" (Matthew 1:21). The word Christ means "the Anointed One" or "the Messiah." He was both human and divine during His years on earth and remains so forever. His Father is our Heavenly Father, God himself. His mother was Mary.

5   Of all the doctrines of the Christian faith, why is salvation the most important? Or, why is it the most important of the four foundational doctrines we are studying?

Salvation saves us from sin, guilt, bondage, fear, despair, spiritual death, and a meaningless life. It provides peace with God (forgiveness), a redeemed life, personal access to God's presence, supernatural strength in suffering, and opportunity for a Spirit-filled life.

6   There is another side of grace. Can we forgive and demonstrate grace to fellow humans who offend or mistreat us?

In Matthew 5:44 Jesus tells us that. Still, it is not often easy to do.

7   Do we find it hard to forgive? Do we have rights that others should not violate?

Rights are civil and secular concepts. The Bible nowhere tells Christians to stand up for their rights in human relationships. The Bible does require that we look out for the interests of our fellow humans, including what is often referred to as their rights. This is the essence of justice, required by God as a basic principle for His creation. The IST is correct in emphasizing that Christians are not to insist on recognition of their own personal rights at the expense of others or relationship.

Affirming and Maintaining Salvation

How do we recall the many salvation blessings we have just been studying? Is salvation an emotional high, which soon passes, leaving one to question if anything special really happened? For some people, unfortunately, that is what eventually happens. But God in His wisdom has made provision for keeping our salvation experience alive and growing. There can be fresh revelations of God's love to us "new every morning" (Lamentations 3:22–23).

In this chapter, we will look at two ordinances that remind us of our wonderful salvation experience. When the new convert experiences water baptism, he or she says to the watching world, "I have accepted Jesus Christ as my personal Savior, and I want to know Him better each day from now on." Each time a believer observes a baptismal service, there is a reminder of the testimony he or she made at a former baptism. Then following our Lord's instructions, we partake of the Lord's Supper, or Holy Communion. This is a regular reminder of what Jesus Christ has done for our salvation.

In the last lesson of this unit, we deal with one of the great *divides* of the evangelical community. We will look closely at the eternal security issue, or the "once-saved, always saved" question. Every believer should have a reasoned answer that lines up with the full teaching of Scripture.

Lesson 4.1   Declaring and Remembering Our Salvation

Objectives

4.1.1   Describe how water baptism symbolizes our new birth at salvation.

4.1.2   Explain why we baptize in the name of the Father, and of the Son, and of the Holy Spirit.

4.1.3   Identify the Old Testament scene in which the Lord's Supper was instituted.

4.1.4   Identify two communion principles taught by Paul to the Corinthians.

Lesson 4.2   The Security of the Believer and Warnings Against Falling

Objectives

4.2.1   Identify Bible verses that emphasize our security in Christ, and explain why we do not believe in eternal security.

4.2.2   Describe how Bible assurances of our salvation and warnings against backsliding are both important.

4.2.3   Explain the five points of Calvinism as taught by the TULIP acrostic.

4.2.4   Identify the basic steps of salvation that can be used in witnessing to sinners.

Declaring and Remembering Our Salvation

A new convert publicly declares he or she is now a follower of Jesus Christ by being baptized in water. All believers regularly partake of Holy Communion to remember the great work Christ did for our salvation. Water baptism and the Lord's Supper (or Holy Communion) are the two **ordinances** of the church. Both are essential to a full appreciation of our salvation.

An ordinance is a divinely established religious custom or practice regarded as an essential spiritual duty. Some churches recognize as many as seven ordinances, which they usually call **sacraments.** Evangelicals and Pentecostals, however, limit the number of ordinances to those established by Jesus and existing in the practices of the church since New Testament times. Included in Jesus' last words to His disciples was this command: "'Therefore go and make disciples of all nations, baptizing them in the name of the Father and of the Son and of the Holy Spirit'" (Matthew 28:19). Paul recorded the words of Jesus at the Last Supper with His disciples: "'This is my body [the bread] which is for you; do this in remembrance of me'" (1 Corinthians 11:24). Then, as He took the cup, He said, "'This cup is the new covenant in my blood; do this, whenever you drink it, in remembrance of me'" (v. 25). We first look at water baptism.

The ordinance of water baptism is administered only once to each believer. As the new convert participates in the rite, he or she announces to all who see or hear of the baptism that a new life in Jesus has begun. The voluntary act boldly states the intent of the baptized Christian to follow Christ in complete obedience from that time on.

The Symbolism of Water Baptism

Water baptism is a simple object lesson portraying the fundamentals of the gospel. Being immersed under the water speaks of Christ's death and burial. The raising of the convert out of the water symbolizes Christ's resurrection and victory over death. In this symbolic act the convert spiritually identifies with Christ and His saving work. Paul speaks of being "buried with him in baptism and raised with him" (Colossians 2:12).

Any believer who sincerely repents of his or her sins and exercises a living faith in Jesus Christ is eligible for baptism. Infants, of course, have no sins of which to repent. Nor can they understand salvation or exercise the faith required. Some churches, teaching that water baptism is required for salvation, baptize infants, thinking that if they should die without water baptism they would not go to heaven. Believing the Bible teaches the need for rational faith that understands salvation, we do not baptize infants. Instead, we dedicate babies. Parents and the entire church are charged with the responsibility of leading the child to a saving knowledge of Jesus Christ at an early age.

A Biblical Pattern

Pentecostal believers almost unanimously practice immersion as the correct form of water baptism. We see all other forms as unscriptural. Other churches follow different traditions; but the Bible, not tradition, should be our pattern. Churches that believe in infant baptism often use sprinkling because immersion would be inappropriate for an infant. Pentecostals oppose both sprinkling and infant baptism because they are based on human tradition rather than on scriptural authority.

Some who practice infant baptism, and similarly sprinkling, point to the conversion of the Philippian jailer. Paul and Silas "spoke the word of the Lord

4.1.1
OBJECTIVE

Describe how water baptism symbolizes our new birth at salvation.

We all Born again in a New creation. All of our past sins have been forgiven. We are to Live a New life in christ free of sin.

to him and to all the others in his house . . . then immediately he and all his family were baptized" (Acts 16:32–33). They conclude that there must have been infants or very small children in the family. But such an argument from omission rather than recorded statement is not justified. The descriptive accounts of water baptism in the New Testament all point to baptism by immersion.

4.1.2
OBJECTIVE
Explain why we baptize in the name of the Father, and of the Son, and of the Holy Spirit.

Baptism in the Name of the Godhead

Several references in the Book of Acts mention baptism in Jesus' name (Acts 8:16, 10:48, 19:5). On the basis of these verses, one Pentecostal group, informally identified as "Jesus Only" believers, baptize in the name of Jesus, without mention of the Father and the Holy Spirit. But the exact command of Jesus to His disciples was "baptizing them in the name of the Father and of the Son and of the Holy Spirit" (Matthew 28:19). How should these passages be brought into agreement?

We believe that when the writer of Acts was referring to water baptism, he was especially focusing on the salvation aspect of new life through Jesus Christ in contrast to John's baptism or a Jewish baptism. Through the Matthew passage, Jesus was giving the disciples the formula He wanted them to use. One of the three Acts passages is contrasting Christian baptism with John's baptism. This passage required simple labels for the baptisms for the sake of comparison and did not intend to offer a theological formula. These labels (John's baptism and that done in Jesus' name) made more sense than to speak of John's baptism and of the Father/Son/Spirit baptism.

Of course, the "Jesus Only" teaching that there is no Trinity, only three different manifestations of Jesus, is more of a theological problem than the water baptism formula. The two ideas are intertwined. It is unclear whether the opposition to the Trinity is based on the water baptism formula interpretation or if Oneness Pentecostals use the Acts statements because of their rejection of the Trinity. But from the earliest days of the Christian church, the concept of the Trinity has been the orthodox belief, with the "Jesus Only" belief a minority position.

We do not accuse those baptized "in the name of Jesus only" of being outside the family of God, though some of the Jesus Only people do teach that Trinitarians are not Christians. Water baptism is simply an outward testimony of an inner spiritual experience of salvation. The spiritual reality is far more important than the symbol testimony to that reality.

Water baptism is an important ordinance of the church. Water baptism is an outward sign of an inward work. In itself it has no saving power. People are baptized because they are saved, not in order to be saved. Although baptism is not absolutely essential to salvation, it is essential to full obedience. As Peter preached on the Day of Pentecost, he charged his listeners: "'Repent and be baptized, every one of you, in the name of Jesus Christ for the forgiveness of your sins. And you will receive the gift of the Holy Spirit'" (Acts 2:38). To refuse to be baptized when there is opportunity makes one disobedient.

> Those who teach that water baptism is a sacrament providing salvation (including infants) interpret this verse to read, "Be baptized . . . for the forgiveness of your sins." We understand the verse to place the emphasis on "Repent," as the context makes clear. To read the verse as sacramentalists interpret it contradicts Ephesians 2:8-9. "It is by grace you have been saved, through faith . . . not by works, so that no one can boast." Both actions—repenting and being baptized—are commands that every obedient believer will fulfill.

Jesus instituted the Lord's Supper or Holy Communion on the eve of His crucifixion. This ordinance is a memorial of Christ's death. The bread represents His broken body, and the wine represents His shed blood.

The Lord's Supper: Passover Replacement

4.1.3
OBJECTIVE
Identify the Old Testament scene in which the Lord's Supper was instituted.

The Lord's Supper as part of the New Covenant took the place of the Old Testament Passover Feast. On the night before the Crucifixion, Jesus and the Twelve were recalling the events of Israel's deliverance from Egypt. Taking up the bread and the wine that were on the table, Jesus gave each a special significance in the redemptive work He was about to do.

"While they were eating, Jesus took bread, gave thanks and broke it, and gave it to his disciples, saying, 'Take and eat; this is my body.' Then he took the cup, gave thanks and offered it to them, saying, 'Drink from it, all of you. This is my blood of the covenant, which is poured out for many for the forgiveness of sins'" (Matthew 26:26–28).

The Seriousness of the Lord's Supper

The ordinance of Holy Communion is a solemn and important ceremony. Those who partake are given special warning to prepare themselves for the holy occasion. "Therefore, whoever eats the bread or drinks the cup of the Lord in an unworthy manner will be guilty of sinning against the body and blood of the Lord" (1 Corinthians 11:27).

1   How often should we remember the death of our Lord in this manner?

This caution should not frighten a Christian into abstaining from the Lord's Supper. The command to partake is still valid. "A man ought to examine himself before he eats of the bread and drinks of the cup" (1 Corinthians 11:28). Partaking of Holy Communion reminds us that our experience of salvation must be kept current. The Christian life is a spiritual walk in which we must continually open our hearts for cleansing.

The Lord's Supper reminds us of Christ's atoning work at Calvary. It looks forward to the Second Coming when our salvation will be perfect and complete. But this ordinance also points to another of the foundational doctrines we will be studying in greater detail: divine healing.

The terrible suffering Jesus endured in His body as He purchased our salvation on the cross was for our physical healing as well as our spiritual restoration. "But he was pierced for our transgressions, he was crushed for our iniquities; the punishment that brought us peace was upon him, and by his wounds we are healed" (Isaiah 53:5). The receiving of the Lord's Supper is an excellent time to reach out in faith for the healing that the believer may need.

> The evangelical and Pentecostal worlds have in recent years been reminded of Christ's great suffering in the film "The Passion of the Christ," released in 2004 and produced by Mel Gibson. It is easy to think lightly of the suffering of Jesus on the cross. But seeing graphic pictures of the beatings and abuse Christ suffered for us has made many believers realize the great price Jesus paid for our salvation.

Until Jesus Comes

4.1.4
OBJECTIVE
Identify two communion principles taught by Paul to the Corinthians.

Paul told the Corinthians: "Whenever you eat this bread and drink this cup, you proclaim the Lord's death until he comes" (1 Corinthians 11:26).

The Bible gives no directive on the frequency for the partaking of communion. It seems appropriate, therefore, to observe the memorial frequently enough that we are regularly reminded of the atoning work of Jesus Christ. On the other hand, it should not be observed so often that it becomes routine and commonplace. Many evangelicals have concluded that once a month gives a proper balance between over use and proper remembering. Some people observe Communion at weddings and special religious occasions as well. The keeping of the Lord's Supper, like the rite of water baptism, will end with the coming of the Lord for His saints (1 Corinthians 11:26). These ordinances are for a testimony now. They are symbols of the reality of our salvation and the return of Jesus for His bride.

The Security of the Believer and Warnings against Falling

One of the great debates in evangelical circles for centuries has been **eternal security** versus the free will of humans. There are verses in Scripture to support both views. Whichever view a person supports, there must be a recognition of the Scripture passages that support the other view. In this lesson, we will look at the biblical passages that are used by each side in the debate. Then we will attempt to provide a position that gives full importance and value to all the biblical references.

> The Assemblies of God position paper, "The Security of the Believer" can be found on the Internet. Enter www.ag.org, and then follow the "Beliefs" and "Position Papers" buttons. The section "Salvation Is Available for Every Man" addresses two questions: (1) "Are some predestined to be saved and others to be lost?" and (2) "Who are the elect?" (written in 1978).

One side in the debate usually does not charge the opposing side as being unsaved. Since we will be spending eternity with all who have accepted Jesus Christ as personal Savior, we should certainly be able to get along here on earth with fellow believers who hold different interpretations on matters not immediately critical to our salvation. However, we must always be alert to interpretations that can lead a person toward backsliding, apostasy, and eternal damnation.

Salvation Cannot Be Taken From Us

Below are the primary verses Calvinists use to support their belief in eternal security. For the sake of focus, verses may not be quoted in their entirety. One can check the entire passage by the reference at the end of quoted verses. Appeal is also made to over twenty-five references to "eternal life" in the New Testament.

"Whoever believes in the Son has eternal life" (John 3:36).

"I give them [my sheep] eternal life, and they shall never perish; no one can snatch them out of my hand. My Father, who has given them to me, is greater than all; no one can snatch them out of my Father's hand" (John 10:28–29).

"For those God foreknew he also predestined to be conformed to the likeness of his Son. . . . And those he predestined, he also called; those he called, he also justified; those he justified, he also glorified" (Romans 8:29–30).

"For I am convinced that neither death nor life, neither angels nor demons, neither the present nor the future, nor any powers, neither height nor depth, nor anything else in all creation, will be able to separate us from the love of God that is in Christ Jesus our Lord" (Romans 8:39).

"In him we were also chosen, having been predestined according to the plan of him who works out everything in conformity with the purpose of his will" (Ephesians 1:11).

What Predestination Means

Eternal security and predestination are companion teachings of Calvinistic belief. In Romans 8 and 9, Paul emphasizes the fact that God took the initiative in planning and providing salvation and a restored relationship. Staunch Calvinists have taken this truth to mean that humans do not have free will and that God predetermines some to be saved and some to be lost.

> The Assemblies of God position paper, "Eternal Punishment" can be found on the Internet. Enter www.ag.org, and then follow the "Beliefs" and "Position Papers" selections.

But such a teaching forgets that God is not willing that any should perish, but that all should come to repentance (2 Peter 3:9). God shows His wrath (Romans 9:22) only on those who reject His provision of salvation. And even then He does so without malice, because He is a God of love (1 John 4:8). Why does not a God of love forgive everyone, even when they do not want or feel a need for forgiveness? Because He is also a God of justice. But His justice is never revenge. His compassionate nature is strained when He must also be a just God.

Warnings against Taking Salvation Lightly

OBJECTIVE

Describe how Bible assurances of our salvation and warnings against backsliding are both important.

The Bible does not teach "once saved, always saved" or "once a Christian, always a Christian." Just as there are Scripture verses that give us assurance of our salvation, there are verses that warn against the great tragedy of falling away from our faith and trust in Jesus Christ as our Savior.

"So, if you think you are standing firm, be careful that you don't fall!" (1 Corinthians 10:12).

"Because of the increase of wickedness, the love of most will grow cold, but he who stands firm to the end will be saved" (Matthew 24:12–13).

"Some have rejected these [faith and a good conscience] and so have shipwrecked their faith" (1 Timothy 1:19).

"'So, because you are lukewarm—neither hot nor cold—I am about to spit you out of my mouth'" (Revelation 3:16).

But the most terrifying passage is found in Hebrews. It speaks clearly of the possibility of apostasy after one has known Jesus Christ as personal Savior. "It is impossible for those who have once been enlightened, who have tasted the heavenly gift, who have shared in the Holy Spirit, who have tasted the goodness of the word of God and the powers of the coming age, if they fall away, to be brought back to repentance, because to their loss they are crucifying the Son of God all over again and subjecting him to public disgrace" (Hebrews 6:4–6).

This may also be related to the unpardonable sin mentioned in the Gospels—a sin that "will not be forgiven, either in this age or in the age to come" (Matthew 12:32). Some people are worried about having committed the unpardonable sin. But if one has that worry, he or she most definitely has not committed that sin. When one is eternally lost after having known salvation, there is no longer any care or concern about getting back into a relationship with God. No matter how far a person has drifted, the Holy Spirit seeks to draw the backslider.

There is no sin God cannot or will not forgive as long as there is a desire to be forgiven, and then a willingness to accept that forgiveness through Jesus Christ.

Assurance and Warning

The divine inspiration of Scripture is nowhere more evident than in the theological debate of the **sovereignty of God** and the free will of humankind. There is a tendency in any debate to push the opposite position to the extreme. Some people need to be assured of their salvation. Others need to be warned that carelessness can jeopardize their relationship with the Lord. Therefore, the Bible contains verses that seem to stress two opposites. But in reality both are true, but wrong when taken to extremes.

God's sovereignty and humankind's free will are both biblical truths. God created humans in His own image (Genesis 1:26–27). No one would deny that God has free will. So in His creative act, God placed a free will in Adam and Eve—and in all their descendants. **Human free will** is not contrary to God's sovereignty. Nor is God's sovereignty diminished by His giving humans free will. God achieves all His purposes without abusing our free will.

There is another way of looking at the seemingly contradictory truths of God's sovereignty and our free will. If we are born-again believers, it is due only to God's love and provision; we can take not even a little credit for our salvation. If we choose by our free will to reject God's provision, we must take total responsibility; God bears not even the slightest blame for our eternal punishment.

Calvinistic Teachings Not Supported by Scripture

4.2.3
OBJECTIVE
Explain the five points of Calvinism as taught by the TULIP acrostic.

The TULIP acrostic of Calvinism helps us understand this theological position accepted by Christians in Reformed churches. "All five points of the TULIP are based on a specific view of God's sovereignty: It neglects the fact that God is sovereign over himself and is thereby able to limit himself in areas of His choice so that we might have true free will, able to choose to become His children, rather than bound to be His puppets" (Railey, Jr. and Aker 1995, 49).

- Total Depravity. A person has no ability to respond to God's offer of salvation. (Scripture records humanity's depravity but invites individuals to respond to God's offer of salvation.)

- Unconditional Election. Sovereign God before the Creation chose (elected) some individuals to be saved without regard to a future decision to accept or reject salvation. (Scripture teaches the elect are those who accept God's salvation.)

- Limited Atonement. Christ died only for those who were unconditionally elected to salvation. (Scripture teaches that Christ died for the entire human race.)

- Irresistible Grace. The people elected cannot resist or reject salvation. (This has no basis in Scripture.)

- Perseverance of the Saints. Once saved, the elect will persevere to the end and enjoy eternal life. (Scripture teaches that believers can fall from grace.)

A Ready Witness

4.2.4
OBJECTIVE
Identify the basic steps of salvation that can be used in witnessing to sinners.

"Always be prepared to give an answer to everyone who asks you to give the reason for the hope that you have. But do this with gentleness and respect" (1 Peter 3:15). To be prepared to fulfill the Great Commission (Mark 16:15, Matthew 28:19–20), you will need a simple biblical framework you can follow, allowing the Holy Spirit to adjust the pattern to meet the needs of the person you are seeking to introduce to Christ.

But first there is some heart preparation to be done. Witnessing to the unsaved is more than a routine to be followed. The heart must beat with a passion prompted by the Holy Spirit. If you have not yet felt that burden, begin praying for a passion to see the lost brought to Christ. Then when that burden is felt, pray regularly for lost souls in your own community and around the world. Be sure to include some lost people in your friendship circle. We cannot win the lost unless we come into contact with them. Be ready to share your own testimony of coming to know God personally. Be able to quote from memory Bible verses describing the steps to salvation.

The Bible describes the sequence of what happens as a sinner changes into a child of God.

1. First, the Holy Spirit convicts of sin and makes a person aware of his or her sinfulness. "And when He [the Holy Spirit] has come He will convince the world of its sin, and of the availability of God's goodness, and of deliverance from judgment" (John 16:8, *The Living Bible*). The Holy Spirit is here now and working to draw men and women to Christ.

2. The sinner admits he or she is lost. "As the Scriptures say, 'No one is good—no one in all the world is innocent.' No one has ever really followed God's paths, or even truly wanted to. Every one has turned away; all have gone wrong. No one anywhere has kept on doing what is right; not one" (Romans 3:10–12, *The Living Bible*). The lost cannot be saved until they admit they are sinners.

3. The sinner repents and asks for forgiveness. Repentance means true sorrow for sin, with a sincere effort to forsake it. Repentance works in three ways: (1) confession of sin to God (Luke 18:13); (2) forsaking sin (Isaiah 55:7); and (3) turning to God (Acts 26:18).

4. The sinner believes that Jesus died for him or her. "Believe in the Lord Jesus, and you will be saved" (Acts 16:31).

5. The sinner confesses Christ. "For it is with your heart that you believe and are justified, and it is with your mouth that you confess and are saved" (Romans 10:10).

6. The Holy Spirit makes the sinner a new person. Christ now lives in the believer. "I have been crucified with Christ and I no longer live, but Christ lives in me. The life I live in the body, I live by faith in the Son of God, who loved me and gave himself for me" (Galatians 2:20).

7. God justifies the believer. "Through him everyone who believes is justified from everything you could not be justified from by the law of Moses" (Acts 13:39).

8. The one who once was lost has now been saved.

In reviewing the eight steps above, notice that only four are actions on the part of the sinner. Points 2–5 are often called the ABC of salvation. After admitting he or she has sinned, the sinner must ask for forgiveness, believe that Jesus died for him, and confess Jesus Christ as Savior. God does all the rest.

T Test Yourself

Circle the letter of the *best* answer.

1. Water baptism by immersion is a testimony that one has
a) received Jesus Christ as personal Savior.
b) received the baptism in the Holy Spirit.
c) accepted the Jesus Only doctrine as truth.

2. Holy Communion should be observed regularly until
a) one has received the baptism in the Holy Spirit.
b) the last rite on a person's death bed.
c) Jesus comes to rapture His followers.

3 Christ's command was to baptize in the name of
a) Jesus only.
b) the Father, and of the Son, and of the Holy Spirit.
c) the Holy Spirit only.

4. The Lord's Supper replaced the Old Testament Feast of
a) the First Fruits.
b) Tabernacles.
c) Passover.

5. The ordinance of water baptism should be observed by
a) parents taking their infants to be baptized.
b) relatives for their deceased loved ones.
c) newly converted Christians as soon after salvation as it is feasible.

6. Calvinists believe that
a) Old Testament believers will go to heaven.
b) humans have free will and can choose to accept Christ as Savior.
c) God in the eternal past determined who would be saved.

7. The Bible contains assurance and warning about a person's salvation because
a) Calvinists and Arminians are both wrong.
b) believers need assurance; others need warning about neglect.
c) the books of the Bible were written by different writers.

8. The "T" in the Calvinistic TULIP acrostic stands for total
a) depravity.
b) dependence.
c) devotion.

9. Predestination is a word that means
a) God has determined that none should perish, but that all will be saved.
b) God has already determined who will be saved and who will not be saved.
c) heaven is our home, not this world.

10. The ABCs of salvation are
a) Always Be a Christian!
b) Admit sinning and ask forgiveness; Believe in Christ; Confess and forsake sin.
c) Accept Christ as Savior; Be a witness for Him; and Conform to His Image.

Responses to Interactive Questions
Chapter 4

Some of these responses may include information that is supplemental to the IST. These questions are intended to produce reflective thinking beyond the course content and your responses may vary from these examples.

1 How often should we remember the death of our Lord in this manner?

The Bible gives no directive on the frequency for the partaking of communion. It seems appropriate, therefore, to observe the memorial frequently enough that we are regularly reminded of the atoning work of Jesus Christ. On the other hand, it should not be observed so often that it becomes routine and commonplace. Many Evangelicals have concluded that once a month gives a proper balance between over use and proper remembering. Some people observe Communion at weddings and special religious occasions as well.

UNIT PROGRESS EVALUATION 2

Now that you have finished Unit 2, review the lessons in preparation for Unit Progress Evaluation 2. You will find it in the Essential Course Materials section at the back of this IST. Answer all of the questions without referring to your course materials, Bible, or notes. When you have completed the UPE, check your answers with the answer key provided in the Essential Course Materials section, and review any items you may have answered incorrectly. Then you may proceed with your study of Unit 3. (Although UPE scores do not count as part of your final course grade, they indicate how well you learned the material and how well you may perform on the closed-book final examination.)

UNIT 3

The Promised Holy Spirit

It was Jesus himself who said, "If you love me, you will obey what I command. And I will ask the Father, and he will give you another Counselor to be with you forever—the Spirit of truth. The world cannot accept him, because it neither sees him nor knows him. But you know him, for he lives with you and will be in you" (John 14:15–17). Love for Jesus and obedience to His commandments are absolutely necessary if we are to receive the special blessings God has prepared for us. The Holy Spirit, as Comforter and Counselor, is at the top of the list of our spiritual blessings.

In this unit of study, we deal with the historical distinctive of the Assemblies of God: the baptism in the Holy Spirit. Since many in the Christian world do not believe in this special after-salvation experience imparting power and holiness, we will give greater attention to this foundational truth of Pentecostals. But we must understand one thing as we begin our study of the Holy Spirit: Though Pentecostals often stress the physical manifestations, the miracles, and the power of the Holy Spirit, we must always remember the gentleness of the Holy Spirit. Some are frightened away from the baptism in the Holy Spirit, with the evidence of speaking in unknown tongues, but the Holy Spirit never forces a person to do what he or she is not willing to do or receive. The Holy Spirit is a gentle Spirit, demonstrating and instilling the fruit of love, joy, peace, patience, kindness, goodness, faithfulness, gentleness, and self-control.

As you study the next eleven lessons, expect the Holy Spirit to empower you to be a more effective witness. Ask Him also to make you more Christlike as He develops in you the fruit of the Spirit.

CHAPTER 5

The Holy Spirit: God's Agent in Today's World

Some Christians take lightly the work of the Holy Spirit today. The Father and the Son have personalities with counterparts in the human family, but the Holy Spirit may seem less important. Church historians have noted that the Christian church of the Middle Ages made very little mention or study of the Holy Spirit. But we are now living in days that could be called the "Age of the Spirit." We are seeing the fulfillment of Joel's prophecy. "I will pour out my Spirit on all people. Your sons and daughters will prophesy, your old men will dream dreams, your young men will see visions. Even on my servants, both men and women, I will pour out my Spirit in those days" (Joel 2:28–29). In the "Age of the Spirit" we should be "People of the Spirit. (The stories of many twentieth-century people of the Spirit are told in Gary B. McGee's *People of the Spirit: the Assemblies of God*, published in 2001 by Logion Press of Gospel Publishing House in Springfield, Mo.)

The two lessons in this chapter deal with two critical matters in the Christian experience: (1) the importance of our belief in the Trinity, and the distinctive work of the Holy Spirit in that Trinity of Father, Son, and Spirit, (2) the nature of the holy life the Spirit desires to produce in each one of us. There are many different ideas as to what constitutes holiness. There is a fine line between true holiness and legalism. One pleases God, while the other does not. We must never allow our sincere desire to please God by holy living to sink into legalism.

Lesson 5.1   The Role of the Spirit in the Trinity

Objectives

5.1.1   Explain how the "Jesus Only" teaching is not compatible with Scripture.
5.1.2   Identify the members of the Trinity and describe their relationship to each other.
5.1.3   List and explain the attributes of God.
5.1.4   Describe the special attributes of the Holy Spirit.

Lesson 5.2   The Spirit's Part in Producing Holy Lives

Objectives

5.2.1   Describe the role of the Holy Spirit in the believer's sanctification.
5.2.2   Explain the principles of progressive sanctification.
5.2.3   Indicate the difference between legalism and living a holy life that pleases God.

The Role of the Spirit in the Trinity

Can we just talk about "God" in the singular as the Islamic faith does when it calls Allah their god? It is useless to try to redefine God in human terms. We must take His divinely inspired Word, the Bible, as the true description of the **Godhead**. To us, God is as the commandment states, "I am the Lord your God, . . . You shall have no other gods before me" (Exodus 20:2–3). Yet that one God consists of three Persons: the Father, the Son, and the Holy Spirit.

The "Jesus Only" Teaching

There are some Christians—even evangelicals and Pentecostals—who do not believe in the Trinity. **Unitarians** deny the divinity of Jesus and say that God is a single Person. This doctrine is not Christian and is not difficult to disprove from the Bible. But what about those persons who do believe that Jesus Christ is divine but still refuse to believe that there are three Persons in the Godhead?

One Pentecostal group that holds this view is referred to as the "Jesus Only" churches. They teach that the three Persons mentioned in the Bible are really only names for different manifestations of one Person. They speak of Jesus as the most important form of God because that is the form in which God revealed himself to humankind.

"Jesus Only" churches further hold that before God appeared on earth in the form of Jesus, His name was the Father. But He stopped being the Father when He became the Son. Then when Jesus ascended into heaven and was no longer walking on this earth, He took on the form of the Holy Spirit. So Jesus was in the form of the Father at one time, the human form of Jesus at another time, and finally in the form of the Holy Spirit as He is today. According to this heretical teaching, the three Persons have never existed at the same time. Can you refute this wrong belief from God's Word?

The Triune God

The best proof that the Trinity is one God in three Persons is the Gospel account of John's baptism of Jesus. You may study the story in Matthew 3:13–17, Mark 1:9–11, or Luke 3:21–22. In this one incident, recorded in detail three times, we find all three members of the Trinity present at the same time: Jesus being baptized, the Holy Spirit descending like a dove, and the voice of the Father expressing approval from heaven. To explain this passage from a Jesus Only perspective, we would have to make Jesus a ventriloquist who bounced His words off the clouds: "This is my beloved Son, in whom I am well pleased."

Some proponents of the Jesus Only position point to Early Church councils, like the Nicene Council (AD 325) and the Council of Constantinople (AD 381), as the beginning of the church's belief in the Trinity. However, they overlook the fact that such councils usually recognized and responded to heretical teachings that were circulating at the time. Instead of promoting new doctrine, these councils reaffirmed biblical truth that had been held from the days of the Early Church.

God's Attributes Applicable to All Three Persons

When we speak of the attributes or characteristics of God, we are describing the qualities of each of the three persons. When we find it necessary to note the unique characteristics of one of the three Persons, we must always include the personal name.

5.1.1
OBJECTIVE
Explain how the "Jesus Only" teaching is not compatible with Scripture.

1   Why do the Father and the Son need another Person to speak for them?

5.1.2
OBJECTIVE
Identify the members of the Trinity and describe their relationship to each other.

5.1.3
OBJECTIVE
List and explain the attributes of God.

The word Trinity does not appear in the New Testament. The word is a theological term, first used during the second century, to describe the obvious "threeness" within the unity of God. The divine God is one being of three distinct Persons. Each One of them expresses the unity of the Godhead. Yet each of the three is very conscious of and dependent upon the other Two. The word *Trinity* is not the same as *tritheism*, or the belief in three gods.

Since God is infinite in His being, and since we are finite, we are not able to know Him exactly as He is. Yet He has told us some things about himself that help us understand in a limited way who He is and what He expects of us. The attributes of God point out various sides of His character.

God is a Spirit.	He thinks, feels, speaks, and can have direct relationship with creatures made in His image. He cannot be seen with natural eyes or perceived by our natural senses. God can manifest himself in bodily form and thus be perceived by humans, but the essence of God cannot be seen (John 1:18; 4:24).
God is Infinite.	He is not subject to natural and human limitations. He is throughout, and greater than, His creation. He is eternal (1 Kings 8:27; Revelation 4:8–10).
God is Omnipotent.	He is all-powerful (Job 42:2; Matthew 19:26; Revelation 19:6).
God is Omnipresent.	His presence is everywhere (Psalm 139:7–10; Jeremiah 23:23–24).
God is Omniscient.	He knows all things. His knowledge is perfect; He does not have to reason, search, or learn gradually (Job 12:13; Job 36:4–5; Proverbs 3:19).
God is All-wise.	In addition to knowing everything, God applies that knowledge in the best possible way to achieve the best possible purposes (Daniel 2:20–22; Ephesians 1:8).
God is Sovereign.	He has the absolute right to govern and deal with His creatures as He pleases (Daniel 4:35; Matthew 20:15; Romans 9:19–21).
God is Holy.	He is morally perfect; He does only righteous acts (Isaiah 6:3; Genesis 18:25).
God is Faithful.	He is absolutely trustworthy; His word will never fail (1 Corinthians 10:13; Matthew 24:35).
God is Merciful.	For one of the most eloquent reminders of the everlasting mercy of God, read Psalm 136. God's mercy was best manifested in sending Christ into the world (Luke 1:78).
God is Love.	This is the attribute that caused God to send His Son to die for our sins (John 3:16).
God is Good.	God is so good in all His dealings with us (Psalm 34:8; 52:9).

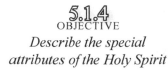

Describe the special attributes of the Holy Spirit

The Holy Spirit: Special and Distinctive Functions

All of the things mentioned above about God are true of the Holy Spirit. But there are specific roles or functions of the Holy Spirit.

The Holy Spirit is described in Scripture as having characteristics we all have: a mind (Romans 8:27), a will (1 Corinthians 12:11), and feelings (Ephesians 4:30). Human-like activities include teaching (John 14:26), witnessing or testifying (Romans 8:16), speaking (Revelation 2:7), and revealing (1 Peter 1:12).

Some of the names by which the Holy Spirit is identified are helpful in calling attention to the distinctive characteristics of the Third Person of the Trinity.

As the Spirit of God, He is an executive carrying out the will of God.

As the Spirit of Christ (Romans 8:9), He comes in the name of Christ and gives glory to the Son.

As the Comforter or Paraclete (John 14:16), He stands beside and sustains believers in their time of need.

As the Holy Spirit, He seeks to impart holiness and sanctification to us.

As the Holy Spirit of Promise (Ephesians 1:13), He is the manifestation of God that was promised throughout the Old Testament.

As the Spirit of Truth (John 14:17), His mission is to reveal Jesus Christ, the Way, the Truth, and the Life.

As the Spirit of Grace (Hebrews 10:29), He imparts grace and power for living a sanctified life.

As the Spirit of Life (Romans 8:2), He gives and preserves both natural and spiritual life.

As the Spirit of Adoption (Romans 8:15), He brings us into the family of God.

These aspects of the Holy Spirit describe what the Holy Spirit is doing in the church today. Capturing the relationship between the Holy Spirit and the church, Dr. Anthony D. Palma (2001) writes, "The Holy Spirit and the Church are inseparable. Wherever the true Church is, there is also the Holy Spirit at work. In its fullest sense, the Church did not come into existence until the Day of Pentecost, because it was on that occasion that the Spirit came upon the assembled body of believers" (55). What an important and wonderful member of the Trinity is the Holy Spirit!

The Spirit's Part in Producing Holy Lives

One might ask why the Holy Spirit is the only member of the Trinity who has the word "holy" in His name. It is not because He is more holy than the Father or the Son. From our last lesson, we learned that God is holy (Isaiah 6:3 and throughout Scripture). So each of the members of the Trinity is holy. Peter called Jesus "the Holy One of God" (John 6:69). And in His great prayer for himself and all believers, Jesus addressed the Father as "Holy Father" (John 17:11). So the Holy Spirit is not more holy than the Father or Jesus. The Holy Spirit is so named for two reasons: (1) to set Him apart from spirits that are not holy, and (2) to identify the believer's increasing sanctification or holiness as His primary ministry (Romans 15:16; 2 Thessalonians 2:13; 1 Peter 1:2).

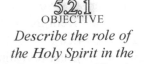

Believers Resembling Jesus

For most people, salvation is an experience that can be identified as to where and when it happened. For others, the experience took place at such an early age that no first time or place can be established. In either case, however, there was a work of the Holy Spirit that brought the believer into the family of God. But there is a work of sanctification that takes place beyond that initial salvation experience.

We should not remain in the same condition in which we find ourselves immediately after conversion. Christ expects us to become more and more like Him. This process by which we become more like Him is called "progressive sanctification." It is distinct from instantaneous sanctification when God declares us holy, or set apart to Him, at the moment of salvation.

As we daily become more like Jesus, there are four things that happen in our lives. First, we more completely present our lives to God. "I urge you, brothers, in view of God's mercy, to offer your bodies as living sacrifices, holy and pleasing to God—this is your spiritual act of worship" (Romans 12:1).

Second, there is growth from spiritual infancy toward spiritual maturity (1 Corinthians 3:1; 2 Peter 3:18). Third, we are continually cleansed and purified from all filthiness of the flesh and the spirit (2 Corinthians 7:1). Finally, we are transformed, day-by-day, into a more Christlike person. The Holy Spirit is the primary Agent in bringing about these changes in our lives.

Progressive Sanctification

The Bible uses several symbols or pictures in helping us to understand the nature of the Holy Spirit. These include, among others, wind (John 3:8), streams of living water (John 7:38-39), anointing oil (1 Samuel 16:13), and a dove (Luke 3:22). Yet the symbol of fire carries with it a special function of the Holy Spirit. At the initial experience of Holy Spirit baptism on the Day of Pentecost, what looked like tongues of fire settled on the heads of those who were about to be filled with the Spirit (Acts 2:3).

John the Baptist foretold the special gift Jesus would give to His followers: "He will baptize you with the Holy Spirit and with fire" (Matthew 3:11). One Pentecostal scholar sees this mention of fire as a reference to a national cleansing, not a personal cleansing. (Menzies 1994, 128). Another Pentecostal scholar views the mention of fire as being **eschatological**, or a judgment sometime in the future (Horton 1976, 85–86). There are other interpretations as well. However, without settling the debate over the meaning of fire in the statement by John the Baptist, we can agree that fire as a symbol stands for cleansing and/or judgment. And from references listed above, we know that sanctification is an important work of the Holy Spirit in the life of the believer. The sin is judged and the believer cleansed as he or she becomes more and more like Jesus. The believer is "set apart" from the remnants of sin in personal behavior and "set apart" to God's use.

Scripture calls all believers to separate from sin. "Christ also loved the church, and gave himself for it; That he might sanctify and cleanse it with the washing of water by the word" (Ephesians 5:25–26, KJV). Throughout Scripture believers are encouraged to "Throw off everything that hinders and the sin that so easily entangles" (Hebrews 12:1). In another place, Paul instructs to "Put off falsehood and speak truthfully to [your] neighbor, for we are all members of one body" (Ephesians 4:25). The sanctifying work of the Holy Spirit encourages and helps us to separate from our sinful failings.

We will never reach complete holiness on this side of eternity, but each day should find us closer to the image of our loving Savior, through the help of the Holy Spirit. Righteous attitudes and behavior, good works (Ephesians 2:10), holiness (1 Peter 1:15), and Christ-likeness should daily replace the sinful things we leave behind. The Holy Spirit sanctifies and leads us in becoming God's holy people.

Avoiding Legalism

5.2.3
OBJECTIVE
Indicate the difference between legalism and living a holy life that pleases God.

Is holiness a set of dos and don'ts that someone else has prescribed? What behaviors are acceptable, and which are sinful? Are some things considered acceptable in some countries or states but wrong in other countries or states? How do you apply biblical principles to contemporary activities that were not known in Bible times? If an activity or behavior was considered wrong in earlier days, was it wrong for all future generations?

Christians have struggled with questions like these for years. The Bible obviously teaches standards of morality and personal relationships. It also gives principles like "Avoid every kind of evil" (1 Thessalonians 5:22) or "Abstain from all appearance of evil" (KJV). But who should define "evil"? Specific things are mentioned in Scripture as evil, and there should be no question about them. But other behaviors are not specifically mentioned in the Bible. How are they to be judged?

2   How do we define holiness?

The difficult task of finding the right answer to these questions is seen in the difference between **legalism** and the freedom the Spirit provides. Legalism in religious circles defines sanctification as complete obedience to some code of law, such as the Old Testament or the New Testament. In its worst form, legalism holds that salvation depends on works (dos and don'ts), rather than on faith, and that is definitely condemned in Scripture (Ephesians 2:8–9). Yet the Bible specifically condemns certain behaviors and describes good deeds we are to do with the help of the Holy Spirit. How do we know which are approved and which are condemned?

If we look at deeper principles of Scripture, we see that the heart and motivation are more important to God than the specific act that may not be clearly condemned as sin. "Man looks at the outward appearance, but the Lord looks at the heart" (1 Samuel 16:7). Understanding that biblical truth, we can then consider three principles of choice that please God.

1. Personal convictions are not always universal commands. The Holy Spirit develops in each believer applications of Scriptural truth. He leads us from one step of commitment and obedience to another step. All believers are not at the same point in their spiritual development. For instance, one younger convert was offended when the Sunday school leadership planned a picnic for the youth and children and included pitching horseshoes as one of the game activities. He was offended because he felt pitching horseshoes was a sin. As he was questioned about his belief, he said that when he was saved, the Holy Spirit convicted him of his horseshoe obsession. It had grown to consume all of his free time. However, this convert's conviction was personal and not intended to be universal. God does deal with us individually on the things that we must surrender to His control.

Another spiritual leader, halfway around the world, was convicted by the Holy Spirit to give up his obsession with tennis. Years later, when the obsession was no longer controlling him, he reported the Spirit had confirmed that he could resume playing tennis to the extent that it did not draw him away from his call to ministry. In such matters of personal conviction, we may need to say, "Others may, I cannot!" But that conviction does not mean that everyone else must have the same convictions.

2. The influence our actions may have on fellow believers must also guide our choices. After Paul had finished telling the Corinthian believers that idols were nothing at all and eating meat offered to idols was not sinful, he explained, "But not everyone knows this. Some people are still so accustomed to idols that when they eat such food they think of it as having been sacrificed to an idol, and since their conscience is weak, it is defiled. But food does not bring us near to God; we are no worse if we do not eat, and no better if we do" (1 Corinthians 8:7–8). Then he concluded with the great principle that should guide our choices in controversial matters. "Be careful, however, that the exercise of your freedom does not become a stumbling block to the weak" (v. 9). Knowledge of our liberty in Christ can puff up, but love and concern for others builds up" (8:1). It is not appropriate to point fingers at a weak brother or sister, claiming our spiritual superiority.

3. The Christian's personal rights are no reason for denying fellow believers their rights. A real mark of spiritual maturity is the move from self-centered concern ("What can the Holy Spirit do in my life to meet my needs?") to concern for ministry to others ("What can the Holy Spirit do through me to meet the needs of others?"). We need to spend more time learning and practicing the concepts of 1 Corinthians 12 and 14, within the love emphasis of chapter 13.

T Test Yourself

CHAPTER 5

Circle the letter of the *best* answer.

1. Pentecostals who do not believe in the Trinity are called
a) Unity Assemblies of God.
b) Jesus Only churches.
c) Three Manifestations of God churches.

2. The best biblical proof of the Trinity is found in
a) the account of Jesus' baptism by John.
b) the outpouring of the Holy Spirit on the Day of Pentecost.
c) the description of Jesus sitting at the right hand of the Father.

3. The work of the Holy Spirit in helping us become more like Jesus is called
a) unification with Jesus.
b) Jesus Only manifestation.
c) progressive sanctification.

4. John's use of fire in predicting a baptism "with the Holy Spirit and with fire" means
a) the national cleansing of Israel.
b) the cleansing or sanctifying work of the Holy Spirit.
c) the end-time cleansing or judgment of all believers.

5. Legalism as a means of righteous living is defined as
a) required obedience to religious law or a moral code.
b) God's act of declaring a person legally justified.
c) a religious discipline that is pleasing to God.

6. The best proof that there are three Persons in the Godhead is that
a) Scripture specifically states, "God is a Trinity."
b) all three Persons are mentioned by name in the New Testament.
c) water baptism in Acts is in the name of Jesus.

7. The Holy Spirit is at work today wherever
a) Satan is doing his evil works.
b) people need healing for sickness or disease.
c) the true Church is found.

8. A genuine mark of spiritual maturity is
a) speaking in tongues.
b) moving from self-centered concerns to ministry and concern for others.
c) living day after day without committing sin.

9. Progressive sanctification is the process of
a) becoming more like Jesus
b) becoming more effective in helping others experience sanctification.
c) becoming more aware of Satan's presence in the world.

10. Holiness is properly defined as
a) what is generally acceptable in a Christian community.
b) an obedient heart that seeks to please God in every action.
c) obedience to a code of conduct.

Responses to Interactive Questions
Chapter 5

Some of these responses may include information that is supplemental to the IST. These questions are intended to produce reflective thinking beyond the course content and your responses may vary from these examples.

1   Why do the Father and the Son need another Person to speak for them?

Student's answer will vary. The Holy Spirit is not separate from the Godhead, but is an active Person within a single Trinity. A possible response to this question is, the Holy Spirit operates in voicing God's communication somewhat like our human voice expresses mental thoughts.

2   How do we define holiness?

Student's answer will vary and will depend on religious training and tradition. Students should infer from the text that holiness includes behavioral and relationship standards. True, biblical holiness is produced from the heart in the lives of believers seeking to please God and represent Him to the world.

CHAPTER 6

The Baptism in the Holy Spirit

The Pentecostal experience, the baptism in the Holy Spirit, was the secret to the powerful growth of the Early Church. It revolutionized believers and sent them as missionaries to the ends of the known world. Over the centuries, the Church drifted from the supernatural anointing that marked the first-century beginning. But once again, in the past one hundred years, the Holy Spirit has been moving as was promised by Joel. "And afterward, I will pour out my Spirit on all people. Your sons and daughters will prophesy, your old men will dream dreams, your young men will see visions. Even on my servants, both men and women, I will pour out my Spirit in those days" (Joel 2:28–29).

The "afterward" speaks of what happens after repentance and restoration of God's people. It also refers to Christ's work of redemption at Calvary. There was a partial fulfillment on the Day of Pentecost and in the early days of the Church Age. The supernatural move of the Holy Spirit in the past century has also been a fulfillment of "those days." Yet there is still much to be fulfilled from Joel's prophecy. Our attention will be focused on what is being fulfilled today.

It is so important to put the events of our spiritual lives in proper order. Salvation comes first. Growth in hunger for God then follows. Finally, the enduement of power comes to equip for effective ministry and give help in living a holy life. If you have not yet received the baptism in the Holy Spirit, be open to what God wants to do in your life as you study this topic. If you have received this wonderful experience, make sure you keep the Spirit relationship strong and growing. There is no limit to what God can do through vessels yielded completely to His control and guidance. Your study can prepare you to lead other believers into this beautiful Pentecostal experience.

Lesson 6.1   An Experience Available to All Believers

Objectives
6.1.1   *Describe the initial outpouring of the Holy Spirit as a pattern for the infilling today.*
6.1.2   *Explain why a person must not give up when praying for the baptism in the Holy Spirit.*
6.1.3   *Identify possible sins against the Holy Spirit.*

Lesson 6.2   Supernatural Evidence of the Spirit's Powerful Presence

Objectives
6.2.1   *Identify the three uses of tongues in the Spirit-filled life, and identify the nature of tongues.*
6.2.2   *Define the importance of this experience in the lives of all believers.*
6.2.3   *Explain the role of tongues in salvation, and the necessity for believers to seek Spirit baptism.*

An Experience Available to All Believers

The world is facing an energy crisis. For decades it was thought that the vast underground supplies of natural gas and oil were inexhaustible. A few voices gave warning of an approaching shortage, but people living in affluence found the caution hard to believe. Now there are struggles between countries over the cost and availability of oil.

We recognize another energy crisis—a spiritual energy crisis. This one is quite different. The supply is unlimited, yet the majority of people fail to draw on the energy source. The problem is a long-standing one—existing for as long as man humanity has been under the curse of sin.

People search for alternative sources of spiritual power and energy—the power of the mind, of non-Christian religions, and even of satanically inspired spirits. Yet the true supply is unlimited; it need only be allowed to work in individual lives. The Bible tells us of the supernatural power and energizing strength available to Christians through the work of the Holy Spirit. But sinners refuse to allow the Spirit to do His work in their lives, and Christians live below the provision of supernatural power that has been made available to them.

The Holy Spirit works in the lives of all believers after conversion to make them more like Jesus. But there is an experience that holds the potential for accelerating the process of making us more Christlike. It is described in Acts 2 and is the distinctive belief of all Christians who call themselves Pentecostals.

Living in the Holy Spirit

6.1.1
OBJECTIVE
Describe the initial outpouring of the Holy Spirit as a pattern for the infilling today.

It seems unbelievable that a dynamic experience like the baptism in the Holy Spirit and the exciting walk that follows would ever lose their vitality. But for many who sit in the pews of our churches, they have. One reason is that the initial experience has been strongly emphasized while the continuing life in the Spirit is overlooked or neglected. Daily communion and praying in the Spirit will keep the Spirit-filled believer "walking in the Spirit" (Galatians 5:25).

There is more to the Pentecostal experience than speaking in tongues at an altar after a soul-stirring sermon. For those who have progressed no further in their spiritual experience, or who have allowed the original fervor to cool to a lukewarm apathy, the doctrine of the Holy Spirit needs to be re-energized.

Every Pentecostal Christian should read the Book of Acts at least once a year. The excitement and vitality of Early Church Pentecost is the best encouragement to living the same life today. All five instances of infilling by the Holy Spirit (Acts 2; 8; 9; 10; and 19) should be studied in-depth in various translations.

The believers in the Early Church were people just like Christians today. They had similar desires, struggles with the flesh, and a need for divine help in their daily lives. We should not place the New Testament saints on a pedestal high above the level of ordinary people. We can identify with them as we read the historical accounts of the Spirit's work among these early believers.

Acts 2 Today

Jesus gave His disciples the promise of a special Person to be with them, because He was soon to leave them. "It is for your good that I am going away. Unless I go away, the Counselor will not come to you; but if I go, I will send him to you . . . . But when he, the Spirit of truth, comes, he will guide you into all truth" (John 16:7, 13). Jesus reaffirmed the promise after His resurrection and just before He ascended into heaven: "But you will receive power when the Holy Spirit comes on you; and you will be my witnesses" (Acts 1:8).

Then it happened! The sound of wind, what seemed to be tongues of fire, the speaking in tongues! The promise had been fulfilled—or so some have thought. Peter's response indicated that "this initial experience was just a beginning." "The promise is for you and your children and for all who are far off—for all whom the Lord our God will call" (Acts 2:39).

1   How is the experience received?

The Baptism is received in much the same way that salvation was received earlier. A right attitude is essential. The believers on whom the Spirit was first outpoured were united in purpose and prayed in one accord. Obedience to God is necessary, because "God has given [the Holy Spirit] to those who obey him" (Acts 5:32). Just as faith is required in salvation, so we must have faith to receive this gift of power and commitment.

6.1.2
OBJECTIVE
Explain why a person must not give up when praying for the baptism in the Holy Spirit.

The Persistent Seeker

Some who have long desired and prayed for the baptism in the Holy Spirit, but have not received, may begin to question if they are really saved. But one can have assurance of salvation, without doubting, until the promised Baptism is received. In the meantime, obedience and motives must be examined. After the believer has asked the Holy Spirit to reveal any sin or relationship that may be standing in the way of receiving the Gift, then the person must examine his or her motive.

Do you want to be filled with the Spirit to have power for living a holy life? To have power for effective witnessing and ministry? Or, is there just a desire to join the fortunate blessed group who can say they have received the experience and spoken in tongues? The Spirit does not fill persons who do not plan to use the Spirit empowerment for the purposes God intended.

In seeking the Baptism, one young man felt increasingly self-conscious of the fact that as the pastor's son he had not received the experience about which his father so faithfully preached. He felt that all the church was watching to see if he would receive. Then he went away to college and attended a struggling new assembly with no more than thirty people in a service. As he had done for years, he continued to go to the altar every Sunday night and pray for the Baptism. His prayer time usually amounted to about twenty minutes, ending with the conclusion that nothing spiritual was happening and it was not to be for that night. On one particular Sunday night, he had prayed the usual twenty minutes. In no special need to get back to the dormitory, he got up from the altar and sat in one of the folding chairs against a wall to the left of the altar. Things were over for this time, but then he thought he would wait a little longer before leaving. As others at the altar were being blessed by the Spirit, he continued praising the Lord. The pressure of having to do something was off, and he felt a desire to tell the Lord how much he loved Him. Before long, the young man was speaking in tongues while still sitting on the chair.

Self-consciousness can delay the infilling. Seeking just to speak in tongues may also hinder. But when the heart so deeply loves the Lord, and has difficulty finding words to express that desire, the Spirit can give the words in a heavenly language. But speaking in tongues is not the end. It is only the beginning of an exciting life guided and empowered by the Holy Spirit. Speaking in tongues is not a badge of spirituality. It is a gift for drawing closer to Jesus. If one has no desire for a deeper spiritual life, there is no need for the Baptism. Yet Scripture commands us to be "filled with the Spirit" (Ephesians 5:18). So if after salvation we are not seeking to be filled with the Spirit, that suggests that our desire to draw closer to Jesus is lacking.

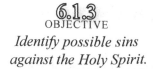
OBJECTIVE

*Identify possible sins
against the Holy Spirit.*

Sin against the Holy Spirit

The work of the Spirit in individual lives can bring great blessing. But there are corresponding responsibilities expected of each person in whom the Spirit moves. We must cooperate with the work the Spirit seeks to accomplish. The Bible lists several ways in which Christians can hinder the move of the Spirit. We can lie to Him as Ananias did (Acts 5:3). We can grieve Him (Ephesians 4:30). We can quench, smother, stifle, or put out the fire or power of the Holy Spirit (1 Thessalonians 5:19). We can resist Him (Acts 7:51). Christians grieve the Spirit when they fail to use the provision of the indwelling Holy Spirit to produce holy and fruitful lives. They quench the Spirit when they do not allow Him to endue them with power for use in His service.

We do not want to be guilty of any of the above sins. If they should happen, we must plead for forgiveness immediately. But most serious of the sins against the Holy Spirit is blaspheming against the Spirit. Every sin and blasphemy can be forgiven, "but the blasphemy against the Spirit will not be forgiven" (Matthew 12:31). Some non-Pentecostals have spoken harshly against the Pentecostal belief in the baptism in the Holy Spirit. Have they committed blasphemy against the Holy Spirit? Dr. Anthony Palma (2001) describes two meanings for blaspheming or sinning against the Holy Spirit: "(a) It consists of knowingly and persistently attributing to Satan what is obviously the work of the Holy Spirit. (b) It is a rejection of Jesus Christ as God's chosen and anointed One for the deliverance of humankind" (Palma 2001, 23).

There may be some relation between the **unpardonable sin** of the Gospel accounts and apostasy in the Book of Hebrews. "It is impossible for those who have once been enlightened, who have tasted the heavenly gift, who have shared in the Holy Spirit, who have tasted the goodness of the Word of God and the powers of the coming age, if they fall away, to be brought back to repentance, because to their loss they are crucifying the Son of God all over again" (Hebrews 6:4–6). Both passages suggest the severe consequence of eternal separation from God. Unfortunately, some sensitive Christians have expressed great fear that they have committed the unpardonable sin or apostasy. But the fact that they have such concerns indicates that the Holy Spirit has not left them. God is still "faithful and just and will forgive us our sins and purify us from all unrighteousness" (1 John 1:9). A person who has actually committed the unpardonable sin or apostasy has no longer any tug in God's direction. He or she wants no relationship with God or His children.

Another area of concern for Spirit-filled believers is the moral failure of some who have publicly and forcefully proclaimed their Spirit baptism experience. When non-Pentecostals view such immorality and lack of integrity, they are not inclined to find anything desirable or necessary in an experience they have tried to discredit. Their negative expressions may be made out of ignorance rather than out of animosity toward the Holy Spirit, but the Pentecostal message is unfortunately compromised. To echo James's words, "My brothers, this should not be" (James 3:10). The Holy Spirit seeks to help us resist temptation and sin, but we must cooperate by living close to Jesus and resisting the assaults of the evil one.

Supernatural Evidence of the Spirit's Powerful Presence

To persons not accustomed to a Pentecostal worship service, a message in tongues they cannot understand may seem frightening. Meaningless sounds suggest to them that the speaker is not in touch with reality. They may even suspect pagan or demonic excesses. However, to the person who believes the Bible and its encouragements to be filled with the Holy Spirit, experiencing the supernatural inspiration of the Holy Spirit is one of the highest moments of the Christian walk.

There is also confusion among non-Pentecostals concerning the significance of tongues. "What is the value of speaking in tongues?" they ask. They confuse the gift of tongues with other uses of Spirit-prompted tongues. This lesson will study this distinctively supernatural manifestation of the Holy Spirit and provide answers a Pentecostal can share with non-Pentecostal Christians.

Purpose of Tongues

Pentecostals recognize in Scripture three distinct uses or purposes of tongues.

1. There is the initial evidence, properly documented in Acts by such statements as "All of them were filled with the Holy Spirit and began to speak in other tongues" (Acts 2:4). They were filled with the Spirit and spoke in tongues. There is no record in Scripture of these tongues being interpreted; though on occasion they were understood by persons present (e.g., the Day of Pentecost).

2. There are devotional tongues, or prayer language, for times when the human intellect falls short of knowing what to ask for in prayer. At such a time, the Spirit prays through the Spirit-filled believer with groans and tongues that cannot be expressed in human language (Romans 8:26). Devotional tongues, of course, do not happen without a first-time initial evidence of tongues. We believe this devotional use of tongues is what Paul was referring to when he told the Corinthians: "I thank God that I speak in tongues more than all of you." (1 Corinthians 14:18). Certainly, Paul was not speaking in tongues more than the Corinthians in public worship services, because he was giving instructions on regulating the public use of tongues (which leads to the third use of tongues).

3. The gift of tongues operates in the public worship service, within appropriate guidelines. It is to this use of tongues Paul is referring in 1 Corinthians 12:30. Some non-Pentecostals loosely call all three of these uses "the gift of tongues" and quote Paul when he asks the rhetorical question, "Do all have the gift of tongues?" The answer to that question is obviously no, but every believer can receive the post-salvation baptism in the Holy Spirit and enjoy the first two uses mentioned above. Let us look at each of the uses in greater detail.

Tongues as initial evidence. The question of initial evidence has caused much controversy and has been a major point of disagreement between Pentecostals and non-Pentecostal evangelicals. The Pentecostal position that speaking in tongues is the initial physical evidence of the baptism in the Holy Spirit is based on the five instances of such infillings recorded in the Book of Acts (chapters 2, 8, 9, 10, 19).

In three of the five records, the believers all spoke in Spirit-given languages upon receiving the Baptism. In the other two instances, the speaking in tongues is implied: (1) Simon the Sorcerer desired to buy the gift because of some obvious external manifestation (Acts 8); (2) Paul obviously had the manifestation at some time because he later testified that he spoke in tongues more than the believers

OBJECTIVE

Identify the three uses of tongues in the Spirit-filled life, and identify the nature of tongues.

2   How do we know when a person receives the **charismatic** impartation of the Holy Spirit?

to whom he wrote (Acts 9; 1 Corinthians 14:18). The Holy Spirit dwells in every believer, but not all believers have been baptized in the Holy Spirit.

Tongues as prayer language. There are times when a believer faces an extreme situation, so critical that he or she does not know how to pray. Praying in tongues at such a time can be the Spirit himself interceding in behalf of the need. This privilege is certainly included in Bible references to praying "in the Spirit" (1 Corinthians 14:14–15; Ephesians 6:18; Jude 20). Since Paul says, "For anyone who speaks in a tongue does not speak to men but to God" (1 Corinthians 14:2), those expressions must be either prayer or praise. So Paul continues, "He who speaks in a tongue edifies himself" (1 Corinthians 14:4). Dr. Palma highlights the value of this prayer language: "When done in private, it [tongues] builds up the one praying, in a manner not explicitly stated in Scripture. Since tongues is a means of spiritual upbuilding (what some would call a means of grace), it is available to all God's children" (Palma 2001, 168).

The gift of tongues. This gift is not available to every Spirit-filled believer, only to those the Spirit chooses to use in edifying the worshipping congregation (1 Corinthians 12:10, 30). Critics of the Pentecostal belief in the baptism in the Holy Spirit point to pagan cults and heathen rites that made use of tongues, ecstatic speech, and trances even at the time the Spirit was outpoured on the Day of Pentecost. (Palma 2001, 225). (Palma notes that New Testament writers recognized such abuses and deliberately avoided the same terminology used to describe the pagan rites. This is especially seen in the account of Paul and the slave girl with "a spirit of divination" in Acts 16:16). Such critics discredit the God-given and inspired tongues by classifying biblical tongues with counterfeit tongues. But we know that Satan goes about as an angel of light, seeking to mislead even the believers. So is it any wonder that Satan would "inspire" counterfeit tongues in an attempt to discredit the real? (cf. 2 Corinthians 11:13–15). Indeed, Satan reigns wherever Christ is not honored and accepted.

Paul had words of caution against the use of tongues without interpretation in public worship. "If the whole church comes together and everyone speaks in tongues, and some who do not understand or some unbelievers come in, will they not say that you are out of your mind?" (1 Corinthians 14:23). The abuse that Paul sought to correct was everyone speaking in tongues at the same time (or individuals in rapid succession) without interpretation.

Human or Heavenly Language

6.2.2
OBJECTIVE
Define the importance of this experience in the lives of all believers.

Critics of the Pentecostal understanding of biblical tongues have described tongues as, among other things, a miracle of hearing, meaningless sounds, and foreign or ancient words spoken from a universal memory bank. There is often a quick assumption that the person speaking in tongues is in a trance. But Scripture clearly identifies tongues as actual languages inspired by the Holy Spirit. Paul mentions speaking "with the tongues of men and of angels" (1 Corinthians 13:1, KJV). There are recorded instances of tongues (never learned by the speaker yet inspired by the Holy Spirit) being heard and understood by native speakers of the foreign language (Harris 1995). Also, the visitors in Jerusalem on the Day of Pentecost "heard them speaking in his own language" (Acts 2:6). But there is also a strong suggestion that tongues may at times be angelic or heavenly languages. If tongues are directed to God (1 Corinthians 14:2), inspired by the Holy Spirit, a heavenly language would seem more appropriate than another human language to address God.

OBJECTIVE
Explain the role of tongues in salvation, and the necessity for believers to seek Spirit baptism.

Encouraging Others

After one has become a Christian, there can be a number of reasons for not immediately receiving this special experience. Some have wanted the Baptism for personal gain (see the account of Simon the Sorcerer in Acts 8:9). Some are not sure that tongues are for today. Others are afraid to let go and let the Holy Spirit take control of their entire being, including the tongue (the most difficult member of the body to control). Others think they have to become better before they can receive the baptism in the Holy Spirit. Of course, if a person has any unconfessed sin, that must be dealt with right away. Others have been taught that the experience is of the devil. Still others are so self-conscious that their attention is focused on themselves rather than on Jesus, the Baptizer.

It is indeed unfortunate that many worshippers sitting in the pews of Pentecostal churches have not received the very experience that gives the church its identity. The normal Christian experience in the Early Church was salvation, followed quickly by the Baptism. We have no record in the Bible of believers waiting for years to be filled with the Spirit. When our focus is on loving Jesus and wanting more of Him, He is just as faithful to fill us as He is to forgive our sins.

Some people receive the Baptism and begin speaking in tongues when a Spirit-filled believer lays hands on the person and joins in prayer for the infilling. The Samaritan converts "received the Holy Spirit" when "Peter and John placed their hands on them" (Acts 8:17). But the laying on of hands is not necessary. The one hundred and twenty believers filled with the Spirit on the Day of Pentecost are proof of that. The Baptism can also be received in private prayer. But that private experience will then become public evidence as the person joins fellow Spirit-filled believers in Pentecostal worship. Of course, there is usually no interpretation of the tongues spoken as evidence of the infilling with the Holy Spirit, or as spoken in private devotions.

Not Required for Salvation

We do not believe, as some Pentecostal churches do, that one must speak in tongues to be a Christian. Salvation comes through faith in Jesus Christ and His sacrificial death for our sins. But we do believe that the baptism in the Holy Spirit is available to all believers, and that it is an enduement of empowerment for holy living and anointed witnessing. It is therefore very important for a fully equipped and effective Christian life.

T Test Yourself

Circle the letter of the *best* answer.

1. The baptism in the Holy Spirit is received
a) in the same way salvation is received, in obedience and faith.
b) by intensely pleading with Jesus for the experience.
c) by making sure the seeker has obeyed Christ's command of water baptism.

2. The events of the Day of Pentecost, according to Peter, were a fulfillment of
a) Joel 2:28–29.
b) Micah 5:2,4.
c) Isaiah 53:4–7.

3. The baptism in the Holy Spirit with the evidence of speaking in tongues
a) is available to Pentecostals, but not to all believers.
b) is received through the good works of the believer.
c) is available to believers today, as it was in the book of Acts.

4. If a person fears having committed the unpardonable sin, he or she should
a) go to confession in a church that believes in venial and mortal sins.
b) know such a person would have no desire to be forgiven, so ask for forgiveness.
c) repent seven times as instructed by Scripture.

5. A Spirit-filled believer should keep his or her experience current and strong by
a) reading the Book of Acts at least once a year.
b) going on a spiritual retreat with Pentecostal believers.
c) daily communion, praying in the Spirit, and walking in the Spirit.

6. Delay in receiving the baptism in the Holy Spirit is often caused by
a) a person thinking he or she is saved, but in reality the person is not saved.
b) self-consciousness rather than God-consciousness.
c) seeking the evidence of speaking in tongues.

7. Blasphemy against the Holy Spirit consists of
a) knowingly and persistently saying the Spirit's work is of the devil.
b) referring to the Holy Spirit with a curse word.
c) misusing the name of the Lord (taking the name in vain).

8. The expressions of tongues that normally are not interpreted are
a) initial evidence and devotional tongues (prayer language).
b) the gift of tongues in a worship service and the use of tongues on the mission field.
c) the native or foreign tongue of a guest speaker and any utterance given by a stranger.

9. The gift of tongues as initial evidence of the baptism in the Holy Spirit is
a) interpreted in all instances so those present can be edified.
b) not interpreted, though some instances have been understood as a foreign, human language.
c) not to be interpreted because the unknown words are spoken in the language of the heavens.

10. We believe Spirit baptism and speaking in tongues are not required for salvation,
a) but we agree with churches that teach that a person is not saved without the Baptism.
b) so our pastors and teachers should not place too much importance on this belief
c) yet we believe we should obey the biblical command to be filled with the Spirit.

Responses to Interactive Questions
Chapter 6

Some of these responses may include information that is supplemental to the IST. These questions are intended to produce reflective thinking beyond the course content and your responses may vary from these examples.

1 How is the experience received?

The Baptism is received in much the same way that salvation was received earlier. A right attitude is essential. Obedience to God is necessary because "God has given [the Holy Spirit] to those who obey him" (Acts 5:32). Just as faith is required in salvation, so we must have faith to receive this gift of power and commitment.

2 How do we know when a person receives the charismatic impartation of the Holy Spirit?

The Pentecostal position that speaking in tongues is the initial physical evidence of the baptism in the Holy Spirit is based on the five instances of such infillings recorded in the Book of Acts (Chapters 2, 8, 9, 10, 19). In three of the five records, the believers all spoke in Spirit-given languages upon receiving the Baptism. In the other two instances, the speaking in tongues is implied: (1) Simon the Sorcerer desired to buy the gift because of some obvious external manifestation (Acts 8); (2) Paul obviously had the manifestation at some time because he later testified that he spoke in tongues more than the believers to whom he wrote (Acts 9; 1 Corinthians 14:18). The Holy Spirit dwells in every believer, but not all believers have been baptized in the Holy Spirit.

The Fruit and Gifts of the Holy Spirit

God does not intend an initial infilling, marked by speaking in tongues, to be the extent of your spiritual experience. After receiving the baptism in the Holy Spirit, we must remain filled with the Spirit as a vital power and presence in our lives. Too many Pentecostals live below the biblical norm of a vibrant and growing walk in the Spirit.

What is the evidence that a Christian is currently filled and cooperating fully with the work of the Holy Spirit? Paul reminds us in 1 Corinthians 13 that we can speak with tongues, possess the gift of prophecy, understand all mysteries and knowledge, have faith that moves mountains—and still be nothing! A great big zero in God's sight.

Jesus said it another way: "By their fruit you will recognize them. . . . Many will say to me on that day, 'Lord, Lord, did we not prophesy in your name, and in your name drive out demons and perform many miracles?' Then I will tell them plainly, 'I never knew you. Away from me, you evildoers!'" (Matthew 7:20, 22–23). So the fruit of the Spirit gives evidence that the Holy Spirit continues to dwell within us in His fullness.

This is not to discredit the operation of the gifts of the Spirit as evidence that the Holy Spirit is working through a consecrated vessel. But the gifts are distributed at the will of the Holy Spirit. Few persons, if any, manifest all of the gifts of the Spirit. But every Spirit-filled believer should be demonstrating, increasingly each day, all the fruit of the Spirit. We will consider the gifts of the Spirit in Lesson 7.2 of this Unit. Though the gifts may seem more exciting to study, there is a greater need for giving attention to the foundational evidences of a Spirit-filled life: the fruit of the Spirit.

Lesson 7.1 **The Fruit of the Spirit: True Evidence of a Spirit-Filled Life**

Objectives

7.1.1 Describe the importance of continuing to live a Spirit-filled life.

7.1.2 Explain how the Holy Spirit develops spiritual fruit in a believer's life.

7.1.3 Describe how a person can determine if the fruit of the Spirit are maturing in his or her life.

Lesson 7.2 **The Gifts of the Spirit: Divine Power for Edifying the Body**

Objectives

7.2.1 Identify the four major Scripture passages that list gifts and ministries of the Holy Spirit.

7.2.2 Compare the necessity of having spiritual fruit to having spiritual gifts.

7.2.3 Define the purpose of the gifts as described in Scripture, and group them according to their use.

LESSON
7.1

The Fruit of the Spirit:
True Evidence of a Spirit-Filled Life

Some Pentecostals seem to believe, "once filled, always filled." We believe, however, that each believer should experience one Spirit baptism, but then many fillings. Our connection with the Holy Spirit must remain strong as our walk with the Spirit matures and becomes more dynamic.

Times of Refreshing

Even Spirit-filled Pentecostals go through times of testing. We would like to live continuously on a mountaintop of spiritual victory and physical wholeness. But our sin-cursed world demands that we carefully guard and nurture our relationship with the Holy Spirit. Then there are times when we are called to engage in spiritual battles that require a special anointing of the Spirit. Peter was filled with the Holy Spirit when he spoke the healing word to the lame man at the temple gate and boldly addressed the faultfinding religious authorities (Acts 4:8). Peter had already received the Baptism, but this was a crisis that needed a powerful assist from the Holy Spirit.

Paul had an experience much like Peter's. "Paul, filled with the Holy Spirit, looked straight at Elymas" (Acts 13:9), rebuking him as "a child of the devil" (v. 10). Believers should not be presumptuous in invoking God's judgment on those who challenge them. But when the Holy Spirit inspires and anoints in a crisis situation, the Kingdom is advanced. We do not know when such confrontations with the devil may occur, but daily communion with the Holy Spirit will keep the Spirit-filled believer prepared for the crisis. And the anointing at the time evil challenges God's work gives evidence of an up-to-date Spirit-filled life.

Developing Spiritual Fruit

Just before the familiar passage on the **fruit of the Spirit**, Paul lists fifteen works of the flesh or the sinful nature. The list concludes with "and the like" (Galatians 5:21). The list of the works of the flesh far exceeds the list of the fruit of the Spirit. Many sins in the list are of the basest nature. But others sound like things we expect to see every day. Many of them are just the opposite of the fruit of the Spirit. We certainly should not expect to see in the church discord, jealousy, anger, selfish ambition, dissensions, factions, or envy. And if we do see any of them, the fruit of the Spirit are badly needed. But the contrast is powerful. "The fruit of the Spirit is love, joy, peace, patience, kindness, goodness, faithfulness, gentleness, and self-control" (v. 22).

If the Holy Spirit is allowed access to a believer's personal life, there should be progress. One may deny the reality of the works of the flesh listed above, sometimes not recognizing them, or choosing rather to justify such responses as normal. But the fruit of the Spirit provide an excellent measuring stick for evaluating one's spiritual progress toward being more and more like Jesus. A study can be made of each of the nine fruit, but brief observations are appropriate here.

Love

Some scholars suggest that Galatians 5:22–23 can be translated: "But the fruit of the Spirit is love: that is, joy, peace, long-suffering, kindness, goodness, faithfulness, meekness, self-control." If one really has divine love, that love will

7.1.1
OBJECTIVE

Describe the importance of continuing to live a Spirit-filled life.

[handwritten: It's like food we must eat daily to stay alive in our flesh. But reading the Bible, prayer, & listening to the holy spirit keeps us alive spiritually]

[handwritten: • Daily communion w/ the Holy Spirit.]

[handwritten: • Scripture teaches us how to speak life, Live out of Spirit filled NOT Flesh, rebuke the evil spirits & Not fall under.]

7.1.2
OBJECTIVE

Explain how the Holy Spirit develops spiritual fruit in a believer's life.

[handwritten: Able to witness to others in accord w/ one's calling walking in obedience to the teachings of the Living word of God.]

1 How does a Christian know when he or she is making spiritual progress?

[handwritten: When we are not living based on our fleshly desires, but choosing to die to ourselves daily.]

take care of all the details. You can check yourself to see if you have godly love by asking if you have joy, peace, patience, kindness, and all the rest, including meekness and self-control. Read 1 Corinthians 13:4–7 in this light. Love is not just one of the fruit of the Spirit, rather it undergirds the rest.

Joy

The joy of the Spirit is much more than natural joy. It exists even in the midst of sorrow and disappointment. In fact, it is birthed in suffering. Jesus himself said that divine joy works that way: "You will grieve, but your grief will turn to joy. A woman giving birth to a child has pain . . . but when her baby is born she forgets the anguish because of her joy that a child is born into the world" (John 16:20–21).

Peace

The peace the Spirit gives is the same kind of peace Jesus promised His disciples: "My peace I give you. I do not give to you as the world gives. Do not let your hearts be troubled and do not be afraid" (John 14:27).

Patience

Tribulation develops perseverance or patience through the work of the Holy Spirit (Romans 5:3–5).

Kindness

Kindness is an attribute of God, but it is not a consistent human trait. This fruit is related to mercy and grace—unmerited or undeserved kindness. We are even to love our enemies by showing kindnesses to them (Luke 6:35). The Spirit wants to develop this Godlike fruit in us.

Goodness

God's goodness is a major theme of Scripture. In a world that epitomizes just the opposite, the Spirit seeks to produce integrity, morality, and deeds of goodness and generosity.

Faithfulness

Christ is our faithful High Priest (Hebrews 2:17), and notice what compassion and sacrifice He demonstrated. The Spirit seeks to develop the same fruit in us. John commended the recipients of his third letter for their "faithfulness to the truth" (3 John 1:3). We should be faithful to our word and obligations. Faithfulness is also a primary virtue of marriage.

Meekness

Like the related fruit of gentleness or kindness, this fruit is humanly impossible to achieve. Society has come to regard meekness as weakness. But in reality, it is inner strength in the face of difficult or undesirable circumstances beyond the control of the Spirit-filled believer. Meekness is not resigning oneself to fate. "The patient and hopeful endurance of undesirable circumstances identifies the person as externally vulnerable and weak but inwardly resilient and strong. Meekness does not identify the weak but more precisely the strong who have been placed in a position of weakness where they persevere without giving up" (Meier 1996, 519).

Self-control

This fruit of the Spirit regulates and binds together all the other fruit. Love without restraint becomes passion. Joy without moderation becomes mirth and hilarity. Peace without temperance becomes idleness. Patience without balance is apathy. Gentleness without temperance is weakness. Goodness without control becomes fawning. Faith without the moderation of reason becomes blind superstition. And meekness without temperance is timidity.

The Holy Spirit seeks to produce all these fruit in the lives of Spirit-filled believers. Some are quick to argue, however, that many non-Pentecostals demonstrate more fruit of the Spirit than do those who claim to be filled with the Spirit. This observation, though sometimes true, does not destroy the validity of the Spirit's work. He works faithfully with the raw material surrendered to Him. How less commendable would be the Pentecostal without the work of the Spirit. And how much more pleasing to God would be the follower who has produced some good natural fruit, if he or she yielded to the full work of the Holy Spirit. For whatever good there is in us, we must give the credit to God. The Spirit has an even greater work to do in each of us. Our part is to place self on the altar and allow the Spirit to make us into reflections of Jesus.

God's Aid in Our Maturity

7.1.3
OBJECTIVE
Describe how a person can determine if the fruit of the Spirit are maturing in his or her life.

Sanctification and separation from worldly values seem to be unnecessary concepts for some believers, especially young people. Parents and church leaders may hear, "What is wrong with . . . ?" or "Why cannot we do it? Everyone else is." Spiritual leaders need the help of the Holy Spirit in giving loving and meaningful answers to such seekers.

There is far more to the Spirit-filled life than "cannots" and "do nots." For everything we are separated from, as the Spirit guides and controls our lives, there is something better in its place. Young people should be taught and shown the joy of walking in the Spirit and of manifesting the fruit of the Spirit in their daily lives. Teenagers may find little attraction in such virtues as patience, gentleness, and meekness. But the Holy Spirit transforms what seems like weakness into supernatural strength. There is power in the fruit of the Spirit.

Most Christians find it difficult to admit weakness or to become vulnerable in front of others. They fear they will lose too much, but the truth is just the opposite. We lose more by not following Christ's teachings, especially His Sermon on the Mount (Matthew, chapters 5–7). The Beatitudes of Matthew 5 tell us the rewards of each Spirit-produced fruit:

- *The meek* will inherit the earth.

- *The gentle* or merciful will be shown mercy.

- *The patient* in persecution will possess the kingdom of heaven.

Earth, heaven, and God's mercy are unbeatable rewards for allowing the Holy Spirit to develop the fruit of meekness, gentleness, and patience in our lives. Do not miss the exciting walk with the Holy Spirit by allowing your spiritual life to stagnate!

Reviving a moment-by-moment walk in the Holy Spirit, with a dynamic growth in spiritual fruit in each Pentecostal believer, would revolutionize our churches. Without such a commitment from our members, business as usual will continue. The churches that have members committed to allowing the Holy Spirit to work in their lives and to use them in the ministries of their churches will see revival and people brought into the Kingdom. Churches where members do not open their arms to the dynamic work of the Holy Spirit will go through the motions, hopefully maintaining current numbers. We too must respond to the charge Jesus gave to the disciples, "Ask the Lord of the harvest, therefore, to send out workers into his harvest field" (Matthew 9:38). May those workers be Spirit-filled and living out the absolutely essential fruit of the Spirit!

The Gifts of the Spirit: Divine Power for Edifying the Body

Some might reason that a person used by the Holy Spirit in special manifestations in the public worship service must have God's approval. Therefore, they feel that being used in such a supernatural way places a stamp of approval on the details of their personal life.

Others are satisfied to be maturing in their Christian lives by producing exemplary fruit of the Spirit. They are satisfied to leave the operation of the gifts of the Spirit to others, while they do their best, with the help of the Holy Spirit, to live lives admired by fellow believers. But the Bible does not give us a choice in the matter. The fruit and the gifts are two sides of the same coin. If either is lacking, the coin is defective. So it is with our spiritual lives.

The traditional list of spiritual gifts is found in 1 Corinthians 12. The nine gifts listed there are a message of wisdom, a message of knowledge, faith, gifts of healing, miraculous powers, prophecy, distinguishing between spirits, speaking in tongues, and interpretation of tongues (v. 8). But the list is not exhaustive. Many more gifts are to be considered as elements of a Spirit-filled life. In this lesson we will consider the evidences of these ministry gifts in the lives of believers today.

Functions and Ministries Imparted by the Holy Spirit

Consider the following chart of the four passages. You will be making repeated references to the chart as we study the gifts of the Holy Spirit.

2   Which are more important in the believer's life—the fruit of the Spirit or the gifts of the Spirit?
All are important to walk
Act upon those gifts we
Can't just walk with one
Without using the other must have them within to be able to operate in them.

7.2.1
OBJECTIVE

Identify the four major Scripture passages that list gifts and ministries of the Holy Spirit.

The Gifts and Ministries of the Holy Spirit			
1 Corinthians 12:8-10	1 Corinthians 12:28-30	Romans 12:4-8	Ephesians 4:11
	Apostles		Apostles
			Evangelists
	Teachers	Teaching	Pastors-Teachers
Word/Message of Wisdom			
Word/Message of Knowledge			
Faith			
Gifts of Healing	Gifts of Healing		
Miraculous Powers	Workers of Miracles		
Prophecy	Prophets	Prophesying	Prophets
Discerning/ Distinguishing Spirits			
Different Kinds of Tongues	Different Kind of Tongues		
Interpretation of Tongues	Interpretation of Tongues		

(continued)

The Gifts and Ministries of the Holy Spirit (continued)			
1 Corinthians 12:8-10	1 Corinthians 12:28-30	Romans 12:4-8	Ephesians 4:11
	Help Others	Serving	
	Gift of Administration	Leadership	
		Encouraging	
		Giving Generously	
		Showing Mercy Cheerfully	

Handwritten note in left margin: (Fruits & gifts of the Spirit.)

Some people speak of the nine fruit of the Spirit (Galatians 5:22–23) and the nine gifts of the Spirit (1 Corinthians 12:8–10) as though the two lists contained a total description of the ministry of the Holy Spirit. But there are other passages that must be considered: 1 Corinthians 12:28–30; Romans 12:4–8; and Ephesians 4:11. There is obvious repetition or overlapping in the lists, as noted on the chart. Notice that prophecy, prophets, or prophesying is mentioned in all four lists; teachers or teaching in three lists; and apostles, healing, miracles, tongues, interpretation, helping, and leadership/administration are mentioned in two lists. Yet the four lists together do not contain all the ministries and gifts of the Holy Spirit. So the ministries of the Holy Spirit are many and extremely varied.

Balancing Fruit and Gifts

The maturing of the fruit of the Spirit is the work of the indwelling Holy Spirit. All believers should have all the fruit of the Spirit; none should be lacking. But no Christian has all of the gifts or ministries of the Spirit. The gifts are given as the Spirit determines (1 Corinthians 12:11). *(Lesson)*

Do not be a Christian who sits back complaining that you do not have any gifts. Some Bible scholars maintain that every Spirit-filled believer should have one or more ministry gifts.

The consensus of New Testament writers, especially Paul, is that every believer is given at least one gift (Rom. 12:6; 1 Cor. 1:7; 3:5; 12:7, 11, 18; 14:1, 26; Eph. 4:7, 11; 1 Pet. 4:10; see also Matt. 25:15). But some maintain that no explicit statement may be found to the effect that every member of the congregation receives a gift. . . . But according to majority opinion on this matter, there should be no passive membership in the body of Christ, for every Christian has been equipped and prepared for service. (Palma 2001, 195–196) *(Lesson)*

The fruit of the Spirit are matters of moral and ethical obligation that should *(Lesson)* mark the Christlike character of every believer. The gifts of the Spirit, in contrast, are anointed ministries that edify the body of Christ. Each member of the body has something to contribute to the spiritual health and well-being of the church.

As it is, there are many parts, but one body. The eye cannot say to the hand, 'I do not need you!' And the head cannot say to the feet, 'I do not need you!' . . . God has combined the members of the body and has given greater honor to the parts that lacked it, so that there should be no division in the body, but that its parts should have equal concern for each other. . . . Now you are the body of Christ, and each one of you is a part of it. (1 Corinthians 12:20–21, 24, 25, 27)

Handwritten margin notes (left column):

722
OBJECTIVE
Compare the necessity of having spiritual fruit to having spiritual gifts.

• To have spiritual gift we must produce fruit w/ them.

• Scripture of the Talents parable - Matt. 25:14-30 Master leaving his house to travel, before leaving he entrusted his property to servants. according to the abilities of each man, 1 servant received 5 talents, 2 2, 3rd only 1. one who received 5 talents traded them for 5 more talents. The one who received 1 talent went to dig in the ground & hid his master's money.

Final Judgement Matt 31-46

Handwritten note at bottom: Reflection: Even if we only have one spiritual gift we must use it otherwise What good is it if we don't operate in our spiritual gifts

3 If every believer should have one or more ministry gifts, which gift or gifts should we desire and seek?

Paul encourages, "Eagerly desire spiritual gifts" (1 Corinthians 14:1). Again he advises, "Eagerly desire the greater gifts" (1 Corinthians 12:31). But Paul does not select from the list on the chart the ones he considers the "greater gifts." Dr. Stanley M. Horton (1976) suggests that the greater or more valuable gift is the one "most needed and most edifying at the time" (219).

The Purpose of the Gifts

7.2.3
OBJECTIVE

Define the purpose of the gifts as described in Scripture, and group them according to their use.

The gifts of the Spirit are to be shared with others. The Spirit-filled believer may edify him- or herself by praying in tongues (1 Corinthians 14:4), but building up the church is the purpose of the gifts.

The gift of tongues refers to inspired tongues, followed by interpretation, in a worship service. Praying in tongues and speaking in tongues at the moment of Spirit baptism (when the tongues are not interpreted) are not listed among the public worship spiritual gifts. They do, however, edify the believer who receives, or has received, the baptism in the Holy Spirit.

The beauty of this truth is that every believer can share with others what God has given him or her. "When you come together, everyone has a hymn, or a word of instruction, a revelation, a tongue or an interpretation. All of these must be done for the strengthening of the church" (1 Corinthians 14:26). Some in that list are recognized as gifts of the Spirit. Others are not on the lists we have looked at, but they are no less gifts if they come from a personal inspiration while responding to the Spirit.

Some gifts seem to be of a permanent nature, for instance, pastors or Bible teachers are recognized for their continued ministry. Some believers seem more sensitive to the prompting of the Spirit in prophecy or other speech gifts. But there are times when the Spirit may prompt a person to edify or bless in a special way that is never duplicated again. No gift is the permanent possession of a person, though some individuals seem to be used more frequently in particular spiritual gifts. But never does the exercise of a gift become the permanent prerogative of one individual. A spirit of love and unity should always guide the operation of the supernatural gifts. *(Lesson)*

Allowing the Holy Spirit to edify the church through one of the gifts fulfills another truth of Scripture: the priesthood of the believer. Peter tells us, "You are a chosen people, a royal priesthood, . . . a people belonging to God, that you may declare the praises of him who called you out of darkness into his wonderful light" (1 Peter 2:9). Ours is a priesthood in which "every believer offers himself and his gifts in personal ministry to Christ and through Christ to others, both in the body of Christ and out of it" (Ouderluys 1975, 215).

Grouping the Gifts of the Spirit

Some Bible scholars group the gifts of the Spirit into two classes: word gifts and deed gifts, or speech gifts and action gifts. However, the five categories suggested by Dr. Anthony Palma (2001) seem more helpful in identifying the significance and uses of the various gifts (206–232).

Gifts of Leadership (to be treated in the next lesson)

Apostles	Prophets	Evangelists
Pastors Teachers	Helps	
Administration	Leadership	

Gifts of Practical Assistance (next lesson also)

Generous Giving   Serving Showing Mercy

Gifts of Revelation

Word of Wisdom   Word of Knowledge

Gifts of Power

Gifts of Healing Faith   Workings of Miracles

Gifts for Worship

Speaking in Tongues   Interpretation of Tongues

Prophecy   Discerning of Spirits

The latter three groups make up the list in 1 Corinthians 12:8–10 and are usually identified as the gifts of the Spirit. They are the more spontaneous and dramatic gifts. As the situation demands or the need arises, especially in the worship service, the Spirit can touch one believer or another to accomplish His work of edifying the entire Body.

1. **The Word of Wisdom**—the supernatural inspiration for speaking the right word at the right time. The "word of wisdom" is literally the "utterance of divine wisdom." "If any of you lacks wisdom, he should ask God, who gives generously to all . . . and it will be given to him" (James 1:5). This gift may also come as a wise word of guidance for a person in a difficult situation.

2. **The Word of Knowledge**—the supernaturally inspired utterance of facts that could only be known by God and revealed to the believer by the Holy Spirit. The word of knowledge suggests insight into divine knowledge, while the word of wisdom is the ability to use knowledge in a wise manner.

3. **Faith**—a special granting of faith to meet an emergency or a critical circumstance with the confidence that miraculous intervention will follow.

4. **Gifts of Healing**—a special surge of divine power that results in the healing of disease, illness, or physical infirmity.

5. **Miraculous Powers (Working of Miracles)**—works of divine power, other than healing, that demonstrate God's intervention in the natural order of things.

6. **Prophecy**—the utterance of a divine truth in a person's own language, as prompted by the Holy Spirit. Since this gift lacks the supernatural physical evidence of other gifts, a word of caution is in order. We should never speak our own thoughts and words and attribute them to God unless we know for certain it is truly the Holy Spirit prompting us. See 1 Peter 4:10–11. Edification of believers and glory to God, not to oneself, must be our guideline.

7. **Discerning of Spirits**—the God-given discernment to detect the difference between words or acts inspired by God, by Satan, or by the human spirit. Through this gift, one may also discern a person's spiritual character. Care must be taken to distinguish this gift from (a) natural insight into human nature or (b) a faultfinding spirit.

8. **Different Kinds of Tongues**—speaking supernaturally in a human or heavenly language never learned by the speaker (1 Corinthians 13:1). Tongues delivered as praise and worship to God or as a definite message for the church must be followed by the supernatural gift of interpretation. This manifestation is the Gift of Tongues (1 Corinthians 12:4, 10). It should be distinguished from tongues as the initial evidence of the Baptism and from private tongues as inspired praise or intercessory prayer addressed to God alone. Only the gift of tongues in the public worship service requires inspired interpretation.

9.   Interpretation of Tongues—Just as the utterance in tongues is not conceived in the human mind, so the interpretation comes from the Spirit rather than from the interpreter's intellect. Tongues plus interpretation are equal to prophecy (1 Corinthians 14:5). Tongues, though, may serve as a sign to the unbeliever (14:22).

Regulating Public Worship Gifts

The manifestations of the Spirit must be regulated according to God-ordained controls so they edify the body of Christ. First Corinthians 14 contains guidelines to assure that the gifts accomplish God's purpose for which they are given. The highlights of the regulations are: (1) All things should be done in a fitting and orderly way and (2) for edification and strengthening the church (1 Corinthians 14:26, 40). Other recommendations in the exercise of the individual public worship gifts are balance of emphasis (vv. 12–15), use of common sense or mature understanding (v. 20), self-control by the Spirit-filled believer (v. 32), and maturing in humility and a teachable spirit (v. 37).

T Test Yourself

Circle the letter of the *best* answer.

1. A Spirit-filled Christian knows he or she is experiencing spiritual growth when
a) the fruit of the Spirit are more in evidence in his or her life.
b) people are healed when he or she prays for them.
c) his or her personal honesty is no longer questioned.

2. The fruit of the Spirit that regulates and binds together all the other fruit is
a) peace.
b) patience.
c) self-control.

3. The Bible contrasts the fruit of the Spirit with the
a) fruit of human effort.
b) works of the flesh or sinful nature.
c) natural goodness in all humankind.

4. Two fruit of the Spirit that suggest human weakness but in reality are strengths produced by the Holy Spirit are
a) love and joy.
b) peace and goodness.
c) meekness and patience.

5. Which of the following Bible passages includes a list of spiritual gifts?
a) 1 Corinthians 12:8–10
b) Philippians 2:5–11
c) 1 John 1:9

6. A Spirit-filled person should
a) speak in tongues daily.
b) speak in tongues and interpret.
c) manifest the gifts and fruit of the Spirit.

7. The gift or ministry of the Spirit included in all four Bible lists is
a) prophecy.
b) tongues and interpretation.
c) teaching.

8. The purpose of the Gifts of the Spirit is to
a) restore unity to a divided church.
b) edify and build up the church.
c) direct the daily decisions of Spirit-filled believers.

9. The gift of prophecy is best defined as
a) a prediction of the future.
b) an utterance of divine truth in a person's own language.
c) a word of wise advice.

10. Public worship gifts must be regulated so that
a) individuals do not become proud of their spirituality.
b) the pastor is seen as the obvious leader of the worship.
c) worship is orderly and appropriate.

Responses to Interactive Questions
Chapter 7

Some of these responses may include information that is supplemental to the IST. These questions are intended to produce reflective thinking beyond the course content and your responses may vary from these examples.

1   How does a Christian know when he or she is making spiritual progress?

The fruit of the Spirit provide an excellent measuring stick for evaluating one's spiritual progress toward being more and more like Jesus.

2   Which are more important in the believer's life—the fruit of the Spirit or the gifts of the Spirit?

The fruit and the gifts are two sides of the same coin. If either is lacking, the coin is defective. So it is with our spiritual lives.

3   If every believer should have one or more ministry gifts, which gift or gifts should we desire and seek?

Paul encourages us to "eagerly desire spiritual gifts" (1 Corinthians 14:1). Again we are advised to "eagerly desire the greater gifts" (1 Corinthians 12:31). Paul does not select the "greater gifts" for us, leaving that for the individual and the Holy Spirit. Dr. Stanley M. Horton suggests that the greater or more valuable gift is the one "most needed and most edifying at the time." Note that the context of 1 Corinthians 12 makes it clear that uninterpreted tongues is not one of the "greater" gifts to be sought.

CHAPTER 8

Leadership Offices and Ministries as Gifts of the Spirit

Spiritual leadership in the Church Age is very different from leadership in the Old Testament. The priesthood in Israel was hereditary. The oldest living son of the high priest inherited his father's position. The tribe of Levi, instead of receiving a portion of land in the Promised Land, had the responsibility of serving as priests and caretakers of the tabernacle and temple. "The priestly service of the Lord [was] their inheritance" (Joshua 18:7).

The earthly ministry of Jesus changed the nature of spiritual leadership. Heredity no longer determines leadership position. Just as Jesus called and commissioned the Twelve, so the Holy Spirit, since the Day of Pentecost, calls and commissions church leaders. While it is appropriate for individuals to desire a ministry of spiritual leadership (1 Timothy 3:1), the actual selection is that of the Holy Spirit, not the wish of the candidate. In the Assemblies of God, the call of the Holy Spirit to divine ministry is confirmed through credentialing by district and national leadership.

Pastors of local Pentecostal churches around the world, as well as district and national leaders who counsel and support local church leaders, may seem like rather common, though very demanding, gifts to the church. Since much of the ministry of these leaders deals with routine matters, there may be a tendency to overlook the anointing of the Holy Spirit. But just as the church leader in public worship must rely on the anointing presence of the Holy Spirit to touch the lives of worshippers, so the leader must rely on the help of the Holy Spirit in the routine administration of church affairs. Poor administration can hinder the move of the Spirit. In this lesson, we will consider some of the requirements, as well as potential pitfalls, of effective spiritual leadership.

Lesson 8.1   Special Callings and Leadership Ministries

Objectives
8.1.1   *Explain whether the church has apostles and prophets today.*
8.1.2   *Explain how pastors, evangelists, and teachers are spiritual gifts to the church.*
8.1.3   *Describe how helps, or serving, are essential support ministries in the church.*
8.1.4   *Describe the ministries of giving generously, showing mercy, and encouraging others.*

Lesson 8.2   Holy Spirit Power in Witnessing

Objectives
8.2.1   *Indicate how Acts 1:8 links Spirit baptism with being effective witnesses, and explain principles of witnessing.*
8.2.2   *Explain the difference between the responsibility to witness and the gift of evangelizing.*
8.2.3   *Summarize the effective witness and evangelism of Pentecostals worldwide.*

Lesson 8.3   Humility and the Miraculous Power of the Spirit

Objectives

8.3.1   Explain how people used by the Spirit may still face challenges for lack of humility.

8.3.2   Describe how the life and teachings of Jesus model humility for His followers.

8.3.3   Indicate the extreme importance of humility in the life of the Spirit-filled believer.

Special Callings and Leadership Ministries

Our last lesson introduced the five categories of spiritual gifts and ministries as suggested by Dr. Anthony Palma. Three of the five categories—gifts of revelation, gifts of power, and gifts for worship—were discussed as well. Those nine gifts are highly regarded by Pentecostals because they clearly represent a supernatural impact on our daily walk with God.

However, those spiritual gifts are most effective as they operate through qualified local church, district, and national leadership. A leader should be the best natural or humanly trained leader possible, through education and study of leadership principles. Then the Holy Spirit can anoint the leader in dynamic, supernatural ways to achieve Kingdom growth.

The leadership books and seminars of John Maxwell have been helpful to many Assemblies of God pastors and leaders. Books on the subject of leadership include *The 21 Indispensable Qualities of a Leader*, *The 21 Irrefutable Laws of Leadership*, *Developing the Leader Within You*, and *Leadership 101*: *What Every Leader Needs to Know*. These books and seminars will provide a church leader with the natural leadership skills that can then be anointed by the Holy Spirit and used in supernatural ways.

Here are the two categories of gifts the Holy Spirit divinely inspires that were not covered in the last lesson.

Gifts of Leadership

Apostles	Prophets	Evangelists
Pastors	Teachers	Helps
Administration	Leadership	

Gifts of Practical Assistance

Generous Giving	Serving	Showing Mercy

8.1.1
OBJECTIVE

Explain whether the church has apostles and prophets today.

Apostolic and Prophetic Ministries in the Assemblies of God

The apostle Paul considered apostles and prophets to be the foundation of the church with Christ Jesus himself as the chief cornerstone. "In him the whole building is joined together and rises to become a holy temple in the Lord" (Ephesians 2:20–21).

The Assemblies of God position paper, "Apostles and Prophets," can be found on the Internet or in the complete collection of position papers, *Where We Stand: The Official Position Papers of the Assemblies of God*. The Internet paper can be found at www.ag.org; then follow the "Beliefs" and "Position Papers" button selections.

1   Are there apostles and prophets today?

In the sense of laying the foundation for the Christian faith of all generations to come, we do not have apostles and prophets today. But in the sense of laying a foundation in countries and cities that have never had the message of the gospel, **apostolic** and **prophetic ministries** are still needed and recognized.

Periodically in the life of the twentieth-century Pentecostal church, voices have been heard saying that God is doing a new thing. He is supposedly raising up apostles and prophets in these last days. The older generation of Pentecostals in the United States recalls this message in the **Latter Rain Movement** of the mid-twentieth century. But that teaching faded, only to resurface as a new revelation of Christ's end-time plan for His church at the end of the century. According to this revived teaching, church organization hinders rather than promotes God's plan for evangelizing the world. So, these voices claim, God is moving the church back to the New Testament pattern of apostles being the highest authority within the church. Thus, in some groups, individuals are assuming the titles of "apostle" and "prophet."

It is important to understand that (1) the Assemblies of God has always recognized the existence and importance of apostolic and prophetic ministries, and (2) there are valid biblical reasons for not instituting a formal process of naming apostles and prophets.

Biblical Apostolic Leadership. A close study of the role of apostles in the New Testament reveals that an apostle:

1. depends totally on the Spirit's empowerment and His supernatural gifts.

2. enlarges the Kingdom by bringing the gospel to unreached peoples.

3. mentors others, helping them to become effective spiritual leaders.

4. plants and nurtures self-supporting and reproducing congregations.

5. models responsibility and accountability without seeking title or office.

6. teaches sound doctrine based entirely on the Word of God.

A person who fulfills all these requirements might well be called an apostle by the total Christian church, yet there would be no seeking for the title. It should also be noted that biblical apostles apparently ministered to the whole Christian community. Yet some groups today name persons as apostles who speak only for their small segment of the Christian faith. Truly apostolic offices, if existing today, might well apply to persons who meet the above requirements and are recognized across denominational and independent Pentecostal and charismatic fellowships.

The Gospel Publishing House (Assemblies of God) has published a book titled, *Smith Wigglesworth: Apostle of Faith*. There is no evidence that Wigglesworth considered himself an apostle or desired that others recognize him as such. Apostolic ministries exist even today, but it rests with those touched by such anointed ministry to recognize the Spirit's special gifting.

Biblical Prophetic Leaders

Prophecy is a gift of the Holy Spirit that should be widely manifest in a spiritual church until Christ returns. The Spirit inspires persons, open and responsive to His promptings, with the verbal gift of prophecy. Paul declared the importance of this gift, "Follow the way of love and eagerly desire spiritual gifts, especially the gift of prophecy" (1 Corinthians 14:1). But the New Testament does not indicate any office of a prophet in the leadership structure of the church. In fact, the message of prophecy must always be tested to be sure it conforms to the authority of Scripture (1 Corinthians 14:29).

Definition of Prophecy

Many non-Pentecostal churches teach that biblical prophecy is simply the delivery of a public sermon. Such teaching and preaching present the gospel with the human intellect, while the gift of prophecy is supernatural revelation. The strong preaching of the sermon is important, but it should not be confused with the supernatural and spontaneous revelation of the prophetic word. The Spirit may anoint the preacher as he or she prepares a sermon, but that is not the word of prophecy. If, in the middle of a sermon, the Holy Spirit interrupts with a prophetic word, members of the congregation will be aware that the Spirit is speaking directly to them. The same would be true when the Spirit prompts a believer in the congregation to speak the word of prophecy.

The gift of prophecy should not be confused with prophecy as a foretelling of end-time events or the future. In fact, foretelling the future is not the primary meaning of the word in the Bible. A biblical prophet was one who spoke God's message to people. The message was often concerned with contemporary problems or warnings. Old Testament prophets called Israel to turn from fleshly pursuits to full obedience to God. But the words, delivered in the language of the people, were God's words, not the thoughts of the prophet.

Leadership Positions in the Church

8.1.2
OBJECTIVE
Explain how pastors, evangelists, and teachers are spiritual gifts to the church.

In the New Testament, *evangelists* did not go from church to church; instead they went where sinners were. The task of the evangelist is to preach the gospel to those who are not yet believers. Like Philip, the evangelist sows the seed and then moves on to sow the seed elsewhere. Other ministries obviously must cooperate to conserve the new harvest.

Pastors are the shepherds of local flocks or congregations. While the primary task of the evangelist is to reach the lost, the primary ministry of the pastor is to expound Scripture to believers. But this does not prevent the pastor from preaching an evangelistic message for unsaved persons who may be present in the congregation. Even after a sermon edifying the believers, an opportunity to accept Christ as personal Savior is always in order. Scripture references to elders or bishops (overseers) are commonly viewed as terms corresponding to pastors.

2   Are the two titles naming the same person (pastor-teachers), or do teachers form a separate class?

Opinion is divided on whether or not the two titles in Ephesians 4:11 are naming the same person or putting teachers in a separate class. But there are enough references to teachers in other biblical passages to indicate a separate function of teaching, even though a pastor also teaches as part of his or her ministry to the body. There are outward similarities between prophecy and teaching; both are spoken in the language of the listeners. But prophecy speaks to the heart, while teaching speaks to the understanding.

Support Ministries

8.1.3
OBJECTIVE
Describe how helps, or serving, are essential support ministries in the church.

The visible and spectacular gifts are sometimes desired to the neglect of ministries that support leadership. Although we can all be examples of Christian character and conduct, not all can be leaders who have the more visible gifts. Love motivates this gift of the Holy Spirit. Serving includes ministries like assisting the needy, helping the physically disabled, or doing any Christian service that contributes to the good of the Christian body. An usher or Sunday school class secretary can perform Spirit-anointed tasks that make the ministry of the church more effective. Because these gifts are included in the lists of ministries of the Holy Spirit, no Spirit-filled believer can claim to be without any gifts.

Church Administration and Leadership

For the most effective and efficient operation of the church, there must be Spirit-directed leadership. The gift of administrations equips a person to guide the financial and management operations of a local church or organization. "The two gifts of helps and administrations may well indicate the functions of deacons and bishops, who are specifically mentioned for the first time in Philippians 1:1. Yet more than likely they were not fixed offices at the time Paul wrote 1 Corinthians" (Palma 2001, 215). These gifts of the Holy Spirit are obviously needed in the Pentecostal mega-churches, but also in the administrative operations of all churches.

The Greek word for "leadership" in Romans 12:8 is also used in 1 Timothy 5:17, where it refers to "elders who direct the affairs of the church." The word has two primary meanings: to direct and to care for or give aid. In combining the two meanings, we see that this gift of the Spirit is compassionate leadership. The church is truly blessed when the leader is not only an accomplished administrator, but also a caring leader.

8.1.4
OBJECTIVE

Describe the ministries of giving generously, showing mercy, and encouraging others.

Unusual Gifts of the Holy Spirit

Tithes and offerings provide the financial support for local, national, and international ministries. But some Spirit-filled believers are blessed with the gift of *generous and hilarious giving.* If God loves a cheerful giver, as Scripture affirms in 2 Corinthians 9:7, then Spirit-inspired giving beyond normal expectations must bring the greatest joy to the generous believer. This bountiful and gracious giving can include personal possessions as well as money. It suggests generous or liberal sharing, without expecting a personal return. Paul commended the saints in Macedonia and Achaia for making a contribution for the poor saints of Jerusalem (Romans 15:26). It was their Spirit-prompted generosity, not their tithes, that helped the poor in the Jerusalem church.

There is a close relationship between a person who gives generously and a person who shows mercy. Both go beyond required duty. And the Holy Spirit prompts the two gifts, both of which have natural counterparts. Showing mercy "involves the personal care of the needy, the sick, the hungry, the naked (those with insufficient clothes), and the prisoners. It is one of the most important of gifts, as Jesus himself indicated" (Horton 1976, 281). Like the ministry of generous giving, showing mercy is to be done cheerfully, not out of a grudging sense of duty.

Encouraging others is another important gift of the Spirit. It involves bringing unity to the Body of Christ by reconciling differences and developing Christian friendships. In a world of self-centered humans, it takes a gift of the Spirit to develop relationships marked by divine love.

The Spirit-filled life is exciting! Each day is a new experience. As we see the Holy Spirit working supernaturally in human relationships, we find ourselves asking, "What beautiful work of the Spirit will I see or be a part of today?"

Holy Spirit Power in Witnessing

It is not unusual for Christians to be challenged with the question, "Do you mean to tell me that Jesus Christ is the only way of salvation, and if I don't believe in Him, I will not go to heaven? Isn't that a snobbish way of looking at all other religions?"

One faithful witness had an answer to the question, "I would not be so presumptuous as to make such a statement for myself. But Jesus did say it. God sent His Son, Jesus, to die for our sins, so either one of them would be entitled to make the statement."

Though it is theologically true that Jesus is the only door to salvation (John 14:6), stating the truth without sensitivity makes one sound "holier than thou." Another way to answer the challenging question is to include Christians along with other religions and say, "All Jews, Hindus, Muslims, Buddhists, and Christians have sinned and are lost. But any of us can be saved by placing our faith and trust in Jesus Christ."

A Key Verse for Pentecostals

The context of Acts 1:8 puts witnessing in proper perspective. The risen Christ was eating with the disciples on one occasion. Jesus wanted to get one thing across to them, but their questioning minds were focused on other things. Jesus told the disciples, "'Do not leave Jerusalem, but wait for the gift my Father promised, which you have heard me speak about . . . . In a few days you will be baptized with the Holy Spirit'" (Acts 1:4–5). But the disciples were thinking about other things, "'Lord, are you at this time going to restore the kingdom to Israel?'" (1:6). Jesus brought their attention back to His message. "'It is not for you to know the times or dates the Father has set. . . . But you will receive power when the Holy Spirit comes on you; and you will be my witnesses in Jerusalem, and in all Judea and Samaria, and to the ends of the earth'" (1:7–8). This promise is still valid.

3 Like the disciples, are you caught up in other things?

Having just finished studying the exciting gifts of the Spirit, we need to keep our priorities straight. Jesus told the disciples they would receive power when they received the Holy Spirit. The purpose of that power was to spread the gospel to the ends of the earth. The gifts of the Spirit equip the church for two purposes: to edify believers and to reach the lost by witnessing of God's full and free salvation. But we must not forget the purpose of edifying the saints. It is not just to make them feel good about themselves. It is to make them more effective witnesses. Of all believers, Pentecostals should be faithful witnesses.

Witnessing about Jesus

Witnessing includes telling sinners how to find forgiveness for their sins. But it also includes telling friends and acquaintances about Jesus and what He means to you right now. First, however, you should become friends if your witnessing is to be effective. An evangelist may come to your community, and many souls may be saved through the message of salvation. But those who come to such outreach ministries usually come because a Christian has shared what Jesus means to him or her, both by word of mouth and by a satisfying lifestyle.

Our witnessing should convey our love for Jesus and the unspeakable joy He has brought into our lives. If that joy and enthusiasm are not there, we must take time to draw closer to Jesus. Calvin Miller (1987) describes how new Christians, still lacking the Bible knowledge we often think is necessary before we can witness, can tell others about Jesus.

Some [Christians] were so new in Christ they had not had the time to learn [a witnessing plan] yet. But they were bubbling over, much like a young woman who has just gotten engaged. She does not have to take a class to learn how to share her good news or how to show her engagement ring to others. She flashes the diamond and excitedly brags about her fiancé because she is full of joy. She is in love. And that is also what happens when we fall in love with Christ. (Miller 1987, 642)

OBJECTIVE

Summarize the effective witness and evangelism of Pentecostals worldwide.

The Evangelist and the Witness

The Holy Spirit desires to bring sinners to Christ more than we do. He stands ready to anoint our efforts as we step out in faith. That does not mean that every person with whom we share Jesus will respond positively. Too many Christians give up on witnessing when the first effort seems to fail. But the more we step out in faith, the greater will be our sensitivity to the prompting of the Holy Spirit directing us to the individuals waiting for a witness.

Bill Bright was personally a great soul winner and inspiration to others to witness. Catch the excitement of this soul winner

Witnessing is an overflow of one's life in Christ. The apostle Paul wrote, 'For Christ's love compels us' (2 Corinthians 5:14). So before we can fulfill the Great Commission to go and make disciples of all nations, we must keep the great command, which is to love. We love God with all our heart, soul, mind, and strength. Then, compelled by his love, we love our neighbors and our enemies, and we tell them about Jesus.

Wherever I go, if I am alone with a person for a couple of minutes, I begin to talk about Jesus. I find there are a lot of "Ethiopian eunuchs" along the way. I got on a plane the other day bound for New Jersey and I was seated next to a young engineer from Oxford. As we talked, he said he wanted to become a Christian. He prayed aloud, and I prayed with him. He was so excited. God had put us together.

I got off the plane in New Jersey, and a porter was waiting for my luggage. I gave him a Four Spiritual Laws booklet and asked if he was a Christian. He said no. I asked him if he would like to be. "I sure would," he replied. He read for a while until he got to a little prayer in the booklet and an explanation on how to pray. The prayer read, "Lord Jesus, I need you. Thank you for dying on the cross for my sins. Come into my life. Forgive my sins. Change my life. Make me the kind of person I should be." I asked him, 'Does that prayer express the desire of your heart?'

'It sure does,' he answered.

'Let's pray,' I suggested, and we did. Again, he was very grateful that I had taken the time to introduce him to the Lord Jesus whom he had wanted to know for a long time. (Bright 1987, 640–641)

You may not have such an experience the first time you witness. But the Holy Spirit was obviously placing people where they would meet Bill Bright. Bright probably had the gift of the evangelist as well as a personal anointing as a witness. But knowing the compassionate heart of God for lost sinners, we know He is looking for witnesses who will speak to the lost in His behalf.

Teamwork

Sometimes we feel all alone trying to save the world with our feeble witness. But just to let you know what a great team of Good News carriers you are part of, look at this chart of the growth of Spirit-filled believers around the world in the last century. And the growth continues.

Worldwide Pentecostal/Charismatic Explosion 1900-2000 (Barrett and Johnson 2002, 301)			
Continent	AD 1900	AD 1970	AD 2000
Africa	901,000	17,049,020	126,010,200
Asia	4,300	10,144,120	134,889,530
Europe	20,000	37,568,700	126,010,200
Latin America	10,000	12,621,450	141,432,880
North America	46,000	24,151,910	79,600,160
Oceania	0	238,240	4,265,520
Global Totals	981,400	101,773,440	612,208,490

These numbers go far beyond the membership of the Assemblies of God around the world. But the Assemblies of God has been used by our Lord in a major way over the past century (since its founding in 1914). Remember how Elisha prayed that his servant would see the invisible (to the human eye) heavenly host filling the hills with horses and chariots of fire to protect Elisha and his servant from the King of Aram (2 Kings 6:15–17). These numbers are not merely statistics. Each individual in the count is part of the host of witnessing, Spirit-filled believers. We know that we are not alone against the forces of Satan that seem at times to be overwhelming God's people. The battle is the Lord's. We are the foot soldiers.

The Assemblies of God regularly updates its ministry statistics on the Fellowship's Web site: www.ag.org.

Assemblies of God USA Statistics (through 2002)	
Credentialed Ministers	32,556
Churches	12,133
Church Membership	1,585,428
Constituency (persons identifying with an AG church)	2,687,366
Assemblies of God World Missions (through 2002)	
World Missionaries	1,880
Countries Served	191
National Ministers/Lay Workers	231,329
Churches and Preaching Points	236,022
Members and Adherents	40,246,064

LESSON 8.3

Humility and the Miraculous Power of the Spirit

If you have been a Christian for any length of time, you have heard of moral or spiritual failure, even among leadership. Today's society delights in pointing an accusing finger at Christians who do not live up to their beliefs and teachings. Meanwhile, little attention is given to the rampant greed and corruption in business, politics, and the general population. The message is clear, "Evangelical and Pentecostal Christians preach and teach integrity and morality, but really they are just like the rest of us." The cause of Christ is hurt, and winning the lost becomes more difficult.

There is little value in recalling names of those who have yielded to temptation. Satan is still attacking Christians, even professing Spirit-filled believers. The New Testament tells us of failures that rocked the young Church. Paul reports that Demas left him, for he loved the good things of this life (2 Timothy 4:10). Ananias and Sapphira (Acts 5), also, did not bring credit to the early Pentecostal church.

Why do we devote an entire lesson to a peril to which Pentecostal believers can unwittingly fall victim? One of the ministries of the Holy Spirit is helping us live holy lives. But if we do not maintain a close relationship with the Spirit, tragedy can happen.

8.3.1
OBJECTIVE
Explain how people used by the Spirit may still face challenges for lack of humility.

Being Used Supernaturally by the Holy Spirit

Feeling the anointing of the Holy Spirit to give a prophetic word, to give an interpretation of tongues, to pray for a terminally ill person and then witness a miraculous healing, or to discern the source of a manifestation can all be exhilarating experiences. But such powerful signs that the Holy Spirit is at work through a Spirit-filled believer can be both a blessing and a challenge.

The blessing is not hard to explain. Seeing God at work saving souls and changing lives through the ministry of others brings a warm response and thankful praise. God is still alive and working in the lives of His people. To see the power of God at work first-hand, rather than through someone else's testimony, is especially edifying. But then comes the challenge. We know it is God who has done the miraculous work. However, it is easy to become haughty, rather than think, "From everyone who has been given much, much will be demanded" (Luke 12:48).

In some instances, blessings are possibly missed because God knows who can handle the success and blessing with humility, and who cannot. Yet we should never be satisfied with unfruitful lives for that reason. Instead, we should work at letting the Holy Spirit produce the fruit of the Spirit in our lives so we can be yielded vessels, as He chooses to move in divine power among His people.

We sometimes wonder why God uses people whom we know are not living the Spirit-controlled life we might expect. And many people are afraid to step out, knowing that they have imperfections and shortcomings in their own lives. But if God had to wait for perfect vessels before He could move supernaturally through humans, there would be no divine intervention in our human lives.

Even the apostle Paul knew he was lacking in several ways. To the Corinthians he wrote, "I came to you in weakness and fear, and with much trembling. My message and my preaching were not with wise and persuasive words, but with a demonstration of the Spirit's power, so that your faith might not rest on men's wisdom, but on God's power" (1 Corinthians 2:3–5). In his second letter to the same church, he quoted some of his critics, "For some say, 'His letters are weighty and forceful, but in person he is unimpressive and his speaking amounts to nothing'" (2 Corinthians 10:10). Yet, today, we view Paul as the epitome of God's presence and power.

So we cannot be judges of who may and may not be used by God in the supernatural gifts of the Spirit, both in worship and in church ministry. All should "eagerly desire the greater gifts" (1 Corinthians 12:31)—but always with humility, recognizing that they are not gifts for our personal use, but the gifts of the Spirit for His use.

The Model for the Spirit-filled Believer

8.3.2
OBJECTIVE
Describe how the life and teachings of Jesus model humility for His followers.

Our goal as Spirit-filled believers is to be like Jesus. In one of the great theological passages of the Bible, Paul tells the Philippian church, "Your attitude should be the same as that of Christ Jesus" (Philippians 2:5). Then Paul proceeds to describe how Jesus humbled himself (2:8), setting aside His divine place with the Father, became a man, and died on the cross. Can you relate that act of humility with a comparable human act, like becoming an ant to communicate with that form of life, if such were possible?

Some Christians, in looking for the easy way to "be like Jesus," find something in the life of Jesus that fits their personality. Jesus expressed divine indignation at the commerce carried on in the Temple. "Jesus entered the temple area and drove out all who were buying and selling there. He overturned the tables of the money changers and the benches of those selling doves" (Matthew 21:12). This one incident in the life of Jesus leads some to justify their fighting, in unchristian ways, those who do not agree completely with their views. But beginning with Paul's statement on Christ's humility in coming to earth to die for our salvation, we must view the entire teaching and life of Jesus. The incident in the temple may have been a one-time lesson for His disciples, rather than a description of what a life "like Jesus" should really be.

Throughout the Gospels, the references to Jesus' humility and meekness are many. The best description of Jesus' humility is found in His own words, "Take my yoke upon you and learn from me, for I am gentle [meek] and humble in heart, and you will find rest for your souls" (Matthew 11:29). Learn—not how to cast moneychangers out of the church, but how to be humble. Even on the cross, where He could have called "twelve legions of angels" to deliver Him (Matthew 26:53), He humbly accepted the abuse and crucifixion that we might have His full and free salvation.

In many ways, humility and meekness are close synonyms. Yet they are both included in lists of Spirit virtues. In making a distinction, the Greek word for *meek* can also mean *"gentle;"* the Greek word for *humble* means literally "lowly, or of low degree."

Power with Humility

8.3.3
OBJECTIVE
Indicate the extreme importance of humility in the life of the Spirit-filled believer.

Paul's admonition that Spirit-filled believers need to be humble is found throughout his letters. "Do nothing out of selfish ambition or vain conceit, but in humility consider others better than yourselves" (Philippians 2:3). James saw the same need for humility: "Humble yourselves before the Lord, and he will lift you up" (James 4:10). Likewise, Peter advised young men, "Clothe yourselves with humility toward one another, because, 'God opposes the proud but gives grace to the humble'" (1 Peter 5:5). Finally, Paul surrounds his call for humility with similar virtues so important to the empowered Spirit-filled life: "As God's chosen people... clothe yourselves with compassion, kindness, humility, gentleness, and patience" (Colossians 3:12). Humility is the essential ingredient for the unity of the church. But it should also be our attitude toward those whose doctrine is different from ours. Non-Pentecostals are seldom persuaded to accept the Pentecostal experience by approaches they conclude are prideful or arrogant.

A gentle, humble attitude, accompanied by the dynamic work of the Spirit, has brought many into the Pentecostal experience.

The accumulated evidence is overwhelming. While some religions increase their numbers by violently killing Christians and others who do not share their beliefs, Christianity has grown through humility in the face of persecution and even martyrdom. The blood of the martyrs, along with the persecution and suffering of the saints, still drives the growth of Christ's Kingdom.

Humility is not sitting on your hands while the world goes by. It is the attitude we must have as we reach out, through the power of the Holy Spirit, to win the lost for Christ. Yet there may be times when the Spirit prompts us to act in ways that challenge Satan and the evil in the world. But these times will be the exceptions, not the rule. Prayer and the guidance of the Holy Spirit are always to be sought. Praying in the Spirit can often change situations that human wisdom and strength can never change.

T Test Yourself

Circle the letter of the *best* answer.

1. Individuals are not addressed as apostles in Pentecostal churches today because
a) apostolic ministries are fulfilled without the need to name apostles.
b) churches that do not have named apostles are not obedient to God's Word.
c) apostolic ministries are no longer needed in modern churches.

2. What are the "unusual" gifts of the Spirit?
a) generous giving, showing mercy, and encouraging other believers
b) evangelists, pastors, and teachers
c) pastor-teachers

3. The key Bible verse identifying witnessing as a Spirit-empowered ministry is
a) Revelation 22:21.
b) John 3:16.
c) Acts 1:8.

4. Not all believers have the gift of the evangelist, but all believers are called to be
a) perfect examples of a Christ-like life.
b) witnesses.
c) students and teachers of Scripture.

5. The most important character trait of a person used supernaturally by the Spirit is
a) discernment.
b) humility.
c) peace.

6. Concerning modern-day apostles, the Assemblies of God believes that
a) apostolic ministries are active, but persons do not assume the title.
b) apostles have been addressed as such from Bible times to this day.
c) apostolic ministries ended with the close of the New Testament.

7. The difference between the gifts of prophecy and teaching is that
a) prophecy predicts the future; teaching deals with the past.
b) prophecy speaks to the heart; teaching speaks to the understanding.
c) prophecy has ceased; teaching is still very important.

8. The gift of generous giving means
a) bountiful giving of money, possessions, and self.
b) faithfulness in paying tithes.
c) assisting the needy and helping the handicapped.

9. Witnessing is defined as
a) explaining to others the beliefs of our church.
b) inviting others to visit our churches for evangelistic campaigns.
c) telling others about our love for Jesus and what He has done for us.

10. Jesus' example—that Spirit-filled believers should imitate—was that He
a) exercised the authority of God on Earth.
b) humbled himself.
c) accepted worship.

Responses to Interactive Questions
Chapter 8

Some of these responses may include information that is supplemental to the IST. These questions are intended to produce reflective thinking beyond the course content and your responses may vary from these examples.

1   Are there apostles and prophets today?

In the sense of laying the foundation for the Christian faith of all generations to come, we do not have apostles and prophets today. But in the sense of laying a foundation in countries and cities that have never had the message of the gospel, apostolic and prophetic ministries are still needed and recognized.

2   Are the two titles naming the same person (pastor-teachers), or do teachers form a separate class?

Opinion is divided on whether or not the two titles in Ephesians 4:11 are naming the same person or putting teachers in a separate class. But there are enough references to teachers in other biblical passages to indicate a separate function of teaching, even though a pastor also teaches as part of his or her ministry to the body.

3   Like the disciples, are you caught up in other things?

Answers will vary, but it is worth consideration.

The Holy Spirit as a Personal Companion

We have studied the dynamic and supernatural activities of the Holy Spirit in the world and in the life of the church. Most of life, however, is a daily walk dealing with routine decisions and activities. Yet choices that seem so insignificant in daily routines can have eternal consequences, for us and for others.

So much depends on what we do and say. There is no time for careless, self-centered actions or words. "'I tell you that men will have to give account on the day of judgment for every careless word they have spoken'" (Matthew 12:36). Those words of Jesus sound terribly severe in our culture of entertainment and recreation. That is not to say we should never do pleasant things. We do best when we have the right balance between working hard for proper goals and resting or renewing our energy for more effective work.

But how do we find the right balance for our moment-by-moment, everyday lives? God has provided for each one of us a Teacher, a Counselor, a Guide, a constant Companion who is in us and beside us to help us make the right choices. In this chapter we will look at these personal ministries of the Holy Spirit and find how we can take advantage of this wonderful provision for making our lives productive and meaningful.

Lesson 9.1   The Holy Spirit: Our Help for Daily Living

Objectives

9.1.1   Explain the biblical meaning of the name "Paraclete."

9.1.2   Explain how the Holy Spirit interprets Scripture and reveals secrets known only to God.

Lesson 9.2   The Church in the Age of the Holy Spirit

Objectives

9.2.1   Identify the Age of the Holy Spirit.

9.2.2   Describe how the church is the temple of the Holy Spirit and a body energized by the Spirit.

9.2.3   Describe the fulfillment today of Joel's prophecy about the outpouring of the Holy Spirit.

9.2.4   Explain the relationship of the Assemblies of God to the Pentecostal Movement and the wider body of Christ.

The Holy Spirit: Our Help for Daily Living

Jesus did say to His disciples, "Unless I go away, the Counselor will not come to you; but if I go, I will send him to you" (John 16:7). Just days after Jesus' ascension into heaven, the Holy Spirit was given in a dynamic experience on the Day of Pentecost. That may sound as though we no longer have Jesus' presence, only that of the Holy Spirit. But that is not true. We have both Jesus and the Holy Spirit as our constant Companions. The Godhead, the Trinity, dwells with us.

The Holy Spirit Our Paraclete

9.1.1
OBJECTIVE
Explain the biblical meaning of the name "Paraclete."

Holy Spirit

Paraclete is not a commonly spoken word in most modern languages. But it is included in dictionaries as a religious term for the Holy Spirit. It is the word Jesus used in telling His disciples He would send a **Counselor**. The word literally means, "one who comes alongside to help." The word is also translated in various versions as Comforter, Helper, and **Advocate** (Bruce 1986, 1255). (Jesus used the word "another" in speaking of the Paraclete [paraklētos], the Comforter, Counselor, Helper, or Advocate. Jesus was and still is the first Paraclete. "If anybody does sin, we have one who speaks to the Father in our defense [*paraklētos*, "Advocate" in many versions]—Jesus Christ, the Righteous One" (1 John 2:1). Jesus has promised not to leave His followers (John 14:18, cf. Hebrews 13:5, 8). Of course, as we learned in our study of the unity of the Trinity, all of God's resources are available for our spiritual benefit.

Teacher, Guide, and Intercessor

9.1.2
OBJECTIVE
Explain how the Holy Spirit interprets Scripture and reveals secrets known only to God.

Names like Comforter, Counselor, and Helper do not need definition. We daily find comfort, counsel, and help in friends and family. The Holy Spirit often fulfills His ministry to us through others. In those cases, our gratitude should be expressed to the individual through whom the help comes. And our praise, worship, and adoration tell God we are thankful for His work in our lives. Reminding ourselves of God's promise to be all these things to us through the Holy Spirit is important.

The Holy Spirit as our Teacher. Jesus told His disciples, "The Holy Spirit, whom the Father will send in my name, will teach you all things" (John 14:26). Jesus was and is the Great Teacher. Nicodemus addressed Him as a teacher early in Jesus' earthly ministry. "You are a teacher who has come from God" (John 3:2). But the Holy Spirit, as an equal member of the Trinity, is also a teacher. Often the Spirit does His teaching through church leaders, both pastors and teachers (1 Corinthians 12:28; Ephesians 4:11). At times, the Holy Spirit, as a teacher, also speaks directly to the learner.

The Holy Spirit is "the Spirit of truth," and as such He leads God's people "into all truth" (John 16:13). Church leaders often must make difficult decisions. Human wisdom is not enough. The young church had to deal with the question of what Gentiles had to do when they became believers. We are not told just how the Holy Spirit taught them in the matter, though James spoke some inspired words. Their conclusion was "It seemed good to the Holy Spirit and to us not to burden you [the Gentile believers]" with requiring circumcision (Acts 15:28). The Holy Spirit is a good teacher. Whether He teaches through the inspired words of others, or speaks to us directly, He confirms the decision to those in tune with Him. The unity of the true body is preserved.

The Holy Spirit as our Guide. Guidance can apply to a variety of things: place of ministry or employment, circumstances for testing or growing, or appropriate

[handwritten margin notes:]
• Peter started the church (Matt 16:18) Acts chpt 3-4 (2:41 Acts)
• (Discipleship) Mentoring, Training, equipping: Leader • Should have seasons & experience in wisdom.

words in a difficult situation. "Jesus was led by the Spirit into the desert to be tempted by the devil" (Matthew 4:1). Just as Jesus passed the test, we too can know the Spirit's presence with us as we go through trials. Strong character develops when we follow the leading of the Spirit.

Many a Spirit-filled believer has faced options for ministry or employment. A right choice makes for a rewarding future. A wrong choice can bring discouragement or grief. Waiting on the Lord, we may hear a gentle voice of the Spirit, "This is the way; walk in it" (Isaiah 30:21).

1   How do we know if the voice we think we hear is that of the Holy Spirit?

Some people have done some very bizarre things, claiming that the Spirit was guiding them. There have even been some false teachers who have prophesied over younger Christians, telling them that they were to marry a certain person or use their financial resources to bless the ministry of the one supposedly prophesying. God expects us to test such "leadings." One young lady was told by an evangelist passing through her church that she should marry a certain young man in the church. Her response, "I have received the baptism in the Holy Spirit. He can tell me directly what He wants me to do." After fifty years of a wonderful marriage to a different man who became a minister, she knows she did not miss the leading of the Spirit. If the advice of the evangelist had been followed, there would have been limited ministry for her.

Another test to determine the true source of a "leading" is consulting with mature, Spirit-filled believers. Someone removed from the situation may have the mind of the Spirit without personal involvement or emotional ties. In some cases, consulting with another person may give one confirmation that the advice is truly from the mind of the Holy Spirit. The Spirit is a faithful guide to those who sincerely desire to follow His leading.

The Holy Spirit as our **Intercessor**. Praying in the Spirit is a great privilege of the Spirit-filled believer. Sometimes we face a situation for which we really do not know how to pray. The choice between two ministry opportunities may cause great uncertainty. Rather than make the decision on the basis of which choice provides the greatest benefits, we want to follow God's will, even if the less desirable choice would be the Spirit's leading. In such a time of indecision, the Spirit intercedes on behalf of the praying believer. "The Spirit helps us in our weakness. We do not know what we ought to pray for, but the Spirit himself intercedes for us with groans that words cannot express" (Romans 8:26). Pentecostals believe "groans that words cannot express" means praying in the Spirit (Ephesians 6:18; Jude 20).

The Holy Spirit: Interpreter of Scripture and Revealer of Secrets

The Holy Spirit is the author and inspiration of Scripture (2 Timothy 3:16, 2 Peter 1:21). ("God-breathed" describes the work of the Holy Spirit. In 2 Peter 1:21, the author uses the phrase "carried along by the Holy Spirit.") But He is also the Interpreter of Scripture. This is important because the Bible is the guide and standard for our daily conduct. Anthony Palma writes, "For the Christian as well as for the sinner, an understanding of the Scriptures comes only to one with a receptive heart. Believers who 'live according to the sinful nature' rather than 'according to the Spirit'" (Romans 8:4) are unable to come to a mature understanding of God's Word. They can digest only spiritual milk, whereas God wishes them to partake of solid food (1 Corinthians 3:1–2; Hebrews 5:11–14)" (Palma 2001, 86).

Prophecy, the word of knowledge, and the discernment of spirits are gifts of the Holy Spirit. Through these and other gifts, the Spirit at times reveals personal inner secrets and sins (1 Corinthians 14:24–25). He also reveals to believers other things known only to God (1 Corinthians 2:9–11). Other passages record this same truth in the life of Jesus. He knew who would betray Him (John 13:11).

Some people have even asked, "Why does the Assemblies of God have such a recent beginning (early twentieth century) when the church traces its beginning back to the time of the New Testament?" The answer is really quite simple. And it holds a warning to the Assemblies of God and all churches in existence today.

As time passes, churches have a tendency to stagnate or lose the passion and fervor that brought them into existence. But God always preserves a faithful group who seek to live according to the Bible. When individuals and groups break away from established churches that no longer adhere completely to the Bible, they are called **restorationists.** They desire to restore Christianity to the New Testament pattern. Since the message of the baptism in the Holy Spirit was no longer a vital teaching and experience in the various churches, Spirit-filled believers were empowered to form Pentecostal fellowships to restore that truth to the Christian church. We who are members of the Assemblies of God should commit to teaching and practicing the dynamic life of the Holy Spirit; if we do not, perhaps some may feel the need to begin a new fellowship that does maintain an emphasis on the works of the Holy Spirit.

2 If the Holy Spirit interprets Scripture with the meaning God intended it to have, why are there so many different churches with conflicting belief statements?

Finally, we must answer the question on the great variety of doctrine in the many Christian churches. As we have already noted, the Spirit guides the true church "into all truth." Paul declared the importance of this work of the Holy Spirit: "Then we will no longer be infants, tossed back and forth by the waves, and blown here and there by every wind of teaching" (Ephesians 4:14). There is one basic truth that is absolutely essential to being part of the family of God. It is not membership in one church, or accepting all the doctrine of one church. We can have fellowship with those who have accepted Jesus Christ as their personal Savior, based on faith in His crucifixion and resurrection for our salvation. Nothing else should be added to that fellowship requirement, "For it is by grace you have been saved, through faith—and this not from yourselves, it is the gift of God—not because of works, so that no one can boast" (Ephesians 2:8–9).

Unfortunately, even those who have in faith accepted Jesus as Savior sometimes argue and debate with other brothers and sisters over some of the issues we have studied in this unit on the Holy Spirit. People are not going to hell just because they do not live the Christian life just as we do. Of course, if they defiantly reject the truth when they know it is truth, they cannot be Christ's disciples. But love between true believers in different Christian traditions can do much to bring the lost to a saving knowledge of Jesus Christ. The world does not need to see Christians fighting with Christians. At times we have to speak out when salvation by faith alone is not taught or practiced. Yet we can do it with love, and with the help of the Holy Spirit we can reach those who only claim the name of Christian. They can come to know Christ as personal Savior.

The Church in the Age of the Holy Spirit

If you were to search the Internet for the "Age of the Spirit," you would find a few references to the Holy Spirit, but many more pointing to the New Age movement. Satan presents a counterfeit spirit to confuse those who do not know the reality of God's Holy Spirit. This vague, imitation spirit has no required standards of conduct, except possibly a fuzzy concept of love without any required behaviors.

9.2.1
OBJECTIVE
Identify the Age of the Holy Spirit.

"The Age of the Holy Spirit"

General theology textbooks usually indicate we are now living in the Church Age. The Church Age began with the outpouring of the Holy Spirit on the Day of Pentecost, marking the beginning of the church of Jesus Christ. "The Church Age" and "The Age of the Spirit," as earthly time periods, will both end at the same time—the Rapture of all believers.

Of course, the Holy Spirit, as a member of the Godhead, has no beginning or end. He is eternal. He is mentioned in the Old Testament, and will be part of the eternal hereafter. Yet the role He has in the Church Age now He did not have before the Day of Pentecost. And His role will again be different after the Rapture of the church. Paul reminds us, "Where there are prophecies, they will cease; where there are tongues, they will be stilled; where there is knowledge, it will pass away" (1 Corinthians 13:8). The gifts of the Spirit are for the present age. They will not be needed in eternity.

9.2.2
OBJECTIVE
Describe how the church is the temple of the Holy Spirit and a body energized by the Spirit.

The Church as Temple of the Holy Spirit

A Temple of the Holy Spirit

Writing to the Corinthian church, Paul said, "Don't you know that you yourselves are God's temple and that God's Spirit lives in you?" (1 Corinthians 3:16). Speaking to the Corinthians as individual believers, Paul emphasizes holiness and moral purity using the temple image. "Do you not know that your body is a temple of the Holy Spirit?" (1 Corinthians 6:19). When Spirit-filled believers gather to worship, that church becomes a temple, just as the individual is also the dwelling place of the Holy Spirit.

Two other passages refer to the church or a local church as the temple of the Holy Spirit. "What agreement is there between the temple of God and idols? For we are the temple of the living God" (2 Corinthians 6:16). Again we read, "In him [Christ the chief cornerstone] the whole building is joined together and rises to become a holy temple in the Lord. And in him you too are being built together to become a dwelling in which God lives by his Spirit" (Ephesians 2:21–22).

Energized by the Holy Spirit

Viewing the church as a human body in which all the parts must work together is especially meaningful. "Each of us has one body with many members . . . We who are many form one body, and each member belongs to all the others. We have different gifts [prophesying, serving, teaching, encouraging, giving, leadership, and showing mercy]." Each must minister his or her part to the body and all its other parts (Romans 12:4,6–8). The same comparison is expanded in 1 Corinthians 12:14–27. A human body is alive only as long as it has breath. The Holy Spirit is the breath of God energizing the church.

The Holy Spirit's Outpouring

The Holy Spirit was present in the Old Testament. But His presence there could only be likened to light rain or raindrops. But God's promise (Joel 2:28) and the fulfillment (Acts 2:17) were an outpouring, a torrential rain, a deluge. And that is what we are seeing in the Age of the Holy Spirit.

The familiar "upon all flesh" of the King James Version is rightly translated "on all people." That does not mean every single person, nor does it mean every individual child of God, but it means that there are Spirit-filled believers in every race, nationality, age group, gender, and social status. And like the provision of salvation, the outpouring is available to every person who desires the blessing.

The Spirit-energized church is marching forward around the world, clad in the full armor of God (Ephesians 6:11–17). The protective armor includes the belt buckle of truth, the breastplate of righteousness, the boots of the gospel of peace, the shield of faith, and the helmet of salvation. The only offensive piece of equipment for carrying the battle to Satan on his own turf is the Sword of the Spirit, the Word of God. As the Holy Spirit anoints the Word, lives are brought into the Kingdom and believers are filled and equipped for mighty spiritual warfare.

Fellowship and the Holy Spirit

The Assemblies of God is a church. But it alone is not "the church." Nor is any other movement or denomination exclusively the church. The universal church consists of all who have accepted Jesus Christ as personal Savior— through faith in His sacrificial death and supernatural resurrection for their salvation—and are currently living an obedient life. All who have done those things are part of the family of God. They are our brothers and sisters, with whom we will be spending eternity.

An important dynamic for fellowship is evident based on the renewed emphasis on the Holy Spirit, with millions of Spirit-filled Christians around the world and many more being added every day. It is significant and in some ways unprecedented, how the Pentecostal emphasis has spread through so many Christian denominations and fellowships, bringing revival and renewal to many of God's people. Of course, there are differences of doctrine and practice in this wide and diverse group of people. In the pursuit of greater unity and fellowship, diversity in various areas can and should be overlooked. Differences that have historically caused division can be challenging, but we must seek greater unity with Christ's followers wherever possible, and faithfully follow the leading of the Spirit that has seen so many souls coming into the Kingdom and into the Pentecostal experience. Avoiding the tendencies of strife or elitism, we should humbly walk in love and in the light of God's Word.

Some critics have seen the Pentecostal message and the baptism in the Holy Spirit as a teaching and an experience dividing the Christian community. They accuse Pentecostals of bringing disunity into the body of Christ. We cannot deny that there has been opposition and ridicule directed at Pentecostals. In the early days of the last century, there were attempts to disrupt Pentecostal services by throwing eggs and rotten vegetables at tents where the Pentecostal message was being introduced to new areas. In some instances there were acts of vandalism. But we owe a great debt of gratitude to those who pioneered and paid the price that we might today have the glorious experience of a personal Pentecost.

Pentecostals are being accepted more kindly today by the Christian community. Some of those who persecuted the early Pentecostals saw the righteous lives of those they persecuted, and later received the experience and joined the ranks of the Pentecostals. Today's secular society rejects Pentecostals and Evangelicals as being bigoted. Speaking out against sin is called "hatred." Jesus warned that His followers would be persecuted for standing up for the righteousness. But we have the promise in the words of Jesus: "Blessed are those who are persecuted because of righteousness, for theirs is the kingdom of heaven" (Matthew 5:10).

Religious history records how revival movements have gradually lost their first love (Revelation 2:4) and settled for ritual routines. Will the Pentecostal Movement do the same? There is one aspect of the Pentecostal Movement that can help avoid the trends of past revivals. The Holy Spirit never backslides or loses His divine love and mission for these end-time days. This is still the Age of the Holy Spirit. And the prophecy of Joel 2:28–29 has had another fulfillment—not just a first-century Spirit baptism of one hundred twenty, but thousands and thousands of believers have since been filled individually or in great outpourings on groups of all sizes.

3   As persecution has diminished, has fervor and commitment for sharing the gospel and the Pentecostal message also lessened?

Spirit-filled believers must faithfully continue to be filled with the Spirit. The connection must never weaken or break. What Paul said to the Galatians, the Spirit speaks to us all today. "Are you so foolish? After beginning with the Spirit, are you now trying to attain your goal by human effort?" (Galatians 3:3). In this Age of the Holy Spirit we must take full advantage of our great Comforter, Counselor, Advocate, Teacher, Guide, and Intercessor. This faithful Friend who comes alongside to help us in our spiritual ministry will never leave us, but we can fail and ignore that powerful Presence. Pray that never happens.

T Test Yourself

Circle the letter of the **best** answer.

1. The Holy Spirit intercedes for us with the Father when we
a) depart this life at death.
b) cannot observe our daily devotional times.
c) pray in the Spirit.

2. Pentecostals understand "groans that words cannot express" to mean
a) identifying with the sufferings of Jesus.
b) praying in the Spirit.
c) urgently pleading for healing.

3. When Jesus referred to the Holy Spirit as the Paraclete, He meant One who
a) represents the Father.
b) tells us about the future.
c) comes alongside to help.

4. The Holy Spirit is described in Scripture as our
a) friend who sticks closer than a brother.
b) faithful partner in times of trouble.
c) teacher and guide.

5. Paul identifies two things as "the temple of the Holy Spirit":
a) the tabernacle in the wilderness and Solomon's temple.
b) the church as the Body of Christ and the body of the individual believer.
c) the earthly Jerusalem and the New Jerusalem.

6. Believers who have been baptized in the Holy Spirit must guard against
a) relying on human effort instead of the power of the Spirit.
b) becoming overconfident in expecting a miraculous move of the Holy Spirit.
c) apostasy, or completely renouncing the work of the Holy Spirit in his or her life.

7. "The Age of the Spirit" began
a) on the Day of Pentecost.
b) when Jesus came into the world as a baby.
c) when Jesus told the disciples to "Receive the Holy Spirit."

8. When Paul likens the believer's body to a temple of the Holy Spirit, he emphasizes
a) God's perpetual presence with us.
b) the security of the believer.
c) holiness and moral purity.

9. The Holy Spirit being poured out "on all people" (Acts 2:17) means
a) there are Spirit-filled believers in every race, nationality, age, and social class.
b) every living person receives the Holy Spirit.
c) every born-again believer receives the baptism in the Holy Spirit.

10. The Pentecostal Movement can be renewed and strengthened primarily by
a) going back to the origins of the revival.
b) reinterpreting God's Word.
c) dependence on the Holy Spirit.

Responses to Interactive Questions
Chapter 9

Some of these responses may include information that is supplemental to the IST. These questions are intended to produce reflective thinking beyond the course content and your responses may vary from these examples.

1 How do we know if the voice we think we hear is that of the Holy Spirit?

The Spirit is a faithful guide to those who sincerely desire to follow His leading. It is important to test such leadings before making imprudent decisions. Spiritual leading should be tested by comparing the content to the Word of God. God's Spirit will never direct Christians to act in any way that contradicts the principles taught in the Bible. Another important test is to consult trusted Christians, such as spiritual leaders, friends, or family. In the multitude of counsel there is wisdom. Spiritual discernment is increased by including other Spirit-filled believers in the process.

2 If the Holy Spirit interprets Scripture with the meaning God intended it to have, why are there so many different churches with conflicting belief statements?

As we have already noted, the Spirit guides the true church "into all truth." Paul declared the importance of this work of the Holy Spirit: "Then we will no longer be infants, tossed back and forth by the waves, and blown here and there by every wind of teaching" (Ephesians 4:14). There is one basic truth that is absolutely essential to being part of the family of God. It is not membership in one church, or accepting all the doctrine of one church. We can have fellowship with those who have accepted Jesus Christ as their personal Savior, based on faith in His crucifixion and resurrection for our salvation. Nothing else should be added to that fellowship requirement, "For it is by grace you have been saved, through faith—and this not from yourselves, it is the gift of God—not because of works, lest any man should boast" (Ephesians 2:8–9).

3 As persecution has diminished, has fervor and commitment for sharing the gospel and the Pentecostal message also lessened?

This is the trend historically with revival movements. However, it can be avoided if Spirit-filled believers faithfully continue to be filled with the Spirit. The connection must never weaken or break. This faithful Friend who comes alongside to help us in our spiritual ministry will never leave us, but we must be diligent not to fail or ignore His powerful Presence.

UNIT PROGRESS EVALUATION 3

Now that you have finished Unit 3, review the lessons in preparation for Unit Progress Evaluation 3. You will find it in Essential Course Materials at the back of this IST. Answer all of the questions without referring to your course materials, Bible, or notes. When you have completed the UPE, check your answers with the answer key provided in Essential Course Materials. Review any items you may have answered incorrectly. Then you may proceed with your study of Unit 4. (Although UPE scores do not count as part of your final course grade, they indicate how well you learned the material and how well you may perform on the closed-book final examination.)

UNIT 4

The Promise of Divine Healing

The doctrine of divine healing has presented more questions for Pentecostal Christians than any of the other three foundational or cardinal doctrines. Believers have no difficulty reading and understanding what seems to be the message of Scripture on divine healing. But problems arise when what we observe in the lives of Christians does not always match the positive statements of God's Word.

We see clear conflict between the obvious promises of healing and the lack of consistent health and healings among Christians. Some seek to "defend" God by blaming the sick for their lack of faith or for harboring sin in their lives. Or they reinterpret Scripture to fit the real-life situation. Some even deny the reality of sickness, claiming that positive thinking or mind control will suppress the imagined pain.

We live in an age of skepticism and unbelief. It even creeps into churches. We spend more time explaining why many are not healed than we spend in encouragement and building faith for healing. Even as the message of healing is proclaimed, doubts may creep in. "How is the pastor [or evangelist] going to explain why Sister Jones, so godly and sincere, is not healed?" "If divine healing is still for today, why does no one with the gift of healing walk the halls of hospitals and send the sick and injured home with new vigor and life?" You may already have your own answers to these questions. We will be looking at God's Word to see how its principles provide some understanding of the issues involved.

Sickness, Death, and God's Response

God invites questions from the honest inquirer, especially from the young Christian who lacks a deeper understanding of the Word. This may explain why some of "the least worthy" or most unlikely persons receive healing while most churches have saints who can claim God's promise of grace in suffering but never receive a complete healing.

There is a fine line between sincere questioning and doubt. This fact seems to be the point of James 1:6—"When he [the person lacking wisdom or answers] asks, he must believe and not doubt, because he who doubts is like a wave of the sea, blown and tossed by the wind." Again we read, "Let us hold unswervingly to the hope we profess, for he who promised is faithful" (Hebrews 10:23). When our questioning reveals a wavering faith, the flow of the Holy Spirit in healing is greatly hindered.

Our study of divine healing in this chapter will recognize that there are times when healing does not come—at least in the manner and at the time we think it should happen. But let that matter rest until later. Open your heart to the truth of God's Word on divine healing without worrying about all the questions at this point.

Lesson 10.1   Sickness and Death: Realities Because of Sin

Objectives

10.1.1 Describe the source and reason for sickness and death.

10.1.2 Explain biblical principles related to demon possession and Christians.

10.1.3 Explain some of the secular and religious objections to the doctrine of divine healing.

10.1.4 List some of the values sickness can have for a Christian.

Lesson 10.2   Claiming the Promise of Health and Healing

Objectives

10.2.1 Explain the ultimate purpose of any healing a believer experiences.

10.2.2 Identify the source of physical healing.

10.2.3 Explain the relationship of doctors and medicine to divine healing.

10.2.4 Describe why God does not heal all who desire to be healed.

LESSON 10.1

Sickness and Death: Realities Because of Sin

Sickness and sin are related, but not in the way some think. We cannot blame every sickness on sin in the life of the sufferer. Health, not sickness, was God's original intention for the human race. But the first act of disobedience in the Garden of Eden brought sickness and physical death on Adam and Eve and all their descendents. "Death [and sickness] came through a man, . . . in Adam all die" (1 Corinthians 15:21–22). Yet we cannot lay all the blame on Adam. Our part in Adam's sin is verified every time we are disobedient to God's standards. Both sickness and death are consequences of the Fall. So humanity's sin explains why sickness is a fact of life.

10.1.1
OBJECTIVE

Describe the source and reason for sickness and death.

Agent of Sickness

Some carry the truth of God's sovereignty to the point of saying, "Since God is all-powerful and Satan is not, God must be responsible for sin." But God does not cause sickness. It is a manifestation of sin in the world. Humankind's free choice to disobey God opens the door to Satan's ugly work.

On the other hand, God does not stand helplessly by while Satan corrupts the world with evil, sickness, and death. Just as God has allowed Satan a limited authority over the world as a direct effect of the Fall, so He permits Satan a limited power to use sickness as part of his evil influence in the world.

Since sickness originates in sin and the work of Satan, it represents a challenge to God's sovereignty. This challenge, though, was answered by Jesus Christ in His healing ministry while on earth and by His healing touch still today. Satan is working in some way in all sickness, for he delights in causing physical suffering and pain.

God is sovereign in all human affairs and especially in the lives of believers. We must therefore conclude that sickness can touch the believer only as God permits it. Yet God is not responsible for illness and suffering. He has divine purposes to accomplish when He allows Satan, through sickness, to afflict the believer temporarily. With God's permission, Satan robbed Job of his wealth, his children, and then his health. If Job had known why he was suffering, it would have answered his questions. But he trusted God, even without an explanation. God works in the lives of believers by turning sickness into an agent for spiritual growth. God has triumphed over the curse Satan brought on the human race.

10.1.2
OBJECTIVE

Explain biblical principles related to demon possession and Christians.

Demons and the Believer

Knowing that Satan is involved in some way in human sickness has wrongly led some to teach that all sickness is caused by demons. They then proceed to cast out the demon of arthritis, cancer, diabetes, or whatever the affliction might be. The New Testament does record instances in which demons caused sickness or disease (Matthew 9:32—a demon-possessed mute; 17:14–18—seizures caused by a demon; Mark 9:20–26—deaf and mute boy suffering convulsions. See also Matthew 12:22 and Luke 13:11, 16). However, there are also many occasions of healing when there is no reference to demons or evil spirits. No demon is mentioned when Jesus touched the man covered with leprosy and said, "Be clean!" (Luke 5:12-13). Another healing by Jesus in which demons were not involved was the paralyzed man let down through the roof by his friends (Luke 5:18–25). Several summary lists of healings include casting out demons and also healings without deliverance from demons (Matthew 4:24, 8:16, 10:1, 8; Mark 1:32–34, 6:13; Luke 6:18, 9:1, 13:32).

It should be noted that not one of the instances of healing by casting out demons involved a follower of Jesus. The deliverance and healing caused many to leave their sins and follow Jesus, but there is no instance in the New Testament of demons being cast out of a believer. This fact is foundational for the Assemblies of God position paper, "Can Born-Again Believers Be Demon Possessed?" (*Where We Stand* 2002). The answer is a firm *no*.

Demons can tempt and trouble Christians. But they cannot know what we are thinking nor take up residence in our lives alongside the Holy Spirit. There is not room for two bitter enemies in the temple of the Holy Spirit (2 Corinthians 6:16). When Satan or his demons attack us, we do not go to someone to have them cast out. Instead, we put on the full armor of God and take our stand against all the schemes of the devil (Ephesians 6:11–17). "Christ's enemies accused Him of having a demon [John 8:48–49]. It is a subtle trick of the devil that makes sincere people accuse Christians today of having a demon. Clearly, there are deliverances, but calling them deliverances from demon possession is unscriptural" (*Where We Stand* 2002, 23).

10.1.3
OBJECTIVE

Explain some of the secular and religious objections to the doctrine of divine healing.

Objections to the Doctrine of Divine Healing

We would not expect an atheist to believe in divine healing. The secular world refuses to accept supernatural miracles if they cannot be reproduced in a medical lab and studied in a test tube. But if such could happen, there would then be no miracle, only a newly discovered human explanation.

Believers not yet grounded in the Word are sometimes influenced by the anti-Christian declarations of highly educated scholars. But the best human mind is no match for the Intelligence Who created the universe. And the believer who has experienced that greatest miracle ever known—the salvation of a sinner—knows in his or her heart that miracles do happen.

Then there are non-Christians who may not deny miracles, but they explain them as magic or illusions to deceive observers. One second-century Greek pagan wrote that Jesus acquired magical powers in Egypt (*Celsus*, Book 1, Chapter 28.). Still today there are those who see Christianity as a mythology to keep people subject to authority.

Karl Marx described religion as "the opiate of the people" in "A Contribution to the Critique of Hegel's *Philosophy of Right*" (February 1844). God won that debate. Christianity is exploding around the world, while communism is fast fading. God still tears down walls of opposition.

Most Christians have little difficulty handling the objections that come from secular critics. The objections from non-Pentecostal Christians, however, can raise serious questions. There is a group of liberal Protestants who give priority to the latest **philosophy** over the truth of Scripture. For them, miracles and healing are not important because they belong to writings from two or more millenniums gone by. These liberals worship at the altar of education and human philosophy. In their opinion, those who believe in divine healing lack their higher level of learning and knowledge.

Some non-Pentecostal Evangelicals consider healing and miracles to be gifts of the Spirit that are no longer in operation. They believe that **charismata** ceased with the completion of the New Testament writings. And since gifts of healings are one of the charismata, or spiritual gifts, such miraculous healing should not be expected. This objection to the doctrine of healing can cause questions in the mind of a younger Pentecostal who observes the upright lives of those who discredit healing. But we must remember that God gives His gifts to those who know they are available and will make use of those gifts for His glory. Many who hold this **cessationist** view are still our brothers and sisters in Christ because they have accepted Jesus Christ as their personal Savior. But they do not teach or believe a **full gospel**.

Other objections to our belief in divine healing come from those who believe God has willed everything, even sickness, for the growth of His children. If that were so, it would be wrong to seek healing. Others teach that believers are sanctified or made holy through sickness and suffering. That may happen as a side effect, but there is no biblical evidence that God sends sickness on His obedient children.

Death Once, Then Judgment

Divine healing is not a means of avoiding the effects of old age or skipping the appointment all living beings have with death (Hebrews 9:27). The gradual deterioration of our bodies (graphically described in Ecclesiastes 12:1–7) is experienced by believers as well as unbelievers. Healing is certainly available to the aged, just as it is for those in the prime of life, but the body part that is healed usually continues to age like the rest of the body. We do not yet have the resurrected and redeemed bodies that will come when the dead in Christ rise (1 Corinthians 15:42–44, 51–54). No matter what we do for this body, no matter how many healings we experience, if Jesus tarries we will all die.

The realities of old age and physical decline do not negate the truth of divine healing. Nor should they discourage us from seeking and expecting healing at any stage of life. Even though outwardly we are wasting away, inwardly we can be renewed day by day (2 Corinthians 4:16). Divine healing or health, though certainly God's desire for us, is not the highest priority Christ has for believers. He seeks first to make us into His spiritual likeness. Our faithful handling of the realities of sickness and eventual death are part of the victory that overcomes the world (1 John 5:4).

Using Sickness

10.1.4
OBJECTIVE
List some of the values sickness can have for a Christian.

Although Satan is the agent of sickness, God is still in control and accomplishes His purposes through the experience. Sickness can serve as *a teacher*, helping us learn important spiritual truths. Paul's thorn in the flesh (2 Corinthians 12:7) served to remind him of the sufficient grace and strength of Jesus Christ. Sickness can also work as *a disciplinarian* to correct or call back from a wrong pathway; for instance, Miriam was temporarily smitten with leprosy (Numbers 12:10) for her murmuring against Moses.

Sickness can function as *a judge* who pronounces a penalty for sin or wrongdoing. King Jehoram (2 Chronicles 21:18–19) was stricken by an incurable disease because of his wicked life and his failure to repent even after the beginning of the sickness. Sickness also serves as *an example* to others of some truth that God desires to illustrate. As in the case of Job, this type of suffering should end when God's purpose is accomplished.

If death is not evidence of Satan's victory, then neither is sickness. "Death has been swallowed up in victory . . . But thanks be to God! He gives us the victory through our Lord Jesus Christ" (1 Corinthians 15:54, 57). Believers can have victory even while they wait for healing. Satan has been defeated; the price has been paid. We wait only for the outward evidence of that already accomplished victory—in the lives of believers now and throughout all creation at the Great Restoration Day.

Claiming the Promise of Health and Healing

God has always been a God who heals. To the Israelites He proclaimed, "I am the Lord, who heals you" (Exodus 15:26). On another occasion He promised a reward for obedience, "The Lord will keep you free from every disease. He will not inflict on you the horrible diseases you knew in Egypt" (Deuteronomy 7:15).

But the best proof that God is by nature a Healer comes in Jesus Christ, the **incarnate** form of Deity. Isaiah prophesied that the Messiah would heal the sick: "By his wounds [stripes, KJV] we are healed" (Isaiah 53:5). In prophetic vision, Isaiah recorded words Jesus would later read and apply to His ministry: "The Spirit of the Sovereign Lord is on me, because the Lord has anointed me to preach good news to the poor. He has sent me to bind up the brokenhearted" (Isaiah 61:1; Luke 4:18). Healing is a part of God's nature.

The Higher Purpose of Divine Healing

10.2.1
OBJECTIVE
Explain the ultimate purpose of any healing a believer experiences.

Healing or health is not an end in itself. To ask for healing merely to escape pain or suffering may reveal a self-centered or selfish motivation. The same principle is true, of course, in all areas of our lives.

God knows our hearts better than we do. Could it be that He withholds some of our desires in order to turn us, in our restlessness and weakness, to Him and to His strength and vast supply? The words of Jesus no doubt apply to physical healing as well as to material blessings: "Seek first his kingdom and his righteousness, and all these things will be given to you as well" (Matthew 6:33).

1   Why do we desire success, material comforts, or security?

Divine healing confirms the *power* of God and the *love* of God. Its focus is the person of Jesus Christ and the advancement of His kingdom. Jesus wants us to be healthy and free from pain, but more than that, He wants us to be like Him—to have His mind and His desires. God created us that we might bring glory and joy to Him. Until we grasp that truth and make it a practical part of our Christian walk, we run the risk of asking with wrong motives. "When you ask, you do not receive, because you ask with wrong motives, that you may spend what you get on your pleasures" (James 4:3). There is no reason to believe that asking for healing is excluded from this statement of truth. Unless our walk with God is close to His heart and His unselfish love, we may not fully comprehend our own motives in asking for anything from God.

Physical Healing in Christ's Atonement

10.2.2
OBJECTIVE
Identify the source of physical healing.

Scripture does not directly state that physical healing of the body was a specific purpose of Christ's crucifixion, death, and resurrection. But there is a strong suggestion that healing was included. Christ's purpose in coming to earth was to deliver His creation from the bondage of Satan and from the effects that bondage has caused. Christ came to "destroy him who holds the power of death—that is, the devil—and free those who all their lives were held in slavery by their fear of death" (Hebrews 2:14–15). The healings and miracles of Jesus were signs that Satan's kingdom was being crushed and that evil, sin, and sickness were to be destroyed by the sacrificial death of Christ.

Since we are redeemed and delivered from the curse of sin and the works of Satan through the death of Christ on the cross, and since sickness is part of the curse of sin, it follows that healing or the conquest of sickness flows from Christ's redemptive work. Both body and soul were contaminated by the Fall. Christ's death provided restoration for both in spiritual and physical healing.

Although the connection between healing and the atoning death of Jesus Christ is clear ("By his wounds we are healed"—Isaiah 53:5), there is an even stronger affirmation of healing in the resurrection of Christ. The death of Christ triumphed over sin, the root of sickness. But the resurrection life of Jesus provides health and life for our redeemed bodies: "If the Spirit of him who raised Jesus from the dead is living in you, he who raised Christ from the dead will also give life to your mortal bodies through his Spirit, who lives in you" (Romans 8:11). The promise is for now as well as for the Resurrection morning.

Response to Healing

2 What should the believer's response be after receiving a verified healing?

After a verified healing, a person should do what he or she did after receiving salvation or any other spiritual blessing. Jesus gave an instruction to the cleansed leper, "Don't tell anyone. But go, show yourself to the priest" (Matthew 8:4). Although the account has some questions that are not answered, we can conclude that "Verify, then testify" is a good path to follow. An Old Testament law required a leper to go to a priest to be pronounced clean (Leviticus 13). That was a step of verification, just as going to a doctor today can confirm that one is cancer free. After a believer has been prayed for and has received healing, confirmation of the restored health will help avoid unnecessary criticism.

Advocates of positive confession turn the "Verify, then testify" pattern around by teaching Christians to "Name it and claim it." (The Assemblies of God position paper, "The Believer and Positive Confession," which refutes this teaching, can be found on the Internet or in *Where We Stand.*) This false doctrine teaches that what a person says determines what the person will receive and become. Verifying your healing before testifying is not a sign of imperfect faith. It simply avoids unnecessary criticism against the Pentecostal message.

Before leaving the biblical account of Jesus' healing the leper, we must look at another aspect of the report.

3 Why did Jesus instruct the leper, "Don't tell anyone"?

Commentator James Shelton notes that it is most likely "Jesus did not want to reveal his identity prematurely since it would—and eventually did—result in his expulsion from the synagogue, forcing his preaching into the open" (Shelton 1999, 176). As His ministry became more visible to religious leaders, opposition grew. Normally, however, the person healed should readily testify to his or her healing. The focus of the testimony, though, must be on the greatness and goodness of God, not on the good fortune of the one healed.

Doctors and Medicines in Divine Healing

10.2.3
OBJECTIVE

Explain the relationship of doctors and medicine to divine healing.

Some people have been known to do rash things in rejecting all medicine and help from physicians. We must not abuse the doctrine of divine healing by a negative attitude toward the medical advances God has permitted and even guided scientists in discovering. Divine healing should not be placed in opposition to or in competition with the medical profession. Doctors have brought help to many sufferers.

Some point to the condemnation of King Asa because "in his illness he did not seek help from the Lord, but only from the physicians" (2 Chronicles 16:12). But the emphasis is not on the fact that he used physicians (who may have been heathen physicians), but that he turned his back on the Lord. He had already refused to rely on the Lord when he turned to Syria for help (2 Chronicles 16:7).

Other Scripture references to physicians are favorable (Jeremiah 8:22; Mark 2:17). Even the reference to physicians in the story of the woman with the issue of blood is not unfavorable. Yes, "She had suffered a great deal under the care of many doctors and had spent all she had, yet instead of getting better she grew worse" (Mark 5:26). But the woman was not told it was wrong for her to go to the physicians. They simply had not been able to help her.

Today, God still performs miracles for persons the doctors have declared incurable. If it were wrong to go to physicians, why would God reward disobedience with the miracle of healing? God may allow His children to find health through the means of medicine or through the touch of miraculous healing. But we must avoid relying on the skill of doctors as a substitute for seeking the help of God. And we should not wait until we have tried all the doctors before we ask God to heal. Ask God first. Then keep asking God for healing as you visit the doctors. Through it all, know that God is the One who heals, whether through a divine touch or through the skills He has given a doctor.

> If you are preparing to be a minister of the gospel who will be leading God's people into experiences of divine healing, there are potential legal problems that can destroy the ministry of an unwise pastor or evangelist. If a person freely chooses to avoid doctors and rely only on God's healing power, and the healing does not come, a spiritual leader cannot be faulted. But if that leader tells an infirmed believer that he or she should rely on God rather than on doctors, and that person dies, a wrongful death lawsuit could be the result. Because this caution is so important, the Assemblies of God has added the following paragraph to its official bylaws:
>
> ### Section 12. Divine Healing and Professional Medicine
> The General Council of the Assemblies of God disapproves of any credentialed minister counseling a believer to exclude medical advice and/or treatment when seeking prayer for physical healing. Assemblies of God ministers shall not represent medical advice and/or treatment as a lack of faith in God's healing power (Bylaws of the Assemblies of God, Article IX, Section 12).

Reasons Why People May Not Be Healed

There is no single answer to the question why individual believers are not healed. Ultimately, only God knows. Someday, when the curtain of time is ripped apart and eternity is revealed, we may be told the answers to our many "whys"— if in fact we still seek answers. Until then we are called to be faithful and to trust God's infinite wisdom. But we can mention a few possibilities, most of which need no explanation.

The primary cause of unanswered prayer is *unbelief* or *lack of faith*. When His disciples asked Jesus why they could not heal the lad suffering from demonic seizures, Jesus said, "Because you have so little faith" (Matthew 17:20).

A person's faith is increased as he or she draws closer to and becomes more intimate with the God of our faith. The Holy Spirit helps us know God better as we devote time and effort to strengthening our relationship with Him.

4   How does one grow in faith?

A hint of doubt or lack of faith may unwittingly creep into our prayer for healing. If our prayer always ends with "If it be Your will," it could reveal an unconscious doubt that God can, or will, heal in this particular situation. Honest submission to God's will is always appropriate, but expecting nothing to happen is doubt, not submission.

Other possible reasons for unanswered prayer for healing might include fear, guilt, willful disobedience, careless health habits, or lessons that still need to be learned before healing comes. There may also be a divine delay in healing to allow others to see the trust and confidence the afflicted person exhibits.

One instance of healing/lack of healing will have to wait until God gives us all the answers. A middle-aged, Spirit-filled woman who was suffering from a debilitating chronic illness, but had a heart for others' suffering, observed a minister suffering from the same illness. His ministry, he confessed, was about to end because he was not able to handle the normal demands. The little lady prayed the prayer of faith for the minister, and he was miraculously healed and his ministry restored for many more fruitful years. The minister testified often of the prayer that had brought his healing. But the woman who prayed the prayer of faith continued to suffer with the affliction. The lesson to be learned from the true incident is that we do not have to be in perfect health to pray for others who need healing. God knows best and always does right.

T Test Yourself

Circle the letter of the *best* answer.

1. Cessationism is defined as the belief that
a) Jesus ceased being the Father when He came to earth as a baby.
b) the gifts of the Spirit, including healing, ended with the first century.
c) all praise and worship will be silenced in heaven for "about the space of half an hour."

2. Sickness and death can be identified with
a) sin in the life of the suffering person.
b) the law of nature that acts impartially on everyone.
c) The Fall of humankind and the resulting evils in the world.

3. Demon powers can inflict limited suffering, but they cannot
a) possess and control a true believer.
b) tempt Christians.
c) afflict or trouble Christians.

4. The secular world does not believe in divine healing because
a) an atheist must see firm evidence of a miracle before believing in healing.
b) the human mind is preferred over a God who cannot be seen.
c) with a closed mind it refuses to accept the reality of supernatural miracles.

5. Though Satan is the agent of sickness, God
a) always heals when His children in faith ask Him to nullify the work of Satan.
b) will ultimately be victorious though Satan is winning right now.
c) can accomplish His purposes through the sicknesses and sufferings of His children.

6. The promise of divine healing for suffering saints means we
a) can avoid the effects of old age.
b) can ask for and expect a healing touch at any stage of life.
c) should always expect spiritual healing but not physical healing.

7. *Full gospel*, a term sometimes used for Pentecostal churches, means
a) "all the gospel, especially salvation, Spirit baptism, healing, and second coming."
b) "a theology based on all four Gospels: Matthew, Mark, Luke, and John."
c) "a fundamental, evangelical church."

8. Divine healing has a higher purpose than removing pain and suffering; it is to
a) confirm the power and love of God.
b) give God satisfaction in healing His chosen people.
c) help those suffering get their minds off their pain and onto Jesus.

9. When a believer has been healed, the proper response is to
a) name it; then claim it.
b) verify, then testify.
c) be quiet and not tell anyone, just as Jesus told the leper He healed.

10. When the disciples could not heal the boy suffering from demonic seizures, what did Jesus identify as the problem (Matthew 17:20)?
a) The boy's house had been swept clean, and the demons had re-entered.
b) The parents had been disobedient, which allowed demons to enter.
c) The disciples had a lack of faith.

Responses to Interactive Questions
Chapter 10

Some of these responses may include information that is supplemental to the IST. These questions are intended to produce reflective thinking beyond the course content and your responses may vary from these examples.

1 Why do we desire success, material comforts, or security?

Student's answer will vary but should include a discussion of human nature to indulge itself in comfort, convenience, and pleasure. Although God intends for our needs to be met in Him and His provisions, we often neglect this relationship and seek fulfillment and satisfaction in other places.

2 What should the believer's response be after receiving a verified healing?

After a verified healing a person should do what he or she did after receiving salvation or any other spiritual blessing—announce the confirmed miracle as testimony to God's love, power, and mercy. After a believer has been prayed for and received healing, confirmation of the restored health will help avoid unnecessary criticism and may encourage others to trust God in periods of suffering.

3 Why did Jesus instruct the leper, "Don't tell anyone"?

According to James Shelton, it is most likely that "Jesus did not want to reveal his identity prematurely since it would—and eventually did—result in his expulsion from the synagogue, forcing his preaching into the open."

4 How does one grow in faith?

By drawing closer to, and knowing intimately, the God of our faith. The Holy Spirit helps us know God better as we devote time and effort to strengthening our relationship with Him.

CHAPTER

Fulfillment of the Promise of Divine Healing

Not a single person in all the recorded miracles of healing in Scripture had the rudeness to demand healing. Those who came to Jesus were desperate, but they did not look on healing as their natural right. For each one it was a gracious privilege.

Just as salvation is by grace through faith (Ephesians 2:8), so the healing ministry of Christ is ours by His grace or unmerited favor. We neither earn nor deserve healing. But God offers it as *the privilege of all believers.* The fact that healing is provided for us does not rule out suffering for the sake of Christ and the gospel. Yet we can boldly proclaim, in the midst of suffering, that God does heal.

Anger at God for the lack of healing is never justified. In humility, we must admit that we do not understand everything about divine healing. As Paul said, we still "see through a glass darkly" (1 Corinthians 13:12, KJV). We do not know why some are healed and others are not. To presume to know why individual Christians are not healed is to assume wrongly the role of God in judging the spiritual condition of people. Even the New Testament records the martyrdom of James as well as the deliverance of Peter. Though we cannot understand some of these conflicting events, our responsibility is to preach the Word and expect signs to follow.

Lesson 11.1   Healing for More than Physical Health

Objectives
11.1.1 Describe salvation in terms of healing.
11.1.2 Describe the need for inner healing.
11.1.3 Explain how the mind affects the body and how abuse of the body can affect the mind.

Lesson 11.2   Appropriating Our Healing

Objectives
11.2.1 Describe how involvement with the community of faith can bring healing.
11.2.2 Explain how faith operates in the process of healing.
11.2.3 Describe the biblical pattern for individual healing.

Lesson 11.3   When Healing Does Not Come

Objectives
11.3.1 Describe the relationship between death and healing.
11.3.2 Describe the biblical way of handling unanswered prayer for healing.
11.3.3 List the spiritual exercises a person must faithfully follow while waiting patiently for healing.

Healing for More than Physical Health

The Statement of Fundamental Truths of the Assemblies of God states: "Divine healing is an integral part of the gospel. Deliverance from sickness is provided for in the atonement, and is the privilege of all believers (Isaiah 53:4–5; Matthew 8:16–17; James 5:14–16)."

Healing was an important part of the earthly ministry of Jesus. His power to heal was a demonstration of His authority to forgive sins (Mark 2:5–12). If God were not able to heal, one area of sin's domain would remain unconquered. At Calvary, Christ made a full atonement for the whole individual.

Healing Body, Soul, and Spirit

11.1.1
OBJECTIVE
Describe salvation in terms of healing.

Theologians are divided on whether humankind consists of body, soul, and spirit or just body and spirit—**trichotomy** or **dichotomy**. In one sense, we can speak of the physical and the non-physical aspects of persons. In that case, the spirit and soul are the same or are both included in the term *spirit*. But since the Bible mentions all three, we are not wrong in recognizing that healing can apply to body, soul, and spirit.

First, salvation is a healing of the soul. (Animals do not have a soul though they do have a non-physical element we call life.) Every single soul needs a healing, a deliverance from sin. The Old Testament records God's words, "The soul who sins is the one who will die" (Ezekiel 18:4). In this verse, *soul* simply means "person." But as Jesus sent out the Twelve, He warned them, "Do not be afraid of those who kill the body but cannot kill the soul. Rather, be afraid of the One who can destroy both soul and body in hell" (Matthew 10:28). (Only God, not the devil, can destroy both body and soul. See Isaiah 8:13.)

Satan cannot destroy both soul and body. He could do to Job only what God allowed (Job 1:12), and God knew Job's soul was safe. Isaiah 8:13 describes God as the one to be feared concerning our eternal destiny: "The Lord Almighty is the one you are to regard as holy, he is the one you are to fear, he is the one you are to dread." Neither Satan nor those who persecute believers can penetrate God's protection for those who fear Him. To fear God is to do His will in obedient service. The believer fears God, but the sinner dreads Him.

Paul expresses the thanksgiving of souls who have been spiritually healed or redeemed. "You were dead in your transgressions and sins" but "God, who is rich in mercy, made us alive with Christ even when we were dead in transgressions—it is by grace you have been saved" (Ephesians 2:1, 4–5). We use the terms "set free," "saved," "redeemed," "justified," and the many others we studied in Unit 1. Add *healing* to that list. What a wonderful spiritual healing happens at the moment of salvation!

The Need for Inner Healing

11.1.2
OBJECTIVE
Describe the need for inner healing.

Most Christians understand the spiritual healing of salvation and the physical healing of the body, but there is another healing or deliverance that is frequently overlooked. The believer suffering an inner bondage may feel pain greater than that of physical suffering. The subject of human emotions and feelings has been given great attention by psychologists, counselors, and psychiatrists. Even Christians can be the victims of abnormal fears and mental or emotional stresses. Christ desires to heal or dispel these afflictions through the application of His atoning work at Calvary. Our minds can be free from devastating fear. If they are not, there is a need for healing. The source of fear is certainly not God, for "God has not given us a spirit of fear, but of power and of love and of a sound mind" (2 Timothy 1:7, NKJV).

Christians suffering with physical sickness sometimes are in need of two healings. They need deliverance from the fear of what the sickness may lead to if healing is not received. The fear of permanent confinement in a wheelchair or bed, or the fear of death at the end of the doctor's diagnosis of "terminal illness," can be replaced by quiet trust in God's Word and His promise of healing.

Christians also need deliverance from emotional scars. The pressures of life's complexities, from childhood through adulthood, leave some people emotionally ill and unable to cope with the normal demands of day-to-day relationships. God says to the emotionally ill and to those beset by daily pressures, "I am the Lord, who heals you" (Exodus 15:26). Even memories that lie buried in the subconscious can be healed by the work of the Holy Spirit.

Mind and Body Dynamics

11.13
OBJECTIVE
Explain how the mind affects the body and how abuse of the body can affect the mind.

God can give complete deliverance from these addictions and other sins at the moment of salvation. But in some cases, though the sinner is forgiven and declared justified, ingrained patterns of behavior come back as strong temptations. The lyrics of popular music and Internet pornography can pollute the mind and even make it sick. Romantic relationships that start with seemingly harmless flirtations can go from bad to worse in a secular society that encourages everyone to seize the pleasures of the moment. Illicit behaviors become habits that bind a person as cruelly as any crippling physical illness. The effects of alcohol and drugs can leave permanent injury and damage the mind.

1   Is there healing for the alcoholic, the drug or pornography addict, the sexual deviant, and the homosexual?

The person who comes to Jesus Christ for salvation and deliverance from such sicknesses can know the healing power of Almighty God. The record of recovery from drug addiction by medical and psychological means is pitifully poor. Yet a miracle of divine grace has more than once delivered a trapped sinner from hellish slavery. Though it often takes patience to help such ill persons find complete deliverance, the church, as God's hospital for a sick world, can do just that with the empowerment of the Holy Spirit.

Paul told the believers in Rome how to meet the healing needs of both the body and the mind. "I urge you, brothers, in view of God's mercy, to offer your bodies as living sacrifices, holy and pleasing to God—this is your spiritual act of worship. Do not conform any longer to the pattern of this world, but be transformed by the renewing of your mind. Then you will be able to test and approve what God's will is—his good, pleasing and perfect will" (Romans 12:1–2). Our young people should be encouraged to follow this advice and so avoid the injury to mind and body that cannot be reversed, unless God grants His healing.

A. B. Simpson, Christian and Missionary Alliance leader in the early twentieth century and strong advocate of divine healing, said, "Divine healing is not giving up medicines, or fighting with physicians, or against remedies. It is not even believing in prayer, or the prayer of faith, or in the men and women who teach divine healing. It is not even believing the doctrine to be true. But it is really receiving the personal life of Christ to be in us as the supernatural strength of our body and the supply of our physical life. It is a living fact and not a mere theory or doctrine" (*The Word* 1887, 75). When Jesus Christ becomes an indwelling and personal reality in the believer, every part of his or her being is affected.

Jesus is the Healer. Before Jesus' earthly ministry and death for our sins, God declared, "I am the Lord, who heals you" (Exodus 15:26). God has always healed. Yet when "the Word became flesh and made his dwelling among us" (John 1:14), divine healing was something humans could understand more clearly. Though we today do not see Jesus as flesh and blood, we know that people just like us did see Him and did have a personal relationship with Him. We can relate to Jesus because He came as one of us. He sympathizes with our weaknesses and infirmities (Hebrews 4:15).

LESSON 11.2

Appropriating Our Healing

As we begin this important lesson on appropriating healing and helping others to appropriate their healing, we should remind ourselves of the role of the Holy Spirit in healing (discussed in Unit 2). We actually have two persons in the Godhead specifically mentioned as having a role in healing. Of course, this does not mean double-strength healing, for there is complete unity in the Trinity. But we do have a host of Scripture passages reminding us that we can expect help from the compassionate and understanding Jesus as well as the help of the Holy Spirit.

"If the Spirit of him who raised Jesus from the dead is living in you, he who raised Christ from the dead will also give life to your mortal bodies through his Spirit, who lives in you" (Romans 8:11). It was through Christ's death that healing was provided, and the Spirit ministers the healing to us. What complete comfort this Comforter brings!

Gifts of healing are among the manifestations of the Spirit provided for the edification and strengthening of the church (1 Corinthians 12:9). Like the other gifts, healings are administered through members of the Body. Yet the operation of the gift through a believer does not make him or her a healer. Just as the operation of the word of wisdom does not make the inspired speaker a perpetually wise person, so it is with the gifts of healing. The Spirit must give a fresh gift of healing for each individual need.

The Christian Community in Divine Healing

11.2.1 OBJECTIVE
Describe how involvement with the community of faith can bring healing.

Human nature places blame for any failure or lack. The failure to receive divine healing is no exception. Many a suffering saint has been subjected to the well-intentioned diagnosis of a healthy observer: "Your faith is too small." But only God knows whose lack of faith is responsible for the delay of healing. Thus, it is necessary that we be sensitive to the needs of others. Paul tells us that when one member of the Body suffers, all members suffer with it. And when one member is honored, all the members rejoice with it (1 Corinthians 12:26).

The call to complete submission, to seek first the kingdom of God, is extended to every generation. But our priorities are too frequently reversed as legitimate things can usurp the rightful priority of the Kingdom. When that happens, the body of Christ is burdened by wavering faith (James 1:6). Questions and doubts disrupt the unified faith that has always characterized the supernatural moves of the Spirit. Unity of mind and heart is essential.

Each of us individually is a member of the Christian community, the body of Christ. We must share in the responsibility for every other member of the Body. If we truly desire to see miracles of healing, we must be willing as a Body to pay the price of setting spiritual priorities in proper order. Seek first our Lord's Kingdom.

11.2.2
OBJECTIVE
*Explain how faith operates
in the process of healing.*

Faith in the Only Source of Healing, Jesus Christ

Many sick persons are waiting for the ministry of the Body in their behalf. Faith is always the key. Yet we sometimes stress faith in such a way that this beautiful gift of God is viewed as a spiritual charm or formula to be invoked when there is a need for healing. In this warped thinking, faith becomes something that Christians work at or activate in order to persuade God to do something for them. The false teaching of positive confession fits this unbiblical definition of faith.

Positive confession was discussed in Lesson 2 of Chapter 10 and in more detail in the position paper, "The Believer and Positive Confession." On the Internet, enter the position paper title in the "search" field. The paper is also included in *Where We Stand*.

Faith is the description of a relationship. For the Christian, it is a relationship to Jesus Christ. Faith is a strong confidence in three things: who God is (Psalm 104:1–5), what He has done (126:3), and what He has said (119:89).

Jesus Christ is the human incarnation of who God is, what He has done, and what He has said. He alone is the source of our faith. As we come to know Him more intimately, our faith in Him grows, and the result of that God-imparted faith is the supernatural visitation of God himself.

11.2.3
OBJECTIVE
*Describe the biblical pattern
for individual healing.*

Following the Biblical Pattern

Healing results from the exercise of divinely initiated faith. *We* cannot create faith. Genuine faith that brings God's intervention into our lives has been, and will always be, a supernatural gift that comes from God. The origin, operation, and effect of that faith are "in accordance with the measure of faith God has given you" (Romans 12:3).

God has ordained some steps for His children to follow in order to move into that place where God can impart faith for the healing.

Call for the support and ministry of the spiritual leaders in the local congregation.

"Is any one of you sick? He should call the elders of the church to pray over him and anoint him with oil in the name of the Lord. And the prayer offered in faith will make the sick person well; the Lord will raise him up" (James 5:14–15).

As we read the healing accounts in the New Testament, we find no mention of healing evangelists holding large meetings and praying for long lines of the sick and infirm. We cannot deny that God has used such services to heal, and just as important, to reach the lost as they see an undeniable demonstration of God's power. Healing comes by faith in Jesus Christ. As the evangelist, under the anointing of the Holy Spirit, preaches the truth of God's Word on healing, faith can rise in the hearts of those who need healing.

Unfortunately, some ill or infirm Christians view the mass healing meeting as the only way to receive healing. They then travel from one meeting to another, hoping that the miracle of healing will become their experience. But the Bible teaches a different pattern that still works alongside the community healing meetings. Call for the elders or spiritual leaders of the church to come and pray the "prayer of faith" (James 5:15, KJV).

The elders, or those mature in faith, can include a pastor, a staff member, or anyone in the church who is used by God as a prayer warrior. But any Spirit-filled believer should be willing to pray for a suffering brother or sister. Would not a local church be blessed to have a whole congregation of people who could touch the throne of God with the prayer of faith! Some may be timid about praying for others, claiming that they do not have the gift of healing. But God heals through the prayer of faith as well as through the more spectacular gift of healing. All believers should be encouraged to step out in ministry to others. You may be the one who prays the prayer of faith when God, according to His will and time, chooses to heal. If He does heal, all the glory goes to Him, not to the person who prays.

The prayer of faith can be with, or without, oil. According to Scripture, in all of His healings, Jesus never anointed with oil. But there is a symbolism to anointing with oil that can be especially meaningful to the sick person. When the Old Testament priests anointed a person for a particular task, that person was set apart to God. So anointing the sick with oil may symbolize him or her being set apart for God's special care.

2   How important is the anointing oil?

may cleansed Jesus feet w/ oil

Humbly strive for personal righteousness and minister to the needs of others in the body of Christ.

"Confess your sins to each other and pray for each other so that you may be healed. The prayer of a righteous man is powerful and effective" (James 5:16).

James gives practical advice concerning prayer for the sick in the local church. The sick can even pray for the physically healthy who may have other needs. Some have wrongly read into James 5:15–16 the assumption that all sickness is the result of sin in the lives of the sick. Instead, James is recognizing that healing should affect the spiritual part of the person as well as the physical part. Both individuals, the one who is sick and the one who prays, should have things right between them and with others in the congregation. To see God's hand outstretched in healing, there should be no suggestion of sin between our Savior and us. The prayer of a righteous believer indeed is powerful and effective. If there should be anything that needs God's forgiveness, He is quick to grant forgiveness to those who ask.

We cannot overemphasize the importance of humility on the part of the person God uses to pray the prayer of faith. All glory belongs to God, not to the one He uses to accomplish His purposes. We can appreciate those yielded to the Holy Spirit's supernatural work, but we still must give all the glory to God.

Give God the opportunity to plant faith through the study and personal application of the Word.

"Faith comes from hearing the message, and the message is heard through the word of Christ" (Romans 10:17).

The writer of Psalm 107 recounts the wanderings, struggles, and victories of the Israelites. Interspersed in the details of their failures and successes, the psalmist four times repeats his theme: "Let them give thanks to the Lord for his unfailing love and his wonderful deeds for men" (vv. 8, 15, 21, 31). God still has unfailing love and does wonderful things for those who accept His Son as their Savior. Near the middle of the Psalm we read, "He sent forth his word and healed them" (Psalm 107:20).

As the children of Israel wandered through the desert for forty years, the word of the Lord came through Moses. That Word became flesh in Jesus, and the disciples basked in His presence, soaking up the Word for three and one-half years. For us today, the Word has been reduced to printed form, but in its pages we come face to face with Jesus—if we take the time to be in His presence.

To the sick and to the one who needs power to pray for the sick, the Word calls: Come, spend time with the Healer. Listen to His voice. Feel the beat of His heart for the hurts and mistakes of His children. Drawing closer to Jesus means seeing the world as Jesus sees it. We then seek His best for those He sends us to help.

LESSON 11.3

When Healing Does Not Come

It would be great if we did not have to deal with the reality that healing does not always come when we ask for it. We have studied some of the causes for lack of healing (Lesson 2), but when all of them have been eliminated as possible causes and healing is still not received, how does a believer respond?

Here, we consider the issue of God's sovereignty and our free will. If every sick person, even every Christian, who was prayed for were actually healed, would not all sick sinners choose to identify with Christians and subsequently be healed? Would such a "conversion" be a true repentance? Of course, a few have received healing and then chose to become Christians, but God must have seen something in their hearts that was reaching out for more than physical healing.

11.3.1
OBJECTIVE
Describe the relationship between death and healing.

The Believer's Immortal Body

In eternity, time and its markers will be no more as "Our earthly bodies, the ones we have now that can die, must be transformed into heavenly bodies that cannot perish but will live forever. When this happens, then at last this Scripture will come true—'Death is swallowed up in victory'" (1 Corinthians 15:53–54, *The Living Bible*). Sickness, disease, and aging will be swallowed up in the same victory.

There is redemption for our souls in this life, a redemption that carries into eternity. The redemption of our physical bodies will take place at the Rapture. Along with all creation, we are waiting for the redemption of our bodies when Jesus comes for all believers, both living and dead (Romans 8:22–23). Healing in this life is a divine ray of sunshine breaking through the storms of life. When the storms are all past, we will live in eternity's full glory. At times the present storm seems unbearable. But God has promised, even without healing, that His grace is sufficient and His power is perfected in our weaknesses (2 Corinthians 12:9). That promise, first given to Paul when God did not remove his "thorn in the flesh" (2 Corinthians 12:7, NKJV), is a promise for all believers.

11.3.2
OBJECTIVE
Describe the biblical way of handling unanswered prayer for healing.

3 Why has God left us with so many unanswered questions concerning those who are not healed?

Share Love, Not Judgment

Why is it that so many people have not received healing? Is it the fault of a church that has not paid the price to have a dynamic healing ministry? Is it the individual's not being open to the Spirit's desire to exercise gifts of healing? Is it something the sick have done, or not done, that has brought on the sickness? Or maybe it is God's fault? There is enough blame to go around.

However, rather than trying to determine who is at fault for the lack of healing, we should examine our own hearts. We serve a God of love, not a God of blame. Instead of looking beyond ourselves for explanations, we should sincerely ask God what He would have us do in lifting the burden of the sick and helping them carry their load. The sick may be in our midst so the healthy can learn compassion, intercession, and service—at the same time the sufferer is learning divine lessons. God taught Paul that divine grace was sufficient. God taught Job humility and submission to His will (Job 42:1–6). In the great family of God, when "one part suffers, every part suffers with it" (1 Corinthians 12:26).

Sickness can be the result of sin in a believer's life, but the one suffering already knows that and has most likely examined his or her heart many times. Suggesting hidden sin can be painful to the individual who has already searched for anything that needs to be set right—with God or with another person. We must be sure we are real comforters, not like Job's condemning comforters.

Coping with Unanswered Prayer

11.3.3
OBJECTIVE

List the spiritual exercises a person must faithfully follow while waiting patiently for healing.

Donald Gee, chairman of the British Assemblies of God in the mid-twentieth century, was known as the "Apostle of Balance." In one of his many writings for Pentecostal magazines, he observed,

> If [God] does not heal us promptly as we might wish, we need not doubt His willingness to answer our prayer. He may be delaying our healing for some very good reason. Personally, I think that the true and wise way of teaching that divine healing is in the Atonement is to keep it exactly parallel with holiness . . . Even though we do not yet see ourselves completely saved from sin, we do not doubt the efficacy of our faith in the Atonement for the salvation of our souls. We know that the consummation of our salvation will come when the Rapture takes place. In the same way, the redemption of our bodies must still await its consummation, and meanwhile they are left subject to weariness, weakness, and certain infirmities until this mortal puts on immortality. (Gee 1956, 18–19)

Though God has promised to save all who come to Him for salvation (Mark 16:16; Acts 2:21; Romans 10:13), there is no promise in the Bible that all sick believers will be healed in this life. Who can argue with God? He has chosen to save sinners by faith alone. He has allowed a reminder of sin's effect in a fallen world, and then He heals as He chooses. No one can claim greater merit or worth to God because he or she receives healing but other believers do not. "God does not show favoritism" (Acts 10:34). Our earth-bound thinking sees favoritism when one receives and another does not. But if you have not received healing yet, you are no less loved or valued by the God of our universe. When we feel overlooked as others receive healing, we must remind ourselves of God's righteousness, fairness, and compassion.

Waiting for Healing

The overwhelming message of Scripture concerning divine healing is clear. It is God's nature to heal. God loves us, and through the identification of Jesus Christ with the human race, He understands and feels the pain and suffering we experience. Healing has been provided in the death and resurrection of Christ. Promise after promise throughout Scripture assures us that God can and will heal. Everyone who places trust in Jesus can be healed. This truth we must affirm with complete confidence if we are to receive healing. Lack of personal healing must never lead us to doubt God's ability or willingness to heal.

This is the point of greatest test for the suffering believer. We must never let go of the confidence that God will heal. But the pain or affliction we experience or see all around us makes unwavering faith difficult, especially in our own strength. We must continually affirm our belief that God is our Healer, and at the same time we must remain faithful, expecting the healing after God's reason for delay has been accomplished. If the healing never comes in this lifetime, our faith and that of fellow Christians must stand firm in the assurance that Sovereign God is accomplishing higher purposes that He chooses not to share with us. Through it all we are learning to trust God completely.

Although God's Word does not explain why healing does not always come the moment it is requested, it does describe the life of faithfulness that waits patiently for the healing.

1. Pray and enjoy communion with God. "Is anyone among you suffering? Let him pray" (James 5:13, NKJV).

2. Walk in obedience to the Word of God. "If you pay attention to these laws and are careful to follow them . . . the Lord will keep you free from every disease" (Deuteronomy 7:11, 15).

3. Wait on the Lord for His strength. "He gives power to the weak, and to those who have no might He increases strength . . . Those who wait on the Lord shall renew their strength; they shall mount up with wings like eagles; they shall run and not be weary; they shall walk and not faint" (Isaiah 40:29, 31, NKJV).

4. Be encouraged in God's faithfulness. "I will sing of the Lord's great love forever; with my mouth I will make your faithfulness known through all generations. I will declare that your love stands firm forever, that you established your faithfulness in heaven itself" (Psalm 89:1–2).

Thank God for His provision of healing. Yet, at its best, it is only restoration to a better plane in a human life of pain, suffering, and eventually physical death—unless Jesus comes before that time. We look forward to a time when there will be no need for healing. All will be perfect and whole. John saw that future day as the time when "no longer will there be any curse" (Revelation 22:3).

T Test Yourself

Circle the letter of the *best* answer.

1. Salvation is a healing of the
a) memories.
b) emotions.
c) soul.

2. Inner healing involves
a) the deliverance of internal organs from diseases such as cancer.
b) deliverance from abnormal fears and mental or emotional distress.
c) salvation or deliverance from sin and wrong attitudes.

3. The entire Christian community is important to a person's healing because
a) other believers must identify the sin that has brought on the sickness.
b) when one member suffers, the whole body suffers and helps bear the burden.
c) healing comes according to the number of people praying for the sick person.

4. Positive confession, in relation to healing, is a false doctrine claiming
a) what a person says determines what he or she receives; name it and you can claim it.
b) a positive attitude always results in healing.
c) that people who do not practice positive confession cannot be healed.

5. The biblical pattern for the healing of sick believers is
a) anointing with oil in a healing campaign prayer line.
b) participation in a service conducted by a well-known faith healer.
c) calling for church elders to anoint with oil and praying the prayer of faith.

6. You can best give God opportunity to plant faith for healing by
a) association with people who encourage the sick to grow in faith.
b) study and personal application of God's Word.
c) getting alone for prayer and meditation on your illness.

7. If a believer dies without receiving the desired healing,
a) the resurrection of the righteous dead (at Rapture) will erase all potential for sickness.
b) healing will be granted to believers at the Great White Throne judgment.
c) he or she will not remember the sickness in heaven.

8. Healthy believers should relate to the sick and suffering by
a) casting out the demon of sickness from the suffering believer.
b) tactfully suggesting that hidden sin might be the cause for the suffering.
c) sharing God's love, not His judgment.

9. The believer can handle unanswered prayer for healing by
a) pleading with healthy Christians for their intercessory prayer support.
b) placing complete trust and confidence in God's faithfulness.
c) committing to ministry more.

10. As a person waits patiently for healing, his or her spiritual duty is to
a) pray and enjoy communion with God.
b) curse the day he or she was born, as Job did when he was suffering.
c) forget the pain and suffering and testify to others that he or she has been healed.

Responses to Interactive Questions
Chapter 11

Some of these responses may include information that is supplemental to the IST. These questions are intended to produce reflective thinking beyond the course content and your responses may vary from these examples.

1   Is there healing for the alcoholic, the drug or pornography addict, the sexual deviant, the homosexual?

First, nothing is impossible with God, so God can, and sometimes does, heal in each of these and other situations. Second, God is sovereign, so God may choose to heal, not heal, heal later, or even heal differently than we expect. Third, we are all tempted and enticed, as James 1:14–15 makes clear (compare with 1 Corinthians 10:13), but sin and its death sentence are not always instantly or immediately imposed. Whether our lusts are for small children or large chocolate cakes we can ask God for help and heed the Scriptural advice, James 1:21–25. Paul's advice to the Corinthians was similar: "Flee from sexual immorality" (1 Corinthians 6:18); "Flee from idolatry" (10:14); and after covetousness, he says, "Flee from all this and pursue righteousness…fight the good fight of the faith." Opposing sin is most often a struggle.

2   How important is the anointing with oil?

The prayer of faith can be with, or without, oil. According to the Scripture, in all of His healings, Jesus never anointed with oil. But there is a symbolism to anointing with oil that can be especially meaningful to the sick person. When the Old Testament priests anointed a person for a particular task, that person was set apart to God. So anointing the sick with oil may symbolize their being set apart for God's special care.

3   Why has God left us with so many unanswered questions concerning those who are not healed?

The sick may be in our midst so the healthy can learn compassion, intercession, and serving one another—at the same time the sufferer is learning divine lessons.

UNIT PROGRESS EVALUATION 4

Now that you have finished Unit 4, review the lessons in preparation for Unit Progress Evaluation 4. You will find it in Essential Course Materials at the back of this IST. Answer all of the questions without referring to your course materials, Bible, or notes. When you have completed the UPE, check your answers with the answer key provided in Essential Course Materials. Review any items you may have answered incorrectly. Then you may proceed with your study of Unit 5. (Although UPE scores do not count as part of your final course grade, they indicate how well you learned the material and how well you may perform on the final examination.)

The Glorious Hope of His Coming

When we stand in the presence of Jesus himself, the fulfilled plan of salvation and of God's dealing with humankind will all be complete. The perfect fellowship for which we were created will be restored—never to be interrupted again. "Therefore encourage each other with these words" (1 Thessalonians 4:18).

The promise of being snatched away from the evil forces that will rule on earth during the Tribulation is clearly stated in the Bible. Yet there are those who do not see the biblical teaching as a literal event. Some have tried to say that Christ returned to earth on the Day of Pentecost as the promised Comforter, but Pentecostals know that the promised Comforter is the Holy Spirit. Critics also attempt to spiritualize Christ's return by suggesting that the second coming occurs when Christ comes for the believer at death. However, the Bible refutes that belief, for both living and dead believers will be "caught up together" at the Rapture (1 Thessalonians 4:17). The event described in Scripture will be a literal event.

Some teach that there will be no Rapture, only a Second Coming. Those who hold this view claim that the church must take control of all the social structures of civilization (e.g., education, arts, sciences, financial systems, and governments), bringing them all under God's control. When that is achieved, Christ will return. This view is sometimes called the "**Kingdom Now**" or "Dominion" teaching. In response to this teaching, Stanley Horton (1996) wrote, "The hope for the Christianization of the world led liberals to develop the so-called gospel, and that has failed and will continue to fail. The millennial kingdom can be brought in only through God's judgment followed by His divine gracious action" (113). Though the roots of the Kingdom Now belief can be traced back for centuries, little evidence exists to support the idea that things are getting better. Rather, they seem to be getting worse as the evil and judgments of the Tribulation approach. We should constantly pray for spiritual victories, but there are terrible days of judgment ahead for those who wickedly oppose God's reign on earth. Thankfully, though, we can trust God's Word on the glorious hope of Christ's return to snatch away His bride from the evil days ahead.

Chapter 12   Living as Though Jesus Would Come Today

Lessons
12.1   Living in the Last Days
12.2   The Blessed Hope of His Coming

Chapter 13   Tribulation, the Day of the Lord, and Christ's Kingdom

Lessons
13.1   Events on Earth and in Heaven During the Tribulation
13.2   Reigning with Christ and the Final Judgment of the Wicked
13.3   Rapture Readiness

CHAPTER 12

Living as Though Jesus Would Come Today

The pastor stood before his congregation preaching his Easter sermon. His voice was strong and composed, even though, as the listeners knew, he had lost his two little children just weeks earlier. Many in the audience had tears in their eyes, but the pastor and his wife remained serene.

"How can they do it?" one listener asked of his neighbor. "It is unbelievable."

"They must really believe what they teach about Easter, the Resurrection, and heaven," said one observer.

"Well, of course. All Christians believe in that."

"But not like the pastor and his wife. They really believe it."

Of course, the young couple felt the loss and grief, the emptiness of a quiet home. But they had a trust that sustained them and made them a blessing to others even while they suffered. They knew there would one day be a resurrection, and they looked forward to the coming of Jesus when that resurrection will take place.

Do you really believe that Jesus could come back for His true followers at any time, even today? When that belief reaches the core of our being, it puts a completely new perspective on the things that happen to us. We celebrate Jesus' first coming at Christmas. At Easter we celebrate His resurrection after dying for our sins at Calvary. And because of those two great events of our Christian faith, we look forward with confidence to His coming back to snatch us away from the problems and evil this world is facing. With this hope within us, we can be victors over anything Satan brings against us.

Lesson 12.1   Living in the Last Days

Objectives

12.1.1 List some of the signs of the times that tell us we may be living in the last days.

12.1.2 Summarize Christ's warnings and instructions on how we should live these days.

12.1.3 Explain the evangelistic purpose for Christ's delay.

12.1.4 Describe the effects of pre-Tribulation Rapture on believers.

Lesson 12.2   The Blessed Hope of His Coming

Objectives

12.2.1 Explain the difference between the Rapture and the Second Coming of Christ.

12.2.2 Describe what will happen at the Rapture to living and deceased Christians.

12.2.3 Indicate how children and youth can be inspired to see the Rapture as the Blessed Hope.

Living in the Last Days

People react differently to the truth that Jesus Christ is coming to earth again. Some are frightened, closing their eyes and ears to news events reminding them how bad things are in the world. Yet they do nothing to get ready to welcome Jesus.

Other people seem unconcerned when someone tells them that Jesus is coming soon and that those who are not ready will be judged and punished. To some it sounds like a fantasy tale from *The Lord of the Rings*. If things are going well for them right now, they are satisfied to let the future take care of itself. They are spiritually asleep when they should be awake and watching for the great event that could occur at any time. This lesson reminds us of the greatest event in the Christian walk. But some things must take place before we can receive our reward for faithfulness.

End-time Signs

The massive stones of the temple were impressive. The disciples could not help calling Jesus' attention to the beautiful buildings (Matthew 24:1). But Jesus' response was not what they expected. "I tell you the truth, not one stone here will be left on another; every one will be thrown down" (24:2). The topic of conversation changed quickly. "Tell us . . . when will this happen, and what will be the sign of your coming and of the end of the age?" (24:3).

A study of Matthew 24:4–38 reveals between twenty-five and thirty signs of the end-time. The most prominent are the appearance of deceivers (v. 5), wars and rumors of wars (v. 6), famine (v. 7), earthquakes (v. 7), persecution and martyrdom (v. 9), believers being hated around the world (v. 10), apostasy (v. 10), false prophets (v. 11), wickedness and evil overcoming love (v. 12), signs and miracles by false prophets (v. 24), sun and moon darkened (v. 29), and people living carelessly as in the days of Noah (v. 38).

Living by Christ's Teaching

The end-time will be full of frightful happenings. Since we will not escape them all, Christ gave instruction on how to live in the last days (Matthew 24).

1. Watch out that no one deceives you (v. 4).

2. Do not be alarmed at the signs; they must happen (v. 6).

3. Stand firm to the end (v. 13).

4. Continue preaching the gospel throughout the world (v. 14).

5. Be ready to flee from evil and persecution (vv. 16-19).

6. Know from the signs that Christ's coming and the end are very near (v. 33).

7. Watch continually for Christ's coming (v. 42).

8. Be ready spiritually for Christ's return (v. 44).

9. Be a faithful and wise servant as you await Christ's coming (vv. 45-46).

There is no sign of the end-time, either in Matthew 24 or elsewhere in the Bible, which must be fulfilled before Jesus returns. The end of day-to-day life as we now know it could be very, very soon.

Continuing Diligence

Some Pentecostal believers in the early twentieth century were so sure that Jesus would return before they would die, so they refused to invest in anything

12.1.1
OBJECTIVE
List some of the signs of the times that tell us we may be living in the last days.

12.1.2
OBJECTIVE
Summarize Christ's warnings and instructions on how we should live these days.

12.1.3
OBJECTIVE
Explain the evangelistic purpose for Christ's delay.

that would have temporal value. They built gospel tabernacles that may have reminded some of the tent tabernacle the Israelites carried with them as they wandered from Egypt to the Promised Land.

What the early pioneers of the Pentecostal faith lacked in finances, they made up in zeal and sacrifice. They used their available resources to do as much for the Kingdom as they could. Today, we have become slack as our buildings have become more respectable. Has the expectation of the second coming faded in our thinking, causing us to lose the urgency to witness and win the lost to Christ? Jesus felt the urgency and expressed it to His disciples, "As long as it is day, we must do the work of him who sent me. Night is coming, when no one can work" (John 9:4). How much more must we work diligently. For every person, there is a night coming when no work can be done. Whether it is at death, or when our opportunity to work is gone, we must work while it is yet day.

Work While Waiting

The born-again child of God may wonder why the rapture has not already taken place. Sinners and scoffers, however, interpret the delay in another manner: "You must understand that in the last days scoffers will come, scoffing and following their own evil desires. They will say, 'Where is this "coming" He promised? Ever since our fathers died, everything goes on as it has since the beginning of creation'" (2 Peter 3:3–4). Peter then proceeds to give two reasons for the delay.

1 If all the signs of Christ's coming have already been witnessed in some fashion, why does the Rapture not take place immediately?

1. God measures time differently than we do. "With the Lord a day is like a thousand years, and a thousand years are like a day" (2 Peter 3:8).

2. God delays His coming because He desires that more will come to repentance through His patience. "The Lord is not slow in keeping his promise, as some understand slowness. He is patient with you, not wanting anyone to perish, but everyone to come to repentance" (2 Peter 3:9). So rather than looking at all the centuries past, when Jesus could have come but did not, we should think of all the people living right now who need an opportunity to receive God's salvation. We must take advantage of the delay and witness to as many souls as possible. If we do the witnessing, the Holy Spirit will convict the sinner of guilt and sin and convince him or her of righteousness and judgment (cf. John 16:8).

12.1.4
OBJECTIVE

Describe the effects of pre-Tribulation Rapture on believers.

Pre-Tribulation Rapture and Believers

Christians around the world right now are being severely persecuted and martyred. Many of them believe the world is already in the Tribulation. But we must be careful to distinguish the tribulation of our everyday trials, distress, suffering, and even individual martyrdom from the Tribulation that begins on earth after believers have been raptured. Paul tells the Corinthians, "I am exceedingly joyful in all our tribulation" (2 Corinthians 7:4, NKJV). The New International Version notes that Paul is not referring to the end-time Tribulation, though the Greek word is the same. It translates the verse, "In all our *troubles* my joy knows no bounds." We can distinguish the two tribulations by capitalizing the Tribulation of the end-time. There is no similarity at all between the two. When the earth is consumed by the judgments of the Great Tribulation, anything we have faced before that time will seem so small, mainly because of the worldwide magnitude of the Tribulation rage and fury.

> Some expositors use the word Tribulation for the entire Seventieth Week of
> Daniel, and the words "Great Tribulation" for the last half of the seven years.
> However, there is not biblical support for such a distinction. So this study will
> use both terms, when capitalized, as the entire seven-year period.

There are other interpretations of when the Rapture takes place. Each one lacks a biblical truth contained in the **Pre-Tribulation** rapture position. It is important to understand the shortcoming of each of the following views.

Mid-Tribulation Rapture—This belief teaches that the rapture of the church will take place in the middle of the Tribulation, coinciding with Antichrist's rescinding his covenant with the Jews (Daniel 9:27). Placing the Rapture at this time, following the confirmation of the covenant at the beginning of Daniel's Seventieth Week, would contradict the warning that "the Son of Man will come at an hour when you do not expect him" (Matthew 24:44).

Post-Tribulation Rapture—This belief teaches that Christians will go through the entire Tribulation. The Rapture and Christ's return to earth to destroy Antichrist are seen as the same event. This view of the Rapture violates God's promise that believers are not appointed "to suffer wrath" (1 Thessalonians 5:9).

These views also have a number of minor variations, and there will probably be more as Jesus tarries His coming. These include a partial-rapture theory, multiple raptures at different times, and a pre-wrath rapture to take place during the last half of Daniel's Seventieth Week. (For detailed treatment of various Rapture theories, from a Pentecostal perspective, see Stanley M. Horton, *Our Destiny: Biblical Teachings on the Last Things* (Springfield, MO: Logion Press, 1996).

12.2.1
OBJECTIVE
Explain the difference between the Rapture and the Second Coming of Christ.

The Blessed Hope of His Coming

Futurism is the fad of the day. People seek out astrologers, fortune-tellers, horoscopes, and other predictors of the future in an attempt to see what tomorrow may hold. Such curiosity opens the door for Satan to gain an evil foothold.

The study of Bible prophecy is right and proper. Yet, such study ought to be done for the right reason—not for sensationalism, but for edification. God's plan for the end-time includes far more than the Second Coming. We should study the prophecies of these coming events so that we will be better men and women as the hour approaches.

Some Bible scholars disagree with dispensational interpretations of end-time prophecies, maintaining that the evidence is not strong enough for such a definitive statement on Daniel's Seventieth Week, the judgments, and the new heavens and the new earth. But these same scholars fail to suggest any better chronology or interpretation of Scripture. The many references to end-time events and details are too specific to be taken as pure symbolism or imaginative **apocalyptic literature**.

The Rapture and the Second Coming of Christ

Jesus Christ is the central figure of prophecy, just as He is the central figure of the entire Bible. To the Christian who truly loves Jesus, the sudden appearance of Christ in the air will hold no fear, dread, or disappointment. The words of Paul concerning this beginning of end-time events should summarize the anticipation of all believers: "We wait for the blessed hope—the glorious appearing of our great God and Savior, Jesus Christ" (Titus 2:13).

Many Christians lack a clear understanding of the second coming of Christ. When we say that the next event in God's timetable of history is the Second Coming, we are using the term in a general sense that includes the rapture of the saints as the first phase of the Second Coming (Number fourteen of the Statement of Fundamental Truths of the Assemblies of God reads, "The second coming of Christ includes the rapture of the saints, which is our blessed hope, followed by the visible return of Christ with His saints to reign on the earth for one thousand years."). At this time, Christ comes and snatches away His church, without actually setting foot on the earth. With the saints removed from the earth, the Great Tribulation comes upon the whole world. At the end of this period of great suffering, Christ returns *with* His saints to confront the Antichrist and his forces at the battle of Armageddon. Since this is the time when Christ physically appears on earth, as He did at the time of His first coming, this event is more exactly the Second Coming to earth, or the Revelation of Jesus Christ. To summarize what we have already studied about the end-time, and to lay the background for events that will still be studied, let us look at a pre-tribulation, pre-millennial "Panorama of Prophecy."

PANORAMA OF PROPHECY

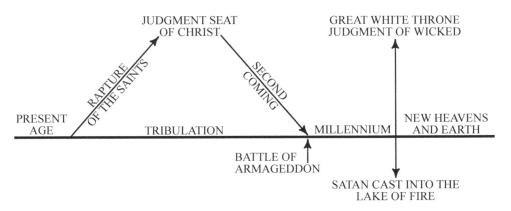

12.2.2
OBJECTIVE

Describe what will happen at the Rapture to living and deceased Christians.

Change at the Rapture

Although there are references throughout the New Testament to the rapture of the saints, two passages describe it in the best detail:

"For the Lord himself will come down from heaven, with a loud command, with the voice of the archangel and with the trumpet call of God, and the dead in Christ will rise first. After that, we who are still alive and are left will be caught up together with them in the clouds to meet the Lord in the air. And so we will be with the Lord forever" (1 Thessalonians 4:16–17).

"Listen, I tell you a mystery: We will not all sleep, but we will all be changed—in a flash, in the twinkling of an eye, at the last trumpet. For the trumpet will sound, the dead will be raised imperishable, and we will be changed" (1 Corinthians 15:51–52).

When the dead in Christ are resurrected with incorruptible bodies at the Rapture, the new bodies will be far different from the old bodies. According to 1 Corinthians 15:52, the bodies of the living saints will be changed too. The Bible does not give a complete description of the new bodies. The full revelation will be a glorious surprise. We get just a peek in the Gospel accounts of Jesus after His resurrection and in 1 Corinthians 15:41–54. These things we do know about the resurrection body:

1. The new body will have a continuing identification with the old body, like a plant that grows from a seed (vv. 37).

2. We will still be individuals in our new bodies (v. 38).

3. Our new bodies will be perfect (v. 49).

We will have to wait to find out what we will really be like until one moment after the Rapture. Now our finite minds cannot understand the description, even if it were given to us in more detail. We have all the information God wants us to have now, and that is all we need to know.

Preparing Youth for the Rapture

One young teenager confided tearfully to her mother, "I do not want Jesus to come until after I get married and have a family." The truth of the Rapture and Second Coming had lodged in her heart. She loved the Lord with her whole heart, but the beautiful things of life also had an attraction. With love, her mother assured her that Jesus would do what was just right for her. She could plan to be part of her own Christian family, and plan it with Jesus. If He should come before she married, He would still allow her to experience the same feelings of joy and happiness that the fulfillment of her Christian family plans would bring.

The youth in our churches should learn that Christ's coming for His children is not an interruption or an end to the enjoyable things of life. To be with Jesus is the capstone or fulfillment of a life completely dedicated to Him in every detail. For very young children, the thought of being "snatched into the air" may be beyond their comfort level. For these age groups, the emphasis might best be placed on heaven and what a wonderful place it will be as we are there with Jesus.

Some young people do not want Jesus to return because they are not ready for His coming. They are not living right, and they want to taste all the pleasures of the world before settling down to get ready. But the things that attract and entice now will become obstacles when the mind starts to turn toward righteous living. "Now is the time of God's favor, now is the day of salvation" (2 Corinthians 6:2).

Christ's coming to rapture those who look for Him must be translated from careful study into personal living. The truth of Christ's return must be more than just a future event. It should be a blessed hope for each Christian. How it will affect those who are not ready should make each Christian a more compassionate and effective witness. The final words of the entire Bible point to Christ's coming back for His saints: "He who testifies to these things says, 'Yes, I am coming soon.'. . . Come, Lord Jesus. The grace of the Lord Jesus be with God's people. Amen" (Revelation 22:20–21).

12.2.3
OBJECTIVE
Indicate how children and youth can be inspired to see the Rapture as the Blessed Hope.

T Test Yourself

Circle the letter of the *best* answer.

1. The Assemblies of God, like most Pentecostal groups, is
a) amillennialist.
b) premillennialist.
c) postmillennialist.

2. The Rapture and the Second Coming of Christ are
a) two names for the same event.
b) two events that take place at the end of the Tribulation.
c) two distinct events, one before and one after the Tribulation.

3. Adults most likely anticipate the Rapture more than children do because
a) adults have faced life's struggles and would welcome going to be with Jesus.
b) adult experiences with temptation cause them to fear moral failure.
c) adults see the Rapture as a way to avoid the difficulties of life.

4. The "Kingdom Now" belief teaches that
a) the world is now being made into Christ's perfect kingdom.
b) the only kingdom of God we will see is already in the hearts of God's people.
c) God's kingdom is both now and not yet; it will be realized in the Millennium.

5. Critics who think a Rapture is a foolish idea are called
a) reprobates.
b) doubters
c) scoffers.

6. In Matthew 24, the most repeated advice about how we should live in end-time is
a) avoid the sin that so easily entangles.
b) watch and be ready.
c) live without the spot or wrinkle of sin.

7. As signs of the approaching Rapture intensify, we must
a) reduce our possessions to bare essentials.
b) study the signs to estimate how close the Rapture may be.
c) work diligently to be ready for His coming.

8. According to Peter, Jesus delays His coming because
a) God is patient and desires more people to come to repentance.
b) time does not exist in eternity.
c) in God's view there is only a blink of an eye from creation to the present time.

9. Which end-time sign is not discussed in Chapter 12?
a) Wars and rumors of wars
b) Famine
c) Re-emergence of Jewish nation

10. The Rapture of the church will involve
a) only the living saints who are expecting Christ to come for them.
b) living believers and believers who died before the Rapture.
c) only the saints from the beginning of time who died before the Rapture.

Responses to Interactive Questions
Chapter 12

Some of these responses may include information that is supplemental to the IST. These questions are intended to produce reflective thinking beyond the course content and your responses may vary from these examples.

1 If all the signs of Christ's coming have already been witnessed in some fashion, why does the Rapture not take place immediately?

First, God measures time differently than we do. "With the Lord a day is like a thousand years, and a thousand years are like a day" (2 Peter 3:8). Second, God delays His coming because He desires that more will come to repentance through His patience (2 Peter 3:9). Third, it is at a time of God's own, sovereign, choosing and even Jesus said He did not know when it would be (Mark 13:32).

CHAPTER 13

Tribulation, the Day of the Lord, and Christ's Kingdom

Since New Testament days, some people have speculated as to the time of the Rapture and the chain of events immediately following the Rapture. Some have even tried to set specific dates, violating the biblical statement that "No one knows about that day or hour, not even the angels in heaven, nor the Son, but only the Father" (Matthew 24:36). One of the more famous efforts at date setting came from William Miller (early nineteenth century), the founder of a religious group called "Millerites." The group numbered between 50,000 and 100,000 members in its best days.

Following intense study of Daniel and Revelation, Miller calculated that Jesus would come back and take His group of followers between March 21, 1843, and March 21, 1844. Many of the followers sold their farms and homes, and left their employment to get ready and to warn others of the coming Rapture. When no Rapture occurred between those two dates, another Rapture date was set for October 22, 1844. Miscalculations of Bible events were blamed for the changes. When the last date passed without any appearance, the group experienced "the great disappointment." Many members left the group, which gradually scattered. Those who remained redefined the Rapture as a spiritual event that took place in heaven.

That was over 160 years ago. Yet people persist in trying to set dates. As recently as 1988, an independent preacher published a pamphlet titled, "88 Reasons Why Jesus Will Return in 1988." Of course, the Bible declaration stands true while date setters are discredited.

Lesson 13.1   Events on Earth and in Heaven During the Tribulation
Objectives
13.1.1 Define the meaning of "The Day of the Lord."
13.1.2 Identify the events that will take place on earth during the Tribulation.
13.1.3 Describe the Antichrist and his role in the Tribulation.
13.1.4 Describe the events that will take place in heaven at the time of the Tribulation.

Lesson 13.2   Reigning with Christ and the Final Judgment of the Wicked
Objectives
13.2.1 Summarize the final conflicts between good and evil, between God and Satan.
13.2.2 Describe the Millennium and Christ's earthly Kingdom.
13.2.3 Explain what will happen at the Great White Throne Judgment.
13.2.4 Describe the beauties of the Holy City and the new heavens and earth.

Lesson 13.3   Rapture Readiness
Objectives
13.3.1 Describe how believers can be assured of making the Rapture.
13.3.2 Explain why we should pray for and expect revival while we look for Christ's coming.

Events on Earth and in Heaven during the Tribulation

We feel sad for those believers who expect to go through most if not all of the Great Tribulation. Their only hope must be that they might die and go into God's presence before **Antichrist** comes on the scene. The suffering of those who will be on earth at the time will be terrible.

Some of the mid-tribulation and post-tribulation proponents understand 1 Thessalonians 5:9—"God did not appoint us to suffer wrath"—to mean "God's wrath," not the wrath of Antichrist and his forces of evil. But in the context of the entire chapter, such a distinction is not justified. We firmly believe through Scripture that true believers will be spared the horrors of the Tribulation.

If the pre-tribulation view of the Rapture is right, that should be incentive enough to live ready to be snatched away at any moment. If the post-tribulation view is right, that should be incentive to those believers to draw ever closer to the only One who can help them through the horrors they expect to face.

As we move into our study for this chapter, here is the segment of the full "Panorama of Prophecy" chart introduced in the lesson 12.2. This segment will be covered in this lesson.

IMMINENT EVENTS IN THE PANORAMA OF PROPHECY

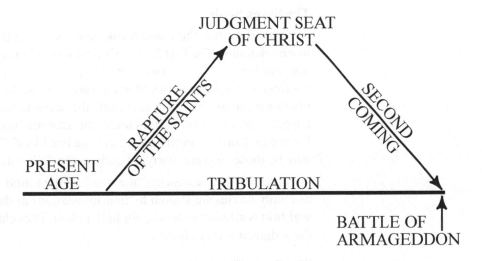

The Day of the Lord

13.1.1
OBJECTIVE

Define the meaning of "The Day of the Lord."

The frequency with which the phrase the Day of the Lord occurs in Scripture gives evidence of its importance in prophecy. Scholars disagree as to its specific meaning. Some apply it to the day of the Rapture, but the use of terms like doom, destruction, wrath, anger, vengeance, and darkness makes that application unlikely. The fearsome terms would certainly describe the terror and judgments of the Tribulation. Yet, it seems contrary to the nature of God to have His day be one of vengeance and destruction.

But it is proper to see the judgments against evil as preparation for something very positive: the establishment of Christ's Millennial Kingdom. Evil must first be destroyed before the time of perfect peace and prosperity on earth becomes a reality.

Paul tells us "the day of the Lord will come like a thief in the night" (1 Thessalonians 5:2; see also 2 Peter 3:10 and Revelation 3:3, 16:15). The same terminology is used in referring to Christ's coming for His saints (Matthew 24:43). It seems best therefore to define the Day of the Lord as that period which begins with the Rapture and the Tribulation and extends through the **Millennium** into the new heavens and earth.

13.1.2
OBJECTIVE
Identify the events that will take place on earth during the Tribulation.

The Tribulation: Seals, Trumpets, and Bowls Judgments (Revelation 6-9, 11, 15, 16)

The Tribulation is a period of seven years, the Seventieth Week of Daniel (Daniel 9:27). It directly concerns Israel and is God's judgment for long apostasy and neglect of the Messiah. During the Tribulation, "All Israel will be saved" (Romans 11:26). The "all" very likely refers to the godly Israelites of the Old Testament as well as those who accept Christ during the Tribulation. The Jews who might not accept Christ during the Tribulation would likely join the forces of the Antichrist and be destroyed in battle by Christ. There will likely be a great number of Jews saved during the Tribulation (Deuteronomy 4:30–31) Revelation 7:1–8 records 144,000 Jews sealed or saved during the Tribulation.

The Tribulation also affects the whole world because of its ungodliness and mistreatment of the Jews. The first half of these seven years will probably be a time of prosperity and acceptance of the Antichrist as the great deliverer from economic chaos. But the latter part of the period will witness the plagues described in Revelation.

The Seven Seals

Jesus is seen as the Lamb breaking the seals on the scroll of God's judgments in Revelation 6. The first four seals reveal four horsemen representing conquest, war, famine, and death. Rather than a sequence of brief judgments, later judgments would seem to add to the earlier ones, thus compounding the intensity of the judgments. The fifth seal shifts the scene to the altar of the heavenly temple. The voices of martyrs under the altar are heard asking, "How long, Sovereign Lord . . . until you . . . avenge our blood?" (Revelation 6:10). These may be those who are martyred early in the Tribulation.

The sixth seal represents "the wrath of the Lamb" (6:16). The earth and the heavenly bodies are shaken to their foundations as darkness prevails. The seventh seal brings silence in heaven for half an hour (Revelation 8:1). There is awe at the judgments yet to follow.

The Seven Trumpets

Seven angels with trumpets announce the future judgments of the wicked earth: hail and fire mixed with blood (Revelation 8:7), a huge burning mountain thrown into the sea turning one-third of the sea into blood (8:8), a great burning star falling on rivers and springs, turning the waters bitter (8:10–11), the sun, moon, and stars partially darkened (8:12). A loud voice interrupts announcing greater woes yet to come: the opening of the abyss or hell, releasing plagues of locusts looking like horses going into battle (9:3–10), releasing four destroying angels leading huge demonic armies to kill one-third of all humans (9:14–16), yet no one repents (9:20–21). After an interlude of time, the seventh trumpet sounds bringing assurance of God's victory and announcing the coming bowl judgments.

The Seven Bowls

The seven bowl judgments are more severe than any of the preceding judgments. Revelation 16 describes the pouring out of the "bowls of God's wrath on the earth" (16:1)—ugly, painful sores or boils received by those who accepted the **mark of the beast** (16:2), seas turned into blood, killing all life in them (16:3), fresh water rivers and springs turn to blood (16:4), increased heat of the sun scorches unrepentant persons (16:8–9), total darkness consumes Antichrist's kingdom (16:10), Euphrates River dries up as preparation for the battle of **Armageddon** (16:12, 16), and the greatest earthquake the world has ever known followed by one hundred pound hail (16:18, 21) complete the bowl judgments.

The Antichrist

13.1.3
OBJECTIVE
Describe the Antichrist and his role in the Tribulation.

The Bible warns against false christs or men who claim to be the Messiah or Deliverer. But this antichrist is *the Antichrist* because he will be Satan's special representative from the pit.

Daniel 9:27 and 2 Thessalonians 2:3–10 contain significant facts about Antichrist and his activity. There is much speculation about the coming Antichrist, but we will stay within the confines of these passages. Daniel notes, "He will confirm a covenant with many for one 'seven.' In the middle of the 'seven' he will put an end to sacrifice and offering." The "seven" (or "week" in some translations) corresponds with the seven years of the Tribulation. The covenant seems to refer to an agreement between the Jews and the Antichrist, permitting the resumption of ancient sacrificial worship.

1 When will the Antichrist appear? What will he be like? And what will he do?

From 2 Thessalonians we learn these facts about the Antichrist. He will be revealed as a "man of lawlessness" and will be "doomed to destruction" (2 Thessalonians 2:3). The Day of the Lord will not come before Antichrist is revealed (2:3). He will set himself up as God sometime after he is revealed (2:4). He will deceive many by "all kinds of counterfeit miracles, signs and wonders" (2:9). He will not be able to accomplish all his evil plans until something that hinders is removed from the world (2:6–7). Though many have speculated about the identity of the hindrance, from the Roman Empire to the Holy Spirit, Stanley M. Horton concludes that the hindering force consists of "the true believers who will be taken out of the way, caught up in the Rapture. This fits the facts indicating that the Rapture will take place before the Antichrist is revealed. As believers we look for Jesus Christ, not the Antichrist" (Horton 1996, 113).

Bible students have noted a satanic trinity in the biblical references to Satan, the Antichrist, and the False Prophet. The evil three carry out their wickedness against God and Israel in an attempt to destroy the kingdom of righteousness. The three are ultimately consigned to the lake of fire.

Earth's Tribulation, Heaven's Celebration

13.1.4
OBJECTIVE
Describe the events that will take place in heaven at the time of the Tribulation.

The rapture of the church marks the beginning of events in heaven for the saints. First is our summons to the *Judgment Seat of Christ,* where our works will be judged. This will be the highest court the Christian ever faces, for each believer has already been declared justified. Everything will be judged—actions, attitudes, motives, stewardship, and handling of suffering. Bad works here are not sins, just worthless deeds. Good works are those worthy of reward, worthy of our hearing "Well done, good and faithful servant!" (Matthew 25:21).

After we have been judged, we are ready to be presented as the perfect bride of Christ, arrayed in "the righteous acts of the saints" (Revelation 19:8). The marriage of the church and the Lamb, the focus of so much biblical imagery and comparison, is finally consummated. After the wedding, of course, follows the **Marriage Supper of the Lamb** (Revelation 19:9). Finally, home at last—forever.

2   What picture comes to your mind when you think of Jesus?

3   Why does Jesus enter Jerusalem on a little donkey and not a high-stepping stallion?

Reigning with Christ and the Final Judgment of the Wicked

Two Bible scenes portray Jesus in very different ways. Picture Number 1: We call it the Triumphal Entry into Jerusalem as the hour of His crucifixion draws nearer. Matthew describes it this way: "See, your king comes to you, gentle and riding on a donkey, on a colt, the foal of a donkey" (Matthew 21:5).

Though Jesus is the Son of God, yet for our sakes He humbled himself (Philippians 2:8). He came not to be served, "but to serve, and to give his life as a ransom for many" (Matthew 20:28). Yet, the crowds thronged this humble figure, shouting out, "Hosanna to the Son of David! Blessed is he who comes in the name of the Lord! Hosanna in the highest!" (Matthew 21:9).

Picture number 2: John records his vision: "I saw heaven standing open and there before me was a white horse, whose rider is called Faithful and True . . . His eyes are like blazing fire, and on his head are many crowns . . . The armies of heaven were following him, riding on white horses and dressed in fine linen . . . On his robe and on his thigh he has this name written: KING OF KINGS AND LORD OF LORDS" (Revelation 19:11, 12, 14, 16). Which is the Jesus you know?

There is beauty in this contrast. We needed a humble Jesus who would come and die to provide our salvation. But we now need a militant Jesus to finally defeat Satan, the one who has made such a mess of this world. Jesus has always been the King of kings, and Lord of lords, even when humbly working out our salvation.

In this lesson we are looking at the following segment of the full "Panorama of Prophecy" chart introduced in Lesson 12.2.

FINAL EVENTS IN THE PANORAMA OF PROPHECY

13.2.1
OBJECTIVE

Summarize the final conflicts between good and evil, between God and Satan.

4   How will the unbelievable destruction and slaughter of the seals, trumpets, and bowls judgments end?

Final Conflict Between God and Antichrist

The unholy trinity will lead the kings of the earth in preparing for war against God. The armies of the Antichrist will gather at Megiddo, about twenty miles southeast of the present day Haifa. Suddenly, Christ will appear, accompanied by a heavenly army of saints and angels. What a one-sided battle! No deaths in Christ's army. The outcome is so certain that an angel, even before the battle begins, calls the vultures of the world for a feast (Revelation 19:17).

Zechariah gives another detail about Christ's return to earth for the final defeat of evil. "On that day his feet will stand on the Mount of Olives, east of Jerusalem, and the Mount of Olives will be split in two from east to west, forming a great valley . . . Then the Lord my God will come, and all the holy ones [the saints in heaven during the Tribulation on earth] with him" (Zechariah 14:4–5). We are not told how the army of saints and Jesus join for the Revelation account.

"The Lord Jesus will overthrow [Antichrist] with the breath of his mouth and destroy by the splendor of his coming" (2 Thessalonians 2:8). The numberless saints and angels coming back with Christ simply add to the grandeur of the scene. They do not fight the battle. Christ himself will destroy five-sixths of the assembled evil forces at Armageddon—with His word and the brightness of His presence. We are on the winning side!

This is not science fiction. It is a climactic struggle between God and the principalities and powers of darkness. When these two worlds collide, the foundations of the earth will be shaken. All men and women will be affected. Revelation 14:20 describes the scene after the battle—"Blood flowed out of the press, rising as high as the horses' bridles for a distance of 1,600 stadia [about 180 miles (Horton 1991, 215)].

Satan will be bound. The significance of this "battle on the great day of God Almighty" (Revelation 16:14) is not in the number killed or in the amount of blood shed. It is in the spiritual victory realized when Satan is bound and cast into the Abyss, or bottomless pit (Revelation 20:3). Satan will no longer be able to deceive the nations and people as he has done since the first sin. For the first time since Lucifer rebelled and fell from heaven (Isaiah 14:12), every hostile force that would challenge Christ's rule over the earth will be suppressed. The other two members of the unholy trinity are at this time cast into the lake of fire from which there is no release (Revelation 19:20).

13.2.2
OBJECTIVE

Describe the Millennium and Christ's earthly Kingdom.

The Millennium

With Satan's influence removed from the earth and Christ's reign of righteousness unopposed, the Millennium will be a time of unsurpassed glory and perfect relationships. References to this future state of perfection are found throughout Scripture. The Old Testament prophets anticipated the day when Israel would again fill a special place of prominence and blessing. The Christian today, tired of the pain and suffering of the curse, also anticipates this time of peace and joy. Consider some of the more significant characteristics of the Millennium, which should not be overlooked.

1. Christ's rule will be over the entire earth (Daniel 7:14), absolute in authority and power (Isaiah 11:4), and completely righteous and just (Isaiah 11:3–5).

2. Israel will enjoy special privileges (Zechariah 10:6, 8, 9, 12), although Gentiles will be active participants and receive blessings as well. "This does not mean there will be competition between Israel and the rest of the church. Each will bless the other, for 'God had planned something

better for us so that only together with us would they be made perfect' (Hebrews 11:40)" (Horton 1996, 209).

3. The curse on the earth will be lifted during the Millennium (Isaiah 35).

4. The normally aggressive nature of animals will be changed (Isaiah 11).

5. Health, healing, and long life will be evident (Isaiah 35 and 65).

6. Jerusalem will become the capital city of the entire world (Isaiah 60:12, 14).

7. Those who refused to receive the mark of the Beast in the Tribulation, and were martyred for that choice, will be resurrected to reign with Christ for the thousand years (Revelation 20:4).

The above description of the Millennium and Christ's earthly kingdom emphasizes a material kingdom rather than a spiritual one. In the Millennium, Christ's kingdom will be both physical and spiritual. Here are some of the spiritual characteristics of that Kingdom.

8. The truth of God will be widespread, "as the waters cover the sea" (Isaiah 11).

9. Righteousness, obedience, and holiness will characterize the Kingdom (Isaiah 62; Zechariah 14).

10. There will be universal peace (Isaiah 2).

11. There will be great joy and happiness (Isaiah 12).

12. The Millennium will be a time of real fullness of the Spirit (Isaiah 32).

This is what Christ's second coming and defeat of Satan will bring to the earth. May it happen soon!

OBJECTIVE
Explain what will happen at the Great White Throne Judgment.

Satan's Last Deception

The Millennium is not forever, just one thousand years. Then there must be another fine-tuning in God's end-time dealing with the earth and its inhabitants before the permanent perfection of eternity begins. During the Millennium there will be normal family relationships with children born to husbands and wives. Before the one thousand years are completed, the children thus born will far outnumber their parents. Some of them will have obeyed Christ because that is the only thing to do. Satan's release will be their test of love, faith, and true loyalty.

Revelation 20:3 describes the release of Satan for "a short time." One last time, Satan will deceive the nations, or peoples, and gather together a group of rebels to oppose God (Revelation 20:7–8) [*Nations* means "peoples," rather than "nationalistic states," and often refers to Gentiles or pagans (Horton 1996, 185)]. He and his followers will do battle with Christ and His faithful. This rebellion will be short-lived. Fire will descend from heaven and devour the opposition (20:9). Satan will finally be cast into the lake of fire permanently (20:10).

13.2.4
OBJECTIVE
Describe the beauties of the Holy City and the new heavens and earth.

The Great White Throne Judgment

After the judgment, fire physically destroys those deceived by Satan at the end of the Millennium; all the wicked who have ever lived on the face of the earth (whose names are not found in the Book of Life) will be dead. Then will follow the resurrection of the wicked dead to stand before the austere Judge from whose presence earth and sky take flight (Revelation 20:11). The books are opened and the wicked are judged according to their works (20:12). Then, like Satan, they are to be thrown into the lake of fire to be tormented day and night forever (20:10, 15).

If we really grasp the power of the scene that awaits sinners at the Great White Throne Judgment, we will be moved to do what we can to help them escape this tragic end. Although the wicked deserve what they get, we should not delight in their end. God certainly does not.

The Holy City

Revelation 20 ends with the Great White Throne Judgment. Chapter 21 begins with John's view of a new heaven and a new earth. The holy city, the New Jerusalem comes down from God out of the new heavens to rest on the new earth.

To discover how the new heavens and earth come about, we must compare this passage in Revelation with Isaiah 65:17 and 2 Peter 3:10–13. Peter gives the best details on how it will happen. "The heavens will pass away with a great noise; and the elements will melt with fervent heat" (3:10, NKJV).

The Bible says nothing more about the origin of the city than that it comes down "out of heaven from God, prepared as a bride beautifully dressed for her husband" (Revelation 21:2). From Revelation 21 and 22 we learn of its majesty, either symbolic or real: brilliant like a precious jewel, clear as crystal, jasper walls, each gate a massive pearl, a main street of pure gold, continually lighted by the Lamb (no night), and a crystal clear river of the water of life flowing from the throne of God. But even more significant is what will be missing from the city: tears, death, mourning, crying, pain, evil persons, night, and the curse humankind had previously lived under.

The description of eternity ends here. And rightly so! We are just introduced to the excitement and magnificence of the forever and ever. Only at that time will we see and hear that which we are told we cannot now grasp: "No eye has seen, no ear has heard, no mind has conceived what God has prepared for those who love him" (1 Corinthians 2:9).

In the "Hallelujah Chorus" of his oratorio *The Messiah,* George Frederick Handel caught some of the overwhelming joy and anticipation that should come to the Christian as he or she contemplates the glorious time we will share with the Father, the Son, and the Spirit:

"The Lord God Omnipotent reigneth!

Hallelujah! Hallelujah!"

LESSON 13.3

5 How should a Christian read the daily news headlines and stories?

Rapture Readiness

This study of end-time events—with emphasis on the soon return of Christ to gather His saints to be with Him forever—should cause us to read today's news with eternity's values in view. What is your reaction when you read or hear of widespread famine, devastating earthquakes, and other natural catastrophes? Do you whisper a prayer for the persons and families going through such a trial and "tribulation"? What about wars and rumors of war? Does the warning of a possible terrorist attack strike fear in your heart?

Your reaction may be the same as that of most readers: "What a tragedy!" The newspaper is then put on the stack of old papers and promptly forgotten. The rush of the day's activity consumes all our thinking.

But before putting the paper down, whisper a prayer of thanksgiving to Jesus. Your gratitude should lie, not in escaping the bad things that could happen to you, but in the assurance that God will begin to straighten out this sin-cursed world as soon as He comes to rapture His faithful followers.

Then the catastrophe you have just read about can be an opener for witnessing today. "What do you make of that earthquake in the East?" Or "What about those poor people in the south being flooded out of their homes?" Your friends may not appreciate your tying every such event to the rapture of the saints, but if a fearful heart responds, the opportunity to share what Jesus means to you is an open door. With the help of the Holy Spirit, seize the occasion.

Run with Perseverance

The joy of anticipating heaven should transform every part of our daily choices and activities. If Jesus "for the joy set before him endured the cross" (Hebrews 12:2), certainly the joy of heaven set before us will give strength for anything we are called upon to face. And it will help us run with patience the race marked out for us, throwing off everything that hinders and the sin that so easily entangles (12:1).

The distinction between "everything that hinders" and "the sin that so easily entangles" is noteworthy. "Hinders" means any kind of weights, encumbrances, that may not be sin but that hinders running the race to win. Athletes shed any unnecessary body weight and carry no baggage in a race. In like manner, Christians must avoid distractions and all hindrances in order to realize the full will of God. "The sin that so easily entangles" us is unbelief (the antithesis of faith) and related sins as discussed in Hebrews, such as spiritual drifting, dullness, prolonged immaturity, and deliberate sinning. These things may tangle the feet and trip a person up so that he or she falls, drops out of the race, and misses the prize. (Adams 1999, 1378)

This awareness should be the true motivation for righteous living—avoiding distractions and subtle unbelief that can so easily creep up on us. Too many Christians find their motivation for holy living in the legalism that proclaims right action, but for the wrong reasons. Once we have grasped the Blessed Hope of the Second Coming and the eternal fellowship with our best Friend, Jesus, our hatred for sin will be more intense and our motivation for holy living will be what it should be. "Dear friends, since you are looking forward to this [the glory of eternity], make every effort to be found spotless, blameless and at peace with him" (2 Peter 3:14).

Church Revivals

Revival in Pentecostal circles means more than merely maintaining a spiritual status quo. It means moving closer to the Jesus whose coming we will welcome. For some, revival means people slain in the Spirit and other physical manifestations. God certainly can do as He pleases in manifesting His presence. And at times people react in different ways when that Presence moves powerfully on them. Someone has likened variety in physical manifestation to the reactions two people might have if both were to accidentally put a finger in a live electrical socket. One might yell and scream, jumping around long after the shock had passed. The other, by nature less demonstrative, might jerk his hand out quickly with only one word, Wow! So it is that different people respond differently to the real presence of God, which naturally is more powerful than a brief electric shock.

Neither the quiet nor the noisy response is biblical evidence of a revival. Instead, the evidence is in lives changed—sinners saved and believers drawing closer to the Lord—and in persons being called into various ministries by the Holy Spirit. Just as the Holy Spirit set Paul and Barnabas apart to a specific ministry that blessed and enlarged the young church, so revival today will witness young men and women called by the Spirit to specific tasks and ministries. Changed lives will

---

13.3.1
OBJECTIVE
Describe how believers can be assured of making the Rapture.

6   What is included in things that hinder and the sin that entangles?

13.3.2
OBJECTIVE
Explain why we should pray for and expect revival while we look for Christ's coming.

mean the fruit and gifts of the Spirit will be more and more manifest in believers' lives. Unity in the body of Christ is another evidence of a revival move by the Holy Spirit. May the Lord revive His church as we await His return.

Relating the Glorious Future

Streets of gold in heaven have special meaning for adults who have struggled for years to earn sufficient money to provide food, shelter, and clothing for a growing family. Gold so plentiful that you walk on it rather than spend it to buy the necessities of life! Heavenly streets of gold are an excellent way to speak of the day when troubles and trials will be left behind.

What do streets of gold, or even getting to be with Jesus, mean to children who still enjoy the benefits provided by their parents? The teacher of a Sunday school class of 12-year-old boys faced the dilemma of translating this message. In the middle of class discussion the teacher asked the boys what they like doing better than anything else. Sports, as might be expected, was the primary interest at their age. So they decided, since it was baseball season, that they liked that better than anything else. Four months later, of course, it would have been football.

"How would you like to play a game of cosmic baseball?" the teacher asked. "The earth could be home plate, Mars first base, Jupiter second base, Saturn third base. Little Mercury could be the baseball. Batter up!" The boys were excited. That kind of a baseball game would make the sandlot game rather tame.

"You can play all the cosmic baseball you want to in heaven." The teacher did not tell the boys though that in heaven they would rather do other things. But at this stage in their spiritual development, resting or visiting with Jesus did not yet have an appeal. It is the task of the preacher and the teacher to make heaven a *want-to-be-there* place.

The same principle applies in our witnessing. We do not win people by quoting cold facts and a few isolated Scripture verses. We introduce them to Jesus in a way that they can get the "feel" of a Friend who loved them so much that He came to die for them.

Carry on with Joy

If our greatest desire is to be like Jesus, heaven will be the fulfillment of that desire. "We know that when he appears, we shall be like him, for we shall see him as he is" (1 John 3:2). When we know that fact, and crave its fulfillment with a real urgency, we can view our entry into heaven, whether by death or by the Rapture, as the crowning day. Today could be that crowning day!

A well-known music composer of a past generation, Stuart Hamblen, became a Christian later in his life. After writing secular music for years, his conversion inspired him to write a song that stirred many hearts for whom heaven had become more theory than reality. Just a few lines here will conclude our study. You can find all the words to "Until Then" (words and music by Stuart Hamblen) on the Internet.

My heart can sing when I pause to remember

A heartache here is but a stepping stone

Along a trail that's winding always upward

This troubled world is not my final home.

But until then my heart will go on singing,

Until then with joy I'll carry on,

Until the day my eyes behold the city,

Until the day God calls me home.

T Test Yourself

Circle the letter of the *best* answer.

1. Daniel's seventieth week is identified as the seven years of
a) famine the Israelites experienced in Egypt.
b) silence in heaven.
c) the Tribulation

2. The creatures that will blow the seven trumpets announcing more judgments are
a) seven angels.
b) seven representatives of Antichrist.
c) seven creatures that rise out of the sea.

3. There have been many antichrists, but *the* Antichrist of Revelation will be
a) Satan himself.
b) the embodiment of evil in the Tribulation.
c) a human being who gathers a following by deluding church leaders.

4. The satanic trinity consists of
a) the Beast, the Antichrist, and Satan.
b) Satan, Antichrist, and a false prophet.
c) the Antichrist, a false prophet, and a false apostle.

5. Two events that will take place in heaven during the Tribulation on earth are the
a) Judgment Seat of Christ and the Marriage Supper of the Lamb.
b) Marriage of the Lamb and Bride, followed by the judgment of false Christians.
c) giving of rewards and hearing the words of Jesus, "Well done, good servants."

6. John describes Jesus as the Rider on a white horse wearing on His robe these words:
a) the Alpha and the Omega.
b) King of Kings and Lord of Lords.
c) Wonderful, Counselor, Prince of Peace.

7. The followers of Christ are not killed in the final battle with Antichrist because
a) Christ fights the battle by himself.
b) the saints will have immortal bodies that cannot be killed.
c) the forces of Antichrist are terrified and try to flee.

8. After his brief release to make his final effort to deceive people, Satan will be
a) cast into the lake of fire permanently.
b) bound and cast into the Abyss or bottomless pit.
c) called before the Great White Throne Judgment and condemned to hell.

9. The Holy City or the New Jerusalem comes to earth from
a) another universe.
b) the original Creation where it has been awaiting Christ's final victory.
c) the new heavens.

10. The greatest need of our world as we await Christ's return at the Rapture is
a) the elimination of poverty around the world.
b) spiritual revival and a renewed emphasis on holy living among believers.
c) a better understanding of end-time events and the nearness of the Rapture.

Responses to Interactive Questions
Chapter 13

Some of these responses may include information that is supplemental to the IST. These questions are intended to produce reflective thinking beyond the course content and your responses may vary from these examples.

1   When will the Antichrist appear? What will he be like? And what will he do?

The Bible warns against false christs or men who claim to be the Messiah or Deliverer. But this antichrist is the Antichrist because he will be Satan's special representative from the pit.

Daniel 9:27 and 2 Thessalonians 2:3–10 contain the significant facts about Antichrist and his activity. There is much speculation about the coming Antichrist, but we will stay within the confines of these passages. "He will confirm a covenant with many for one 'seven.' In the middle of the 'seven' he will put an end to sacrifice and offering." The "seven" (or "week" in some translations) corresponds with the seven years of the Tribulation. The covenant seems to refer to an agreement between the Jews and the Antichrist permitting the resumption of ancient sacrificial worship.

From 2 Thessalonians we learn these facts about the Antichrist. He will be revealed as a "man of lawlessness" and will be "doomed to destruction" (2 Thessalonians 2:3) during the time known as the Day of the Lord (2:8). The Day of the Lord will not come before Antichrist is revealed (2:3). He will set himself up as God sometime after he is revealed (2:4). He will deceive many by "all kinds of counterfeit miracles, signs and wonders" (2:9). He will not be able to accomplish all his evil plans until something that hinders is removed from the world (2:6–7). Though many identifications have been suggested over the centuries, from the Roman Empire to the Holy Spirit, Stanley M. Horton concludes that the hindering force consists of "the true believers who will be taken out of the way, caught up in the Rapture. This fits the facts indicating that the Rapture will take place before the Antichrist is revealed. As believers we look for Jesus Christ, not the Antichrist" (Horton 1996, 113).

Bible students have noted a satanic trinity in the biblical references to Satan, the Antichrist, and the False Prophet. The evil three carry out their wickedness against God and Israel in an attempt to destroy the kingdom of righteousness. The three are ultimately consigned to the lake of fire.

2   What picture comes to your mind when you think of Jesus?

Answers will vary. Some biblical pictures are as follows: Picture Number 1: We call it the Triumphal Entry into Jerusalem as the hour of His crucifixion draws nearer. Matthew describes it this way: "See, your king comes to you, gentle and riding on a donkey, on a colt, the foal of a donkey" (Matthew 21:5).

Picture Number 2: John records his vision: "I saw heaven standing open and there before me was a white horse, whose rider is called Faithful and True . . . His eyes are like blazing fire, and on his head are many crowns . . . The armies of heaven were following him, riding on white horses and dressed in fine linen . . . On his robe and on his thigh he has this name written: KING OF KINGS AND LORD OF LORDS" (Revelation 19:11, 12, 14, 16).

Of course, the Bible provides many other powerful images of Jesus, including those of blessing children, teaching hungry seekers, calming the storm, healing the sick, and so forth. The above response represents the focus of the IST for this section.

3   Why does Jesus enter Jerusalem on a little donkey and not a high-stepping stallion?

Zechariah 9:9 tells of a promised king to come to Jerusalem on the colt of a donkey. Jesus did exactly that as Matthew 21:1–11 shows. It was as a figure of humility and gentleness before the sacrificial offering of His life. It was also a common mount for kings and other royalty in peacetime. But when Christ returns in Revelation 19:11–16 He returns as a conquering king and rides a great white horse.

4   How will the unbelievable destruction and slaughter of the seals, trumpets, and bowls judgments end?

"The Lord Jesus will overthrow [Antichrist] with the breath of his mouth and destroy by the splendor of his coming" (2 Thessalonians 2:8). The numberless saints and angels coming back with Christ simply add to the grandeur of the scene. They do not fight the battle. Christ himself will destroy five-sixths of the assembled evil forces at Armageddon—with His word and the brightness of His presence. We are on the winning side! Also read Revelation 19:15 and following.

5   How should a Christian read the daily news headlines and stories?

We should read today's news with eternity's values in view.

6   What is included in things that hinder and the sin that entangles?

The distinction between "everything that hinders" and "the sin that so easily entangles" is noteworthy. "Hinders" means any kind of weights, encumbrances, that may not be sin but that hinder running the race to win. Athletes shed any unnecessary body weight and carry no baggage in a race. In like manner, Christians must avoid distractions and all hindrances in order to realize the full will of God. "The sin that so easily entangles" us is unbelief (the antithesis of faith) and related sins as discussed in Hebrews, such as spiritual drifting, dullness, prolonged immaturity, and deliberate sinning. These things may tangle the feet and trip a person up so that he or she falls, drops out of the race, and misses the prize. (Adams 1999, 1378)

UNIT PROGRESS EVALUATION 5 AND FINAL EXAMINATION

You have now concluded all of the work in this independent-study textbook. Review the lessons in this unit carefully, and then answer the questions in the last unit progress evaluation (UPE). When you have completed the UPE, check your answers with the answer key provided in Essential Course Materials at the back of this IST. Review any items you may have answered incorrectly. Review for the final examination by studying the course objectives, lesson objectives, self-tests, and UPEs. Review any lesson content necessary to refresh your memory. If you review carefully and are able to fulfill the objectives, you should have no difficulty passing the closed-book final examination.

Taking the Final Examination

1. **All final exams must be taken closed book**. You are not allowed to use any materials or outside help while taking a final exam. You will take the final examination online at www.globaluniversity.edu. If the online option is not available to you, you may request a printed final exam. If you did not request a printed final exam when you ordered your course, you must submit this request a few weeks before you are ready to take the exam. The Request for a Printed Final Examination is in the Forms section of Essential Course Materials at the back of this IST.

2. Review for the final examination in the same manner in which you prepared for the UPEs. Refer to the form Checklist of Study Methods in the front part of the IST for further helpful review hints.

3. After you complete and submit the online final examination, the results will be immediately available to you. Your final course grade report will be emailed to your Global University student email account after your Service Learning Requirement (SLR) report has been processed.

4. If you complete the exam in printed form, you will send your final examination, your answer sheets, and your SLR report to Berean School of the Bible for grading. Your final course grade report will be sent to your GU student email account. If you do not have access to the internet, your grade will be sent to your mailing address.

🔍 Glossary

Chapter

advocate	— a legal term identifying a person who pleads the case for another person.	9
Antichrist	— a false Christ revealed in the Tribulation; claims to be God and demands worship.	13
apocalyptic literature	— writings that predict or reveal future events related to the end of the world.	12
apostasy	— a deliberate denial or abandonment of an individual's faith (cf. Hebrews 3:12).	4
apostolic ministry	— a leadership ministry recognized by an entire movement; demonstrates supernatural gifts, brings Christ to unreached peoples, models responsibility and accountability, and teaches sound doctrine; title of "Apostle" never to be self-assigned.	8
Armageddon	— Site of the final battle when Christ completely defeats Satan and Antichrist at the end of the Tribulation.	13
Arminians	— people who believe the theological position of Jacobus Arminius who opposed the absolute *predestination* taught by John Calvin and maintained that salvation was offered to all. This is the position of the Assemblies of God.	3
atheistic evolution	— a theory that denies the existence of God and assumes that plants, animals, and humans have developed out of earlier forms through changes in succeeding time periods.	2
Bible doctrine	— biblical teachings arranged in a systematic form	1
Calvinists	— people who believe the theological teaching attributed to John Calvin. They emphasize the sovereignty of God, the depravity of humankind, and predestination (each person's ultimate destiny is foreordained). The five points of Calvinism, often called the TULIP list, are listed here: Total depravity (Original sin makes everyone corrupt and unable to know or obey God). Unconditional election (God alone chooses who will be saved). Limited atonement (Christ died only for those destined to be saved). Irresistible grace (If God chooses a person to be saved, he or she cannot resist) Perseverance of the Saints (Those whom God chooses will always remain saved.).	
cardinal	— of basic importance, foundational, primary, chief, main, essential.	1

Chapter

cessationism	— belief that supernatural gifts of the Spirit, including healing, ended with the first century.	10
charismata	— Greek word for spiritual manifestations or the gifts of the Spirit	10
charismatic	— a special dynamic activity of the Holy Spirit; applied to persons who have experienced the baptism in the Holy Spirit but choose not to be called Pentecostals, who have more church structure.	6
Counselor	— one who gives advice or counsel.	9
Daniel's Seventieth Week	— the final "week" of seven years coming at the end of the Church Age (rapture of the saints); identifies the Great Tribulation for premillennialists.	13
Day of the Lord	— period of time, from the Rapture through the Tribulation and Millennium and into the new heavens and earth.	13
dichotomy	— divisible into two parts; as applied to humans—body and soul	11
doctrine	— something taught or held to be true, a statement of faith.	1
edify	— to build up, uplift, enlighten, or improve.	7
eschatology, eschatological	— study of the future destiny of humankind and the world; end-time events.	5
eternal security	— the belief that salvation cannot be forfeited, regardless of a person's decisions, actions, or lifestyle; also called once-saved-always-saved doctrine	4
evangelicals	— protestants emphasizing (1) the authority of Scripture, (2) salvation by faith in the atoning death of Jesus Christ through personal conversion, and (3) the importance of personal relationship with God rather than formal ritual.	1
free will	— freedom of humans to make choices that are not determined by divine intervention	2
fruit of the Spirit	— virtues that in their fullest expression can only be produced by the Holy Spirit; human effort produces only a suggestion of the fruit of the Spirit.	7
Full Gospel	— all the gospel; usually identifies those who believe and teach some or all of the following: salvation, the baptism in the Holy Spirit, divine healing, second coming of Christ.	10
futurism	— a view of life that values the future over the past or the present; frequently leads non-Christians into astrology, horoscopes, and visiting fortune-tellers.	12
Godhead	— term for God as existing in three persons.	5
human free will	— the freedom to accept or reject God's offer of salvation.	4
incarnate, incarnation	— Christ becoming a human being without giving up His deity.	10
inerrant	— free from error.	1
inspired	— influenced, moved, or guided by divine inspiration.	1
intercessor	— one who intercedes for another; a mediator.	9

Chapter

justification	— declaration that a person is just or righteous; a legal term for releasing one from the guilt of sin.	3
Kingdom Now	— a false teaching that the world can and is now being made into Christ's kingdom, as preparation for Christ's return to rule and reign on earth.	12
Latter Rain Movement	— reference to outpouring of the Spirit (Joel 2:28); name applied to a mid-twentieth century Pentecostal Movement that broke away from established Pentecostal churches, advocating an independent and autonomous local church structure; forerunner of today's charismatic movement.	8
legalism	— required adherence to religious law or a moral code.	5
mark of the beast	— name, or number of the name, of Antichrist; everyone required to receive the mark on the right hand or forehead; number identified as 666; without the mark people cannot buy or sell.	13
Marriage Supper of the Lamb	— celebration in heaven uniting Christ and His Church; at the same time, the Tribulation is taking place on earth.	13
Millennium	— future reign of Christ on earth after the Battle of Armageddon; literally means one thousand years.	13
Millennium theories		12
Amillennialism	— a false teaching that there will not be a future thousand-year reign of Christ on earth. The belief does not accept as literal the Bible reference to one thousand years.	12
Premillennialism	— literal understanding of Scripture that Jesus will personally return to earth, with the previously raptured saints, to establish His kingdom on earth for one thousand years.	12
Postmillennialism	— false teaching that the Millennium is an extension of the Church Age; believes that Christ rules during the one thousand years, but is not physically present.	12
omnipotent	— all-powerful.	2
omnipresent	— everywhere present.	2
omniscient	— all-knowing.	2
ordinance	— a divinely established religious custom or practice regarded as an essential spiritual duty.	4
Paraclete	— John's identification of the Holy Spirit; literally means "one who comes alongside to help."	9
philosophy	— system of reasoned values and reality; general beliefs and attitudes of an individual.	10
plan of salvation	— God's plan for saving a person from the power and effects of sin through the sacrifice of His Son Jesus, thus restoring fellowship and a personal relationship with God; the steps a sinner must go through to receive that salvation.	2
predestination	— the belief that because God knows events before they happen, our eternal destiny is predetermined and we cannot change what God has foreordained.	4

Chapter

prophetic ministry	— speaks God's Word to His people; not viewed as an administrator; message to be tested to make sure it conforms to the authority of Scripture (1 Corinthians 14:29).	8
Rapture theories		12
Pre-Tribulation	— the belief that the rapture of the church will take place before the Great Tribulation.	12
Mid-Tribulation	— the belief that the rapture of the church will take place in the middle of the Great Tribulation.	12
reconciliation	— the act of reconciling or restoring to fellowship, settling differences.	3
redemption	— the act of redeeming, winning/buying back, or freeing from the consequences of sin.	3
regeneration	— the act of being created again, to change drastically for the better as a result of the work of the Holy Spirit.	3
repentance	— the act of repenting, turning from sin, and committing yourself to change for the better.	3
restorationist	— a person who believes a church should be restored to New Testament standards.	9
sacrament	— a religious rite that provides saving grace.	4
salvation	— God's act of saving humans from the power and effects of sin.	3
sanctification	— state of being made holy, set apart for the use intended by God.	3
security of the believer	— confidence that a person cannot lose his or her salvation, or assurance that a person's salvation is secure.	3
self-gratification	— any act of pleasing self or of satisfying a person's own desires.	3
sin	— the willful or voluntary rebellion against God's holy law. Sin can be found in what we are (mind, heart, and attitudes), what we do (sinful acts), and what we fail to do (falling short in doing right).	2
sovereignty of God	— supreme power and authority; God's right to choose according to His own nature and will.	4
theology	— the study of God or our understanding of God and His relations with humankind.	1
trichotomy	— divisible into three parts; as applied to the nature of humans—body, soul, and spirit.	11
unitarians	— people who believe that God exists as only one person.	5
unpardonable sin	— a sin that will not be forgiven.	6

 # Reference List

Adams, Wesley. 1999. *Full Life Bible Commentary to the New Testament,* edited by French L. Arrington and Roger Stronstad. Grand Rapids: Zondervan Publishing House.

Barrett, D. B. and T. M. Johnson. 2002. Global Statistics. In *The New International Dictionary of Pentecostal and Charismatic Movements.* Edited. by Stanley M. Burgess. Grand Rapids: Zondervan Publishing House.

Bright, William. 1987. Ways to Witness. In *Practical Christianity*, edited by LaVonne Neff. Carmel, NY: Guideposts.

Bruce, F. F. 1986. *The International Bible Commentary.* Grand Rapids: Zondervan Publishing House.

Celsus. Quoted in Origen's *Against Celsus.* Book 1, Chapter 28.

Eutsler, Steve. 1993. Why Are Not All Christians Healed? *Paraclete* (Spring): 15–23.

Gee, Donald. 1956. If Not Healed . . . *The Pentecostal Evangel*, 19 February, 18–19.

George, Timothy. 2000. The Big Picture: Does God Have a Plan for the World? In *This We Believe: The Good News of Jesus Christ for the World*, edited by John N. Akers, John H. Armstrong, and John D. Woodbridge. Grand Rapids: Zondervan Publishing House.

Harris, Ralph W. 1995. *Acts Today: Signs and Wonders of the Holy Spirit.* Springfield, MO: Gospel Publishing House.

Horton, Stanley M. 1991. *The Ultimate Victory: An Exposition of the Book of Revelation.* Springfield, MO: Gospel Publishing House.

———. 1976. *What the Bible Says about the Holy Spirit.* Springfield, MO: Gospel Publishing House.

———. 1992. *El Espíritu Santo revelado en la Biblia,* edición revisada. Deerfield, FL: Editorial Vida.

———. 1996. *Our Destiny: Biblical Teachings on the Last Things.* Springfield, MO: Logion Press, Gospel Publishing House.

Kennedy, John W. 2004. Euphemisms Tempt Christians to Conveniently Shed Sin, Guilt. *Today's Pentecostal Evangel*, 30 May, 6–7.

Kuizenga, John E. 1956. Sin. In *The International Standard Bible Encyclopedia*, edited by James Orr. Grand Rapids: Wm. B. Eerdmans Publishing Co., 2798–2802.

Lemmel, Helen H. 1922. *Turn Your Eyes Upon Jesus.* Copyright renewed by Singspiration Music in 1950.

Lincoln, Abraham. 1863. Lincoln Prayer Proclamation. www.presidency.ucsb.edu/ws/index.php?pid=69994 or http://showcase.netins.net/web/creative/lincoln/speeches/fast.htm.

Marx, Karl. 1844. A Contribution to the Critique of Hegel's *Philosophy of Right.* Germany.

McGee, Gary B. 2004. *People of the Spirit: The Assemblies of God.* Springfield, MO: Gospel Publishing House.

Meier, Samuel A. 1996. Meekness. In *Evangelical Dictionary of Biblical Theology*, edited by Walter A. Elwell. Grand Rapids: Baker Books.

Menzies, Robert P. 1994. *Empowered for Witness: The Spirit in Luke-Acts.* Sheffield, England: Sheffield Academic Press.

Menzies, William W. 1993. *Bible Doctrine: A Pentecostal Perspective.* Springfield, MO: Logion Press, Gospel Publishing House.

Miller, Calvin. 1987. What to Say in Witnessing. In *Practical Christianity*, edited by LaVonne Neff. Carmel, NY: Guideposts.

Mullen, Bradford A. 1996. Sanctification. In *Evangelical Dictionary of Biblical Theology*, edited by Walter A. Elwell. Grand Rapids: Baker Book House Co.

Ouderluys, Richard C. 1975. The Purpose of Spiritual Gifts. *Reformed Review* 28 (Spring): 215.

Palma, Anthony D. 2001. *The Holy Spirit: A Pentecostal Perspective.* Springfield, MO: Login Press, Gospel Publishing House.

Railey, Jr., James H. and Benny C. Aker. 1995. Theological Foundations. In *Systematic Theology*, rev. ed., edited by Stanley M. Horton, Springfield, MO: Logion Press, Gospel Publishing House.

Reston, James. 1974. *New York Times.*

Shelton, James. 1999. Matthew. In *Full Life Bible Commentary to the New Testament.* Grand Rapids: Zondervan Publishing House.

Simpson, A. B. 1887. *The Word, the Work, and the World.* July/August.

Turner, David L. 1996. *The Evangelical Dictionary of Biblical Theology*, edited by. Walter A. Elwell. Grand Rapids: Baker Book House.

Webster's Third New International Dictionary, unabridged 2002. Merriam-Webster Web site. Available from www.unabridged.merriam-webster.com.

Witherington, III, Ben. 2004. Why the 'Lost Gospels' Lost Out. *Christianity Today,* June, 30.

Wolff, Jonathan. Karl Marx. In *The Stanford Encyclopedia of Philosophy.* (Fall 2003 edition). Edited by. Edward N. Zalta. http://plato.stanford.edu/archives/fall2003/entries/marx/.

Yancey, Philip. 1977. *What's So Amazing About Grace?* Grand Rapids: Zondervan Publishing House.

Essential Course Materials

CONTENTS

CHECKLIST OF MATERIALS TO BE SUBMITTED TO BEREAN SCHOOL OF THE BIBLE

at Global University; 1211 South Glenstone Avenue; Springfield, Missouri, 65804; USA:

Service Learning Requirement Report (required)
Round-Tripper Forms (as needed)
Request for a Printed Final Examination (if needed)

Service Learning Requirement Assignment

BEREAN SCHOOL OF THE BIBLE

SLR INSTRUCTIONS

This Service Learning Requirement (SLR) assignment requires you to apply something you have learned from this course in a ministry activity. Although this assignment does not receive a grade, it is required. You will not receive credit for this course until you submit the satisfactorily completed SLR Report Form. This form will not be returned to you.

Seriously consider how you can design and complete a meaningful ministry* activity as an investment in preparing to fulfill God's calling on your life. If you are already involved in active ministry, plan how you can incorporate and apply something from this course in your ongoing ministry activity. Whether or not full-time ministry is your goal, this assignment is required and designed to bring personal enrichment to all students. Ask the Holy Spirit to guide your planning and completion of this ministry exercise.

> * Meaningful ministry is defined as an act whereby you give of yourself in such a way as to meet the needs of another or to enhance the well-being of another (or others) in a way that exalts Christ and His kingdom.

You will complete the SLR by following these instructions:

1. Complete a ministry activity of your choice that you develop according to the following criteria:

   a. Your ministry activity must occur during your enrollment in this course. Do not report on activities or experiences in which you were involved prior to enrolling in this course.

   b. Your ministry activity must apply something you learned in this course, or it must incorporate something from this course's content in some way. Provide chapter, lesson, or page number(s) from the independent-study textbook on which the activity is based.

   c. Your ministry activity must include interacting with at least one other person. You may choose to interact with an individual or a group.

   d. The activity you complete must represent meaningful ministry*. You may develop your own ministry activity or choose from the list of suggestions provided in these instructions.

   e. Consider a ministry activity outside your comfort zone such as sharing the message of salvation with unbelievers or offering loving assistance to someone you do not know well.

2. Then fill out the SLR Report Form following these instructions OR online by accessing the online course. Students who will take the final exam online are encouraged to complete the online report form.

3. Sincere reflection is a key ingredient in valid ministry and especially in the growth and development of your ministry knowledge and effectiveness.

4. Global University faculty will evaluate your report. Although the SLR does not receive a grade, it must be completed to the faculty's satisfaction before a final grade for the course is released. The faculty may require you to resubmit an SLR Report Form for several reasons, including an incomplete form, apparent insincerity, failing to interact with others, and failure to incorporate course content.

Do NOT submit your SLR notes, essays, or other documents; only submit your completed SLR Report Form. No prior approval is needed as long as the activity fulfills the criteria from number one above.

Suggested SLR Ministry Activities

You may choose to engage in any valid and meaningful ministry experience that incorporates this specific course's content and interacts with other people. The following list of suggestions is provided to help you understand the possible activities that will fulfill this requirement. Choose an idea that will connect well with your course material. You may also develop a ministry activity that is not on this list or incorporate content from this course in ministry activity in which you are actively involved at this time:

- Teach a class or small group of any size.
- Preach a sermon to any size group.
- Share the gospel with non-believers; be prepared to develop new relationships to open doors to this ministry. We strongly encourage you to engage in ministry that may be outside your comfort zone.
- Lead a prayer group experience or pray with individual(s) in need, perhaps over an extended period.
- Disciple new believers in their walk with Jesus.
- Interview pastors, missionaries, or other leaders on a topic related to something in your course (do not post or publish interview content).
- Intervene to help resolve personal conflicts.
- Personally share encouragement and resources with those in need.
- Organize and/or administer a church program such as youth ministry, feeding homeless people, transporting people, visiting hospitals or shut-ins, nursing home services, etc.
- Assist with starting a new church.
- Publish an online blog or an article in a church newsletter (include a link in your report to the content of your article or blog).
- For MIN327 only: present a summary of risk management to a church board or other leadership group; interview community business people regarding their opinion of church business practices.

To review sample SLR Reports and to access an online report form, go to this Web address: library. globaluniversity.edu. Navigate to the Berean School of the Bible Students link under "Quick Link." Another helpful resource is our GlobalReach Web site: www.globalreach.org. From that site you can download materials free of charge from Global University's School for Evangelism and Discipleship. These proven evangelism tools are available in many languages.

BSB SERVICE LEARNING REQUIREMENT (SLR) REPORT

Please print or type your responses on this form, and submit the form to Berean School of the Bible. Do not submit other documents. This report will not be returned to you.

THE 114 Introduction to Pentecostal Doctrine, Third Edition

Your Name... **Student Number** .... **Date** ....

1. Ministry activity date .... **Description of ministry activity and its content:** Briefly describe your ministry activity in the space provided. (You are encouraged to engage in ministry such as sharing your faith with unbelievers, or other activities that may be outside your comfort zone.)

....

....

....

Identify related course content by chapter, lesson, or page number. ....

....

2. Results: What resulted from your own participation in this activity? Include descriptions of people's reactions, decisions to accept Christ, confirmed miracles, Spirit and water baptisms, life changes, etc. Describe the individuals or group who benefited from or participated in your ministry activity. Use numbers to describe results when appropriate (approximate when unsure).

....

....

....

....

Record numbers here: Unbelievers witnessed to?...................... New decisions for Jesus?......................

Holy Spirit baptisms?...................... Other?..

3. Reflection: Answer the following questions based on your experience in completing this assignment:

Did this activity satisfy an evident need in others? How so? ....

....

Were you adequately prepared to engage in this activity? Why or why not? ....

....

What positive or negative feelings were you aware of while you were completing this activity? ....

....

In what ways were you aware of the Holy Spirit's help during your ministry activity? ....

....

What would you change if you did this ministry activity again? ....

....

What strengths or weaknesses within yourself did this assignment reveal to you?...................................

....

....

Did you receive feedback about this activity? If so, describe: ....

....

....

Unit Progress Evaluations

The unit progress evaluations (UPEs) are designed to indicate how well you learned the material in each unit. This may indicate how well prepared you are to take the closed-book final examination.

Taking Your Unit Progress Evaluations

1. Review the lessons of each unit before you take its unit progress evaluation (UPE). Refer to the form Checklist of Study Methods in the How to Use Berean Courses section at the front of the IST.

2. Answer the questions in each UPE without referring to your course materials, Bible, or notes.

3. Look over your answers carefully to avoid errors.

4. Check your answers with the answer keys provided in this section. Review lesson sections pertaining to questions you may have missed. Please note that the UPE scores do not count toward your course grade. They may indicate how well you are prepared to take the closed-book final examination.

5. Enter the date you completed each UPE on the Student Planner and Record form, located in the How to Use Berean Courses section in the front of this IST.

6. Request a printed final examination **if** you cannot take the final examination online. You should do this a few weeks before you take the last unit progress evaluation so that you will be able to take the final examination without delay when you complete the course.

UNIT PROGRESS EVALUATION 1

THE114 Introduction to Pentecostal Doctrine, Third Edition
(Unit 1—Chapter 1)

*[handwritten: • Statement As of God³
• cardinal
• Doctrine
• Theology ⁴]*

MULTIPLE CHOICE QUESTIONS

Select the best answer to each question.

1. The apostle Paul expressed the importance of sound doctrine by
   a) quoting Jesus' references to sound doctrine.
   b) specifically requiring sound doctrine in his Pastoral epistles.
   c) appealing to the Old Testament prophets in support of sound doctrine.
   d) pronouncing anathema on those who preached envy and strife.

2. Which of the following is a cardinal doctrine of the Assemblies of God?
   a) The deity of Jesus
   b) The baptism in the Holy Spirit
   c) Sanctification
   d) The Trinity

3. The official document of the Assemblies of God that is our basis for unity is called the
   a) Bylaws of the General Council of the Assemblies of God.
   b) Amendment for Doctrinal Unity.
   c) Statement of Fundamental Truths.
   d) official creed of the Assemblies of God

4. The word *Theology* literally means
   a) the study of God
   b) the study of religions.
   c) the study of doctrines.
   d) divine philosophy.

5. Systematic study of doctrine is important to
   a) help the student memorize Scripture's warnings.
   b) withstand temptation by sharpening a person's thinking skills.
   c) protect us from unbalanced and wrong interpretations of Scripture.
   d) compensate for the prayer and Bible study no longer provided in public schools.

6. Bible Doctrine is defined as
   a) theology, or specifically the study of God.
   b) Bible teachings arranged in a systematic form.
   c) the teachings of the founder of a religion.
   d) the Bible itself.

7. Which best defines a cardinal doctrine?
   a) Held as true by the Catholic church
   b) A doctrine over-arching a single category of doctrines
   c) Doctrine specifically based on the words of Jesus
   d) A foundational doctrine

8. Which best distinguishes theology from doctrine?
   a) Theology includes doctrine
   b) Any scholar can write theology, but the church approves doctrine
   c) Theology is based on the Bible, but doctrine is derived from practice
   d) Specialized training is required to write theology than to formulate doctrine

9. Why is there is a great need for doctrinal study today?
   a) It is absolutely essential for Christians to witness or lead sinners to Christ.
   b) Paul told Timothy, "Study to show yourself approved by God."
   c) Many Christians lack an understanding of the Bible and its doctrines.
   d) Today nearly everyone can read, while many in the past could not.

10. Which defines the relationship of doctrine to service?
    a) It is the message, not the presentation, which serves others.
    b) Be accurate, be correct, if you want to teach others.
    c) Be personally blameless if you would instruct others.
    d) Your example must match your words if you would witness to others.

11. Strong Christian character requires
    a) teaching our children and youth the beliefs of our church.
    b) teaching our youth that testing that demonstrates integrity and honesty.
    c) consistently living out biblical belief and doctrinal understanding over time.
    d) making valiant attempts to obey the law of God.

12. If God loves us, why would He forbid certain things we may want to do?
    a) God forbids everything Satan promotes.
    b) Denying one's own desires brings harmony among others.
    c) Adam and Eve sinned and this placed all of us under God's curse.
    d) God knows what is best and what will bring ultimate happiness.

13. What purpose does the study of Bible doctrine serve? Doctrine
    a) becomes a guide for conduct.
    b) explains emotional response.
    c) exercises our intellect.
    d) restores the morality of biblical times.

14. Natural law, to those who do not believe in God, means that
    a) mere mortals can distinguish between right and wrong without the aid of a deity.
    b) the moral teachings of the Bible are completely against human nature.
    c) one cannot know right from wrong by observing nature.
    d) people groups must have written legal codes.

15. Human philosophy opposes God by
    a) elevating human reason above the rules given by a god.
    b) requiring a defense of God's character.
    c) seeking to prove that God's Word is a reflection of man's thinking.
    d) allowing God to be merely a first cause in the creation.

16. Two belief systems that do not accept any religious faith or doctrine are
    a) communism and Islam.
    b) natural law and human philosophy.
    c) atheism and Catholicism.
    d) post-modernism and high church Anglicanism.

17. According to the Bible, natural law
    a) belongs to the kingdom of Satan.
    b) is a secondary means of salvation.
    c) is a part of God's law, not separate from it.
    d) is formulated by professional scientists.

18. Natural law cannot be the standard for righteous living because
    a) the "Declaration of Independence" is not a biblical document.
    b) the human race is fallen and cannot be righteous by natural law alone.
    c) everyone interprets natural law in different ways.
    d) all people who believe in natural law become Satan worshippers.

19. Human philosophy cannot restore fellowship with God because
    a) human reason places itself above God's wisdom.
    b) human reason is the highest form of intelligence in the universe.
    c) minds that teach human philosophy already believe in God.
    d) human reason rejects the concept of evil.

20. How should we interpret the occasional errors that are found in modern biblical texts?
    a) We understand that only original manuscripts were without error.
    b) We cannot allow any truth that discredits the Bible.
    c) Recognize that human error and God's truth are incompatible.
    d) We should delete any apparent error when the scriptures are translated.

21. Which statement is the best definition of wisdom?
    a) Advanced learning
    b) Learning that is adequate to be successful teaching others
    c) Knowledge with depth as well as breadth
    d) Knowledge guided by understanding and moral integrity

22. We can trust God's Word, the Bible, because
    a) blind faith is all that God asks.
    b) archaeological studies concur with theological studies.
    c) the Bible is the oldest morality text the world has produced.
    d) the Bible makes credible and internally consistent statements.

23. The Bible is different from all other books in the world in that it
    a) is the oldest book in the world.
    b) was written by many different people.
    c) was written in both Hebrew and Greek.
    d) it is the inspired word of God to humankind.

24. We understand the term inspiration to mean that the Bible
    a) contains information not found in any other book.
    b) includes the highest forms of literature and sublime moral teaching.
    c) was dictated word-for-word by God to many different writers.
    d) is divinely inspired and free from error.

25. Belief that the Bible is inspired and inerrant is important because
    a) God is trustworthy; human reason is fallen and unreliable.
    b) no one would read the Bible if it were not inspired and inerrant.
    c) the many other inspired and inerrant books do not tell us about God.
    d) our culture is losing its appreciation for poetry and literature.

After answering all of the questions in this UPE, check your answers with the answer key. Review material related to questions you may have missed, and then proceed to the next unit.

UNIT PROGRESS EVALUATION 2

THE114 Introduction to Pentecostal Doctrine, Third Edition

(Unit 2—Chapter 2–4)

• God's sacrifice
• salvation, God's Love
• free will
• Apostasy

MULTIPLE CHOICE QUESTIONS

Select the best answer to each question.

1. God's plan of salvation includes the fact that nature will
   a) forever groan as in pains of childbirth.
   b) gradually improve through scientific advances in horticulture.
   c) welcome city dwellers back to righteous country living.
   d) be restored to its original perfection when Satan is forever bound.

2. When we say humans are created with a free will, we mean
   a) we have a choice in our eternal destiny.
   b) humans can do anything they wish to do.
   c) are not subject to the will of a sovereign God.
   d) humans can do anything they are physically able to do.

3. Because God is spirit rather than human, evidence of His existence comes through
   a) mental telepathy.
   b) philosophy.
   c) faith.
   d) apostolic succession.

4. Salvation requires that a person believe that
   a) the Bible is the greatest book ever written.
   b) the teachings of Jesus surpass the best of human philosophy.
   c) Jesus performed the miracles that are attributed to him.
   d) Jesus is the divine Son of God.

5. The image of God in all humans refers to our being
   a) intellectually gifted and able to relate to God and others.
   b) endowed with a superior intellect like God's.
   c) physically a replica of what God looks like.
   d) a little lower than the angels.

6. Every sin has consequences. The result of Adam and Eve's sin was
   a) the loss of the ability to tell right from wrong.
   b) the complete loss of God's image in humankind.
   c) the fall of all creation, including the loss of human innocence.
   d) that their oldest son became a murderer.

7. Christians are promised protection from Satan's deceit because
   a) Satan, though omnipresent, is not omnipotent.
   b) Jesus defeated Satan once and for all when Satan fell from heaven.
   c) God's sovereignty determines who will fall victim to Satan's wiles.
   d) like Peter, we too have Jesus interceding for us.

8. One of the greatest demonstrations that God is love is seen in the fact that
   a) God created both sinners and those who return His love.
   b) Jesus did not lash out at those who insulted and persecuted him.
   c) God will eventually provide eternal life to everyone (universalism).
   d) God hates sin, but loves the sinner.

9. Jesus had to die as a Sacrifice for our sins because
   a) without the shedding of blood there is no forgiveness.
   b) the animal sacrifices of the Old Testament were not pleasing to God.
   c) God had to die like an Old Testament sacrifice to provide salvation.
   d) Roman law required that a crucified person be officially pronounced dead.

10. Apostasy is defined as
    a) committing the unpardonable sin.
    b) turning one's back on God after knowing the reality of His personal presence.
    c) refusing to accept God's offer of salvation.
    d) the total depravity of human kind.

11. When we say that Jesus was both human and divine, we mean that
    a) His spirit was divine but his body was human.
    b) He was 100 percent human and 100 percent divine.
    c) He was 50 percent human and 50 percent divine.
    d) none of the above because God cannot have two natures.

12. Jesus was like no other person who has walked on earth in that He
    a) gathered a huge following during His 3½ years of ministry.
    b) was human at birth but became divine when He was baptized in water.
    c) laid down his life and took it up again.
    d) returned to heaven without dying.

13. Christ's suffering for our salvation (led like a lamb to slaughter) was predicted by
    a) David.
    b) Isaiah.
    c) Malachi.
    d) John the Baptist.

14. Christ's resurrection is essential to our faith because
    a) Easter is more important than Good Friday.
    b) without the Resurrection Christianity could have no miracles.
    c) without the Resurrection the miracle of salvation would lack its power.
    d) the Resurrection was witnessed by over 500 people.

15. The bedrock or most important truth of our Christian faith is
    a) divine healing.
    b) the baptism in the Holy Spirit.
    c) salvation.
    d) the second coming of Christ to earth.

16. Salvation as regeneration means being
    a) adopted.
    b) reinstated.
    c) justified.
    d) born again.

17. Regeneration as an aspect of salvation means
    a) the new birth.
    b) the third generation of a Christian family.
    c) seeing salvation in a new light.
    d) moving up on the socio-economic scale.

18. The process of sanctification, or progressive sanctification, takes place
    a) only after one is baptized in the Holy Spirit.
    b) throughout a believer's entire lifetime beginning with salvation.
    c) only after one is baptized in water.
    d) throughout a believer's lifetime beginning with Spirit baptism.

19. Sanctification is both instantaneous and also
    a) progressive.
    b) impossible to achieve.
    c) regressive.
    d) a second definite work of grace.

20. The biblical mode of water baptism is
    a) by immersion.
    b) by sprinkling.
    c) by pouring.
    d) all of the above.

21. Holy Communion should be observed regularly until
    a) one has received the baptism in the Holy Spirit.
    b) the last rite on one's death bed.
    c) Jesus comes to rapture His followers.
    d) one is sanctified.

22. Christ's command was to baptize in the name of
    a) Jesus only.
    b) the Father, the Son, and the Holy Spirit.
    c) the Holy Spirit only.
    d) Jesus and the holy apostles.

23. Jesus assured His followers their salvation was secure when he said
    a) "He who stands firm to the end will be saved."
    b) "No one can snatch them out of my hand or my Father's hand."
    c) "I am going to the Father."
    d) "I am going to prepare a place for you."

24. Calvinists believe that
    a) Old Testament believers will go to heaven.
    b) humans have free will and can choose to accept Christ as Savior.
    c) God in the eternal past determined who would be saved.
    d) all humankind will ultimately be saved.

25. The Bible contains assurance and warning about one's salvation because
    a) Calvinists and Arminians are both wrong.
    b) believers need assurance; others need warning about neglect.
    c) the books of the Bible were written by different writers.
    d) not all individuals have sufficient faith.

After answering all of the questions in this UPE, check your answers with the answer key. Review material related to questions you may have missed, and then proceed to the next unit.

UNIT PROGRESS EVALUATION 3

· Communion
· Calvinists

THE114 Introduction to Pentecostal Doctrine, Third Edition
(Unit 3—Chapter 5–9)

· Salvation
· Sanctification ·
· HS Baptism
· Spirit filled
· Tongues · Holyness

MULTIPLE CHOICE QUESTIONS

Select the best answer to each question.

1. The work of the Holy Spirit helping us become more and more like Jesus is called
   a) unification with Jesus.
   b) Jesus Only manifestation.
   c) instantaneous sanctification.
   d) progressive sanctification.

2. A genuine mark of spiritual maturity is
   a) speaking in tongues.
   b) moving from self-centered concerns to ministry and concern for others.
   c) living day after day without committing sin.
   d) having the gift of prophecy.

3. Holiness is properly understood as
   a) what is generally acceptable in a Christian community.
   b) an obedient heart that seeks to please God in every action.
   c) obedience to a code of conduct.
   d) a technical Old Testament term.

4. The best proof that there are three Persons in the Godhead is
   a) that Scripture specifically states, "God is a Trinity."
   b) the description of Jesus sitting at the right hand of the Father.
   c) that water baptism in Acts is in the name of Jesus.
   d) the account of Jesus' baptism by John.

5. The baptism in the Holy Spirit is received
   a) by beginning to make sounds that may sound like tongues.
   b) by intensely pleading with Jesus for the experience.
   c) by making sure one has obeyed Christ command of water baptism.
   d) in the same way salvation is received, in obedience and faith.

6. The baptism in the Holy Spirit, with the evidence of speaking in tongues
   a) is available to Pentecostals, but not to all believers.
   b) should cause us to highly revere the New Testament saints who first received it.
   c) occurs today much in the manner described in Acts 2.
   d) can, in rare instances, be experienced before salvation.

7. A Spirit-filled believer should keep his or her experience current and strong by
   a) reading the Book of Acts at least once a year.
   b) going on a spiritual retreats with Pentecostal believers.
   c) daily communion, praying and walking in the Spirit.
   d) taking a seminary course in pneumatology.

8. Paul identifies the tongues that must be interpreted as
   a) prophecy.
   b) distinguishing between spirits.
   c) the gift of tongues edifying the worshipping congregation.
   d) the private use of tongues when one prays in the Spirit.

9. A Spirit-filled Christian knows he or she is experiencing spiritual growth when
   a) the fruit of the Spirit are increasingly evident in his or her life.
   b) people are healed when they are prayed for.
   c) his or her personal honesty is no longer questioned.
   d) is elected to the office of deacon or elder.

10. A Spirit-filled person should
    a) speak in tongues daily.
    b) speak in tongues and interpret.
    c) expect to receive visions and revelations.
    d) manifest the gifts and fruit of the Spirit.

11. The gift or ministry of the Spirit included in all four Bible lists is
    a) prophecy.
    b) tongues and interpretation.
    c) teaching.
    d) healing.

12. The purpose of the Gifts of the Spirit is to
    a) restore unity to a divided Church.
    b) edify and build up the Church.
    c) direct the daily decisions of Spirit-filled believers.
    d) insure accuracy in interpreting the Bible

13. The gift of prophecy is best defined as
    a) a prediction of the future.
    b) an utterance of divine truth in a person's own language.
    c) a word of wise advice.
    d) speaking on behalf of someone else.

14. Special, but unusual, gifts of the Spirit include
    a) generous giving and showing mercy.
    b) evangelists, pastors, and teachers.
    c) pastor-teachers.
    d) anticipating future events.

15. Concerning modern-day apostles, the Assemblies of God believes that
    a) apostolic ministries are active, but persons do not assume the title.
    b) apostles have been addressed as such from Bible times to this day.
    c) apostolic ministries ended with the close of the New Testament.
    d) many people not called apostles today will be called such in heaven.

16. The difference between the gifts of prophecy and teaching is that
    a) prophecy predicts the future; teaching deals with the past.
    b) prophecy speaks to the heart; teaching speaks to the understanding.
    c) prophecy has ceased; teaching is still very important.
    d) teaching is based on what God said; prophecy is what God is saying.

17. Not all believers have the gift of the evangelist, but all believers are called to be
    a) perfect examples of a Christ-like life.
    b) witnesses.
    c) students and teachers of Scripture.
    d) Ministers of the Word.

18. Witnessing is defined as
    a) explaining to others the beliefs of your church.
    b) inviting others to visit your church for evangelistic campaigns.
    c) telling others about your love for Jesus and what He has done for us.
    d) Observing carefully what goes on in church services.

19. Jesus' example, one that Spirit-filled believers should imitate, was how He
    a) exercised the authority of God on Earth.
    b) humbled himself.
    c) accepted worship.
    d) washed the disciples' feet.

20. The right heart attitude of one used by the Spirit in supernatural gifting is
    a) humility.
    b) thankfulness.
    c) pride in being chosen as God's instrument.
    d) compassion for those not so chosen.

21. The Holy Spirit can reveal secrets known only to God through
    a) gifts of prophecy or discernment of spirits.
    b) the preaching ministry.
    c) the gift of tongues.
    d) working of miracles.

22. When Jesus referred to the Holy Spirit as the Paraclete He meant One who
    a) represents the Father.
    b) tells us about the future.
    c) comes alongside to help.
    d) mediates between God and humanity.

23. Paul identifies the temple of the Holy Spirit as the
    a) tabernacle in the wilderness.
    b) body of the individual believer.
    c) New Jerusalem.
    d) Word of God as interpreted by the Holy Spirit.

24. When did the Age of the Spirit begin?
    a) When the Spirit descended on Jesus at His baptism
    b) When Jesus came into the world as a human child
    c) When Jesus told the disciples to receive the Holy Spirit (John 20:22).
    d) On the Day of Pentecost.

25. What is meant in Acts 2:17 that the Holy Spirit
was poured out on all people?
   a) Every born-again believer receives the
      baptism in the Holy Spirit
   b) Every living person receives the Holy Spirit
   c) There are Spirit-filled believers in every race,
      nationality, age, and social class.
   d) All believers receive the Holy Spirit at the
      time of their conversion.

- gifts ministry
- Acts 2:17
- Heart, gifting
- HS, helper
- Age of the spirit

After answering all of the questions in this UPE, check your answers with the answer key. Review material related to questions you may have missed, and then proceed to the next unit.

UNIT PROGRESS EVALUATION 4

THE114 Introduction to Pentecostal Doctrine, Third Edition
(Unit 4—Chapter 10–11)

- Sickness
- Gospel
- Healing

MULTIPLE CHOICE QUESTIONS

Select the best answer to each question.

1. Sickness and death can be identified with
   a) sin in the life of the suffering person.
   b) the law of nature that acts impartially on everyone.
   c) the Fall of humankind and the resulting evils in the world.
   d) terminal illness that is genetically or biologically transmitted.

2. Demon powers can inflict limited suffering, but they cannot
   a) possess and control a true believer.
   b) tempt Christians.
   c) afflict or trouble Christians.
   d) exist in an atmosphere of prayer and worship.

3. The secular world does not believe in divine healing because
   a) an atheist must see firm evidence of anything he or she is asked to believe.
   b) the human mind is preferred over a God who cannot be seen.
   c) it cannot be proven that illness is healed solely as a result of prayer.
   d) it has a closed mind regarding the reality of supernatural miracles.

4. Though Satan is the agent of sickness, God
   a) always heals when His children in faith ask Him to nullify the work of Satan.
   b) will ultimately be victorious over Satan.
   c) accomplishes His purposes through the sickness and suffering of His children.
   d) has banished Satan from the earth during the church age.

5. The promise of divine healing for suffering saints means
   a) we can avoid the effects of old age.
   b) only spiritual healing is really effective.
   c) we should always expect spiritual healing but not physical healing.
   d) we can ask for and expect a healing touch at any stage of life.

6. Full Gospel refers to
   a) all the gospel, especially salvation, Holy Spirit baptism, healing, and second coming.
   b) a theology based on all four Gospels: Matthew, Mark, Luke, and John.
   c) a fundamental, evangelical church.
   d) the Pentecostal denomination: The Church of the Four Square Gospel.

7. A person seeking healing should consider doctors and medicines
   a) as hindrances to divine healing.
   b) as agents God may use in healing.
   c) as substitutes for faith in God for healing.
   d) only if the doctor is a believer.

8. One of the best reasons to believe that Jesus heals today is that
   a) most Christians are healed of their sicknesses.
   b) Enoch was translated and went to heaven without dying.
   c) healing is provided in Christ's Atonement.
   d) God told Old Testament Israel, "I am the Lord who heals you."

9. Divine healing has a higher purpose than removing pain and suffering. Divine healing
   a) confirms the power and love of God.
   b) gives God an opportunity to heal His chosen people.
   c) helps those suffering to get their minds off of their pain and onto Jesus.
   d) extends the life of those with especially effective ministries.

10. When a believer has been healed, the proper response is to
    a) clearly identify the condition and then claim healing.
    b) verify, then testify.
    c) be quiet and not tell anyone, just as Jesus told the leper He healed.
    d) obtain certification of healing from a minister and a medical doctor.

11. When the disciples could not heal the boy
    suffering from demonic seizures, what did Jesus
    identify as the problem (Matthew 17:20)?
    a) The boy's house had been swept clean, and the
       demons had re-entered.
    b) The parents had been disobedient, which
       allowed demons to enter.
    c) The boy had unbelief and could not receive the
       healing.
    d) The disciples had a lack of faith.

12. Divine healing of a believer requires
    a) trust in Christ, who is the source of our faith.
    b) a sinless and victorious life.
    c) an understanding of the realities of sickness
       and death.
    d) an unwavering positive confession.

13. We develop the moment-by-moment communion
    with Jesus for healing
    a) by spending less time with family and friends.
    b) when cutting back on the times we assemble
       with God's children in worship.
    c) in encouraging others to help the needy and
       less fortunate so we can focus on God.
    d) through guarding our time to meditate on
       Jesus through reading God's Word.

14. Salvation is a healing of the
    a) memories.
    b) emotions.
    c) mind.
    d) soul.

15. Inner healing involves
    a) the deliverance of internal organs from
       diseases such as cancer.
    b) deliverance from abnormal fears and mental or
       emotional distress.
    c) salvation or deliverance from sin and wrong
       attitudes.
    d) deliverance from the psychosomatic causes of
       the disease.

16. The only source of physical healing is
    a) faith that one is going to be healed.
    b) faith in the power of Faith.
    c) some understanding of the nature of the
       condition.
    d) faith in Jesus Christ.

17. Faith that results in divine healing is
    a) something the sick person must initiate.
    b) ineffective if the sick person cannot exercise
       his or her faith.
    c) a gift imparted by God to the sick person.
    d) able to be exercised by those especially gifted
       as healers.

18. The entire Christian community is important to a
    person's healing because
    a) other believers may be able to identify the sin
       that has brought on the sickness.
    b) when one member suffers, the whole body
       suffers and helps bear the burden.
    c) healing comes when many people are praying
       for the sick person.
    d) the ministry of healing must be supervised by
       an ordained minister.

19. The biblical pattern for the healing of sick
    believers is
    a) calling for church elders to anoint with oil and
       pray the prayer of faith.
    b) participating in a service conducted by a well-
       known faith healer.
    c) anointing with oil in a healing campaign
       prayer line.
    d) obtaining medical treatment first, then call for
       the elders of the church.

20. One can best give God opportunity to plant faith
    for healing by
    a) association with people who encourage the
       sick to grow in faith.
    b) study and personal application of God's Word.
    c) getting alone for prayer and meditation on
       one's illness.
    d) obtaining the help of one who is known to be
       gifted as a healer.

21. The redemption of our physical bodies will take
    place at
    a) death, the end of this earthly life.
    b) the Battle of Armageddon.
    c) the Rapture of the Church,
    d) at the resurrection of the wicked dead.

22. If a believer dies without receiving the desired
    healing,
    a) ultimate healing will come at the resurrection
       of the righteous.
    b) healing of the body will not be necessary after
       physical death occurs.
    c) he or she will not remember the sickness in
       Heaven.
    d) healing will be granted to believers at the
       Final judgment.

23. Healthy believers should relate to the sick and suffering by
   a) casting out the demon of sickness from the suffering believer.
   b) tactfully suggesting that hidden sin might be the cause for the suffering.
   c) sharing God's love, not condemning with His judgment.
   d) sending cards and letters.

24. The believer can handle unanswered prayer for healing by
   a) asking healthy Christians for their intercessory prayer support.
   b) placing trust and confidence in God's faithfulness.
   c) asking God if one's faith for salvation is sometimes not answered.
   d) realizing that God always heals.

25. As you wait patiently for healing, these spiritual duties should be fulfilled:
   a) pray and enjoy communion with God.
   b) follow Job's example and "curse" (strongly regret) the day of one's birth.
   c) forget the pain and suffering and testify to others that healing has taken place.
   d) command the illness to depart until it does.

- Believers, healing, Communion
- Salvation, Faith, redemption
-

After answering all of the questions in this UPE, check your answers with the answer key. Review material related to questions you may have missed, and then proceed to the next unit.

UNIT PROGRESS EVALUATION 5

THE114 Introduction to Pentecostal Doctrine, Third Edition
(Unit 5—Chapter 12–13)

· Rapture
· Apocalyptic
· Kingdom Teaches
· Assem of God
· Heaven
·

MULTIPLE CHOICE QUESTIONS

Select the best answer to each question.

1. Apocalyptic literature is defined as
   a) writings revealing future events.
   b) accounts describing catastrophes in human history.
   c) fictional stories like Star Wars or The Lord of the Rings.
   d) documents containing coded images of the future.

2. Kingdom Now teaches that
   a) the world is now being made into Christ's perfect Kingdom.
   b) the only Kingdom of God we will see is already in the hearts of God's people.
   c) God's Kingdom is both now and not yet; it will be realized in the Millennium.
   d) there is a distinction between the Kingdom of Heaven and the Kingdom of God.

3. The Assemblies of God holds which view regarding the millennium?
   a) Amillennial
   b) Premillennial
   c) Postmillennial
   d) Antimillennial

4. What do we call critics of the Rapture of the Church?
   a) Reprobates
   b) Doubters
   c) Scoffers
   d) Habitual sinners

5. The Assemblies of God, like most Pentecostal groups, believe in a
   a) pre-tribulation Rapture.
   b) mid-tribulation Rapture.
   c) post-tribulation Rapture.
   d) postponement of the tribulation.

6. In Matthew 24, the most repeated advice about how we should live in end times is
   a) forsake the sin that so easily entangles.
   b) watch and be ready.
   c) live without the spot or wrinkle of sin.
   d) avoid even the appearance of evil.

7. As signs of the approaching Rapture intensify, we must
   a) reduce our possessions to bare essentials.
   b) study the signs to estimate how close the Rapture may be.
   c) work diligently be ready for His coming.
   d) use Biblical numerology to calculate the time of the Rapture.

8. Why, according to Peter, does Jesus delay His coming?
   a) God is patient and desires more to come to repentance.
   b) Time does not exist in eternity.
   c) In God's view, it is but a blink of an eye from Creation to the present time.
   d) The Sanctuary must be prepared in heaven.

9. Which best describes the Assemblies of God teaching regarding the Rapture?
   a) A partial rapture, the Rapture of Overcomers
   b) Multiple raptures
   c) A Rapture of all true believers, both living and dead, at a definite point in time
   d) The pre-wrath Rapture during the last half of Daniel's 70th week

10. Heaven is more attractive to adults than it is to children or youth because
   a) all adults long to be in God's presence forever.
   b) children think of heaven as an unknown place without their parents.
   c) youth are not mature enough to understand heaven.
   d) adults have faced the pains and struggles of life; the younger often have not.

11. The Rapture of the Church will involve
   a) only the living saints who are expecting Christ to come for them.
   b) living believers and believers who have died before the Rapture.
   c) only the saints from the beginning of time who have died before the Rapture.
   d) believers who are alive at the time of the Rapture.

[handwritten margin notes: •Satanic Trinity •Christ •7seals •tribulation •New Jerusalem]

12. The Rapture and the Second Coming of Christ are
    a) two names for the same event.
    b) two events that take place at the end of the Tribulation.
    c) two distinct events, one before and one after the Tribulation.
    d) unrelated events.

13. Paul tells us that the Day of the Lord will come like
    a) a huge burning mountain thrown into the sea.
    b) a lion lying down with a lamb.
    c) a thief in the night.
    d) a beast rising out of the sea.

14. The seven seals on the scroll of God's judgments are broken by
    a) the death angel.
    b) the Lamb.
    c) the false prophet.
    d) no one, for nobody was found that was worthy to break the seals.

15. The Day of the Lord extends into
    a) the new heavens and earth.
    b) the first half of the Tribulation.
    c) the first half of the Millennium.
    d) the second half of the Tribulation.

16. The satanic trinity consists of
    a) the Beast, the Antichrist, and Satan.
    b) Satan, Antichrist, and a false prophet.
    c) the Antichrist, a false prophet, and a false apostle.
    d) Caiaphas, Annas, and Judas.

17. Two events that will take place in heaven during the Tribulation on earth are the
    a) Rapture and the Apocalypse.
    b) Marriage of the Lamb and Bride followed by the judgment of false Christians.
    c) giving of rewards and hearing the words of Jesus, "Well done, good servants."
    d) Judgment Seat of Christ and the Marriage Supper of the Lamb.

18. John describes Jesus as the rider on a white horse wearing on His robe the words
    a) The Alpha and the Omega.
    b) Wonderful, Counselor, Prince of Peace.
    c) King of Kings and Lord of Lords.
    d) The Son of Man.

19. The Holy City is described in the Bible as a
    a) royal chariot that swings low to the earth.
    b) magnificent tent adorned with majestic jewels and precious metals.
    c) bride beautifully dressed for her Bridegroom.
    d) husband coming to be reunited with his wife after a long separation.

20. The followers of Christ are not killed in the final battle with Antichrist because
    a) they will be protected by their breast plates of righteousness.
    b) the saints will have immortal bodies that cannot be killed.
    c) the forces of Antichrist are terrified and try to flee.
    d) Christ himself fights the battle.

21. After his brief release to make his final effort to deceive people, Satan will be
    a) given a final opportunity to repent.
    b) bound and cast into the Abyss or bottomless pit.
    c) permanently cast into the lake of fire.
    d) called before the Great White Throne Judgment and condemned to hell.

22. The Holy City or the New Jerusalem comes to earth from
    a) another universe.
    b) the original Creation where it has been awaiting Christ's final victory.
    c) another galaxy where it has been inhabited by the angelic host.
    d) the new heavens.

23. The greatest need of our world as we await Christ's return at the Rapture is
    a) the elimination of poverty and terrorism around the world.
    b) the conversion of the monotheistic but non-Christian religions.
    c) a better understanding of end-time events and the nearness of the Rapture.
    d) spiritual revival and a renewed emphasis on holy living among believers.

24. What is the sin that so easily entangles?
    a) Lust and sexual impurity
    b) Unbelief and related sins like spiritual drifting and failure to mature in Christ
    c) Telling half-truths to protect one's personal image
    d) Putting oneself before others

25. What should believers do in preparation for the Lord's return?
   a) Diligently attempt to determine the day and hour of His coming
   b) Watch and be ready at any time
   c) Be sure that one's understanding of eschatology (the doctrine of last things) is correct
   d) Be especially concerned about the political climate of the Middle East.

After answering all of the questions in this UPE, check your answers with the answer key. Review material related to questions you may have missed. Review all materials in preparation for the final exam. Complete and submit your SLR assignment and take the closed-book final examination.

Taking the Final Examination

1. **All final exams must be taken closed book.** You are not allowed to use any materials or outside help while taking a final exam. You will take the final examination online at www.globaluniversity.edu. If the online option is not available to you, you may request a printed final exam. If you did not request a printed final exam when you ordered your course, you must submit this request a few weeks before you are ready to take the exam. The Request for a Printed Final Examination is in the Forms section of Essential Course Materials at the back of this IST.

2. Review for the final examination in the same manner in which you prepared for the UPEs. Refer to the form Checklist of Study Methods in the front part of the IST for further helpful review hints.

3. After you complete and submit the online final examination, the results will be immediately available to you. Your final course grade report will be emailed to your Global University student email account after your Service Learning Requirement (SLR) report has been processed.

4. If you complete the exam in printed form, you will send your final examination, your answer sheets, and your SLR report to Berean School of the Bible for grading. Your final course grade report will be sent to your GU student email account. If you do not have access to the internet, your grade will be sent to your mailing address.

- Statement of Fundamental Truths = Salvation, Baptism, Holy Spirit, Divine Healing, second coming Christ
- Tenants of faith =
- 16th Fundamentals Truth =
- Doctrine/Theology = Bible doctrine = study of God, Taught, Biblical Teaching ↑ teaching

- Sacrament = Visible sign & pledge of invisible grace ordained by Christ.
- Consecrate = Sanctify
- Saint = Holy one
- Sanctification = Cooperative effort between God & believers
- Ordinance = Symbolic practice ordained by God, but is optional.

- Regeneration = New Birth
- Sanctification =
- Immersion
- Communion = proclaim's Lords death until he returns
- Calvinists = pre-destined, God in the eternal past determined who would be saved.
- Apostasy = Denial or abandonment of an individual's faith or turning one's back on christ.
- progressive Sanctification = Holiness

- Water Baptism = Immersion
- Decision of salvation was based upon indiv. Free will = Arminios

- prophecy/word of knowledge = Encourage & Edification
- Gifts = yield, Act upon the prompts of the Spirit

- what Theological term is used to describe the restoration of Fellowship w/ God when one is saved? reconciliation → Reconciliation ↑

- Fruit of Spirit =
- Name Immanuel = God w/us

- Primary reason Jesus came to this world and died on the cross? To save people from their sin
- Believers on old Testament were forgiven based upon Blood Jesus would later shed.
- Bible says Believers are saved by Faith = Alone
- Assem. of God is the decision of salvation based upon? God's sovereignty & a person's free will
- Biblical pattern of water Baptism is = immersion
- ways a believer can take Communion in an unworthy manner are by = irreverence, self centered, divisive attitude
- Holy spirit is a person = Believers can have a relationship w/him.
- Joel 2:28 = God will pour out his spirit on All people.
- Baptism of HS = Separate exp. following salvation.
- which verse in the Book of Acts affirms that Baptism of the HS is to empower believers in ministry. 1:8
- Evidence of the HS is Separated 3x's of Acts = Speaking in other tongues.
- Gentile believers @ Cornelious Home had received the Baptism of HS was = Heard them sp. in other tongues.
- Speaking in tongues = Serves initial Physical evidence of the Baptism of the HS, a gift of the spirit, Praying in private for sp. growth.
- Eph. 5:18 HS = Something needed by All believers who would always be filled w/ HS.
- Benefit of speaking in tongues edifies = The person speaking in tongues.
- Evidence Gentile believers at cornelius home had received the Baptism of the HS = Heard them speak in tongues
- Baptism of HS = separate exp. following Salvation.
- ways a believer can take Communion in an unworthy manner = irreverance, Self-centered, divisive attitude
- significance of communion is Past, present & future.
- God offers believers forgiveness because of = the Atonement

Answer Keys

- **Compare your answers to the Test Yourself quizzes against those given in this section.**

- **Compare your answers to the UPE questions against the answer keys located in this section.**

- **Review the course content identified by your incorrect answers.**

ANSWERS TO TEST YOURSELF

THE114 Introduction to Pentecostal Doctrine, Third Edition

Answers below are followed by the number of the objective being tested. For any questions you answered incorrectly, review the lesson content in preparation for your final exam.

Chapter 1
1. B 1.1.1
2. B 1.1.2
3. C 1.1.2
4. A 1.1.3
5. C 1.2.2
6. B 1.3.1
7. B 1.3.1
8. A 1.3.1
9. C 1.4.2
10. A 1.4.2

Chapter 2
1. B 2.1.1
2. C 2.1.1
3. A 2.1.1
4. C 2.1.1
5. C 2.1.2
6. A 2.1.3
7. A 2.2.1
8. C 2.2.3
9. B 2.3.2
10. A 2.3.2

Chapter 3
1. C 3.1.1
2. B 3.1.1
3. A 3.1.2
4. B 3.2.1
5. C 3.2.2
6. A 3.2.2
7. C 3.3.1
8. C 3.3.2
9. B 3.3.1
10. A 3.5.1

Chapter 4
1. A 4.1.1
2. C 4.1.4
3. B 4.1.2
4. C 4.1.3
5. C 4.1.1
6. C 4.2.1
7. B 4.2.2
8. A 4.2.3
9. B 4.2.1
10. B 4.2.4

Chapter 5
1. B 5.1.1
2. A 5.1.2
3. C 5.2.1
4. B 5.2.1
5. A 5.2.3
6. B 5.1.2
7. C 5.1.4
8. B 5.2.3
9. A 5.2.1
10. B 5.2.3

Chapter 6
1. A 6.1.1
2. A 6.1.1
3. C 6.1.1
4. B 6.1.3
5. C 6.1.1
6. B 6.1.2
7. A 6.1.3
8. A 6.2.1
9. B 6.2.1
10. C 6.2.3

Chapter 7
1. A 7.1.2
2. C 7.1.2
3. B 7.1.2
4. C 7.2.3
5. A 7.2.1
6. C 7.2.2
7. A 7.2.1
8. B 7.2.3
9. B 7.2.3
10. C 7.2.3

Chapter 8
1. A 8.1.1
2. A 8.1.4
3. C 8.2.1
4. B 8.2.2
5. B 8.1.2
6. A 8.1.1
7. B 8.1.2
8. A 8.1.4
9. C 8.2.2
10. B 8.3.2

Chapter 9
1. C 9.1.1
2. B 9.1.1
3. C 9.1.1
4. C 9.1.1
5. B 9.2.2
6. A 9.1.2
7. A 9.2.1
8. C 9.2.2
9. A 9.2.3
10. C 9.2.4

Chapter 10
1. B 10.1.3
2. C 10.1.1
3. A 10.1.2
4. C 10.1.3
5. C 10.1.4
6. B 10.2.3
7. A 10.1.3
8. A 10.2.1
9. B 10.2.2
10. C 10.2.4

Chapter 11
1. C 11.1.1
2. B 11.1.2
3. B 11.2.1
4. A 11.2.2
5. C 11.2.3
6. B 11.2.3
7. A 11.3.1
8. C 11.3.2
9. B 11.3.3
10. A 11.3.3

Chapter 12
1. B 12.1.1
2. C 12.2.1
3. A 12.2.3
4. A 12.1.1
5. C 12.1.3
6. B 12.1.2
7. C 12.1.2
8. A 12.1.3
9. C 12.1.1
10. B 12.2.2

Chapter 13
1. C 13.1.1
2. A 13.1.1
3. B 13.1.3
4. B 13.1.2
5. A 13.1.4
6. B 13.2.1
7. A 13.2.1
8. A 13.2.2
9. C 13.2.3
10. B 13.3.2

UNIT PROGRESS EVALUATION ANSWER KEYS

THE114 Introduction to Pentecostal Doctrine, Third Edition

Answers below are followed by the number of the objective being tested. For any questions you answered incorrectly, review the lesson content in preparation for your final exam.

UNIT PROGRESS EVALUATION 1

1.	B	1.1.1	14.	A	1.3.1
2.	B	1.1.1	15.	A	1.3.2
3.	C	1.1.3	16.	B	1.3.3
4.	A	1.1.3	17.	C	1.3.1
5.	C	1.2.1	18.	B	1.3.1
6.	B	1.1.1	19.	A	1.3.2
7.	D	1.1.2	20.	A	1.4.1
8.	B	1.1.3	21.	D	1.4.1
9.	C	1.2.1	22.	D	1.4.1
10.	D	1.2.2	23.	D	1.4.2
11.	C	1.2.2	24.	D	1.4.2
12.	D	1.2.2	25.	A	1.4.2
13.	A	1.2.2			

UNIT PROGRESS EVALUATION 2

1.	D	2.1.3	14.	C	3.3.2
2.	A	2.1.1	15.	C	3.3.1
3.	C	2.1.1	16.	D	3.4.1
4.	D	2.1.2	17.	A	3.4.1
5.	A	2.2.2	18.	B	3.5.1
6.	C	2.2.3	19.	A	3.5.1
7.	D	2.3.2	20.	A	4.1.1
8.	D	2.3.3	21.	C	4.1.4
9.	A	3.4.2	22.	B	4.1.2
10.	B	3.1.1	23.	B	4.2.1
11.	B	3.2.2	24.	C	4.2.3
12.	C	3.2.2	25.	B	4.2.2
13.	B	3.2.1			

UNIT PROGRESS EVALUATION 3

1.	D	5.2.1	14.	A	8.1.4
2.	B	5.2.3	15.	A	8.1.1
3.	B	5.2.3	16.	B	8.1.2
4.	D	5.1.2	17.	B	8.2.2
5.	D	6.1.1	18.	C	8.2.2
6.	C	6.1.1	19.	B	8.3.2
7.	C	6.1.1	20.	A	8.3.1
8.	C	6.2.1	21.	A	9.1.2
9.	A	7.1.3	22.	C	9.1.1
10.	D	7.2.1	23.	B	9.2.2
11.	A	7.2.1	24.	D	9.2.1
12.	B	7.2.3	25.	C	9.2.3
13.	B	7.2.3			

UNIT PROGRESS EVALUATION 4

1.	C	10.1.1	14.	D	11.1.1
2.	A	10.1.2	15.	B	11.1.2
3.	D	10.1.3	16.	D	11.2.2
4.	C	10.1.4	17.	C	11.2.3
5.	D	10.1.4	18.	B	11.2.1
6.	A	10.1.4	19.	A	11.2.3
7.	B	10.2.3	20.	B	11.2.3
8.	C	10.2.2	21.	C	11.3.1
9.	A	10.2.1	22.	A	11.3.1
10.	B	10.2.2	23.	C	11.3.2
11.	D	10.2.4	24.	B	11.3.2
12.	A	11.2.2	25.	A	11.3.3
13.	D	11.1.3			

UNIT PROGRESS EVALUATION 5

1.	A	12.2.1	14.	B	13.1.2
2.	A	12.1.1	15.	A	13.1.1
3.	B	12.1.1	16.	B	13.1.2
4.	C	12.1.3	17.	D	13.1.3
5.	A	12.1.4	18.	C	13.2.1
6.	B	12.1.2	19.	C	13.2.3
7.	C	12.1.2	20.	D	13.2.1
8.	A	12.1.4	21.	C	13.2.3
9.	C	12.1.4	22.	D	13.2.3
10.	D	12.2.3	23.	D	13.3.2
11.	B	12.2.2	24.	B	13.3.1
12.	C	12.2.1	25.	B	13.3.1
13.	C	13.1.1			

Forms

The following pages contain two course forms: the Round-Tripper and the Request for a Printed Final Examination.

1. For students who do not have access to email, we are including one **Round-Tripper** for your use if you have a question or comment related to your studies. If you do not have access to the internet, you will want to make several photocopies of the Round-Tripper before you write on it. Retain the copies for submitting additional questions as needed. Students who have access to email can submit questions at any time to bsbcontent@globaluniversity.edu.

2. Students who do not have access to the internet-based tests may request a printed final examination. For faster service, please call Enrollment Services at 1-800-443-1083 or fax your **Request for a Printed Final Examination** to 417-862-0863.

ROUND-TRIPPER

**THE114 Introduction to Pentecostal Doctrine,
Third Edition**
Date ....

Your Name .... Your Student Number ....

Send questions and comments by email to bsbcontent@globaluniversity.edu. If you do not have access to email, use this form to write to Berean School of the Bible with questions or comments related to your studies. Write your question in the space provided. Send this form to Berean School of the Bible. The form will make its return, or round-trip, as Berean School of the Bible responds.

YOUR QUESTION:

FOR BEREAN SCHOOL OF THE BIBLE'S RESPONSE:

PN 03.21.01

 GLOBAL
UNIVERSITY

1211 South Glenstone Springfield, MO 65804
1-800-443-1083 * Fax 1-417-862-0863
www.globaluniversity.edu

BEREAN SCHOOL OF THE BIBLE
REQUEST FOR A PRINTED FINAL
EXAMINATION
NOTE: All final exams are to be taken closed-book.

Final examinations are available online at www.globaluniversity.edu.

Taking the test online gives immediate results and feedback. You will know your test grade and which learning objectives you may have missed.

Students who do not have access to the internet-based tests may request a printed final examination. For faster service, please call Enrollment Services at **1-800-443-1083** or fax this form to **417-862-0863**.

If preferred, mail this form to:
   Berean School of the Bible, Global University
   Attn: Enrollment Services
   1211 South Glenstone
   Springfield, MO 65804

Please allow 7–10 business days for delivery of your final examination. **You may only request an exam for the course or courses in which you are currently enrolled.**

_____
Student Number

_____
Name

_____
Address

_____

_____
City, State, Zip Code

_____
Phone

_____
Email

Certified Level	Licensed Level	Ordained Level
☐ BIB114 Christ in the Synoptic Gospels	☐ BIB115 Acts: The Holy Spirit at Work in Believers	☐ BIB313 Corinthian Correspondence
☐ BIB121 Introduction to Hermeneutics: How to Interpret the Bible	☐ BIB117 Prison Epistles: Colossians, Philemon, Ephesians, and Philippians	☐ BIB318 Pentateuch
☐ BIB212 New Testament Survey		☐ BIB322 Poetic Books
☐ BIB214 Old Testament Survey	☐ BIB215 Romans: Justification by Faith	☐ MIN325 Preaching in the Contemporary World
☐ MIN171 A Spirit-Empowered Church	☐ MIN123 The Local Church in Evangelism	☐ MIN327 Church Administration, Finance, and Law
☐ MIN181 Relationships and Ethics in Ministry	☐ MIN223 Introduction to Homiletics	☐ MIN381 Pastoral Ministry
☐ MIN191 Beginning Ministerial Internship	☐ MIN251 Effective Leadership	☐ MIN391 Advanced Ministerial Internship
☐ THE114 Introduction to Pentecostal Doctrine	☐ MIN261 Introduction to Assemblies of God Missions	☐ THE311 Prayer and Worship
☐ THE142 Assemblies of God History, Missions, and Governance	☐ MIN281 Conflict Management for Church Leaders	
☐ THE211 Introduction to Theology: A Pentecostal Perspective	☐ MIN291 Intermediate Ministerial Internship	
	☐ THE245 Eschatology: A Study of Things to Come	

Signature_____   Date_____